Peter Berresford Ellis

THE CELTIC EMPIRE

The First Millennium of Celtic History
*c.*1000 BC—51 AD

CONSTABLE · LONDON

First published in Great Britain 1990
by Constable and Company Limited
3 The Lanchesters, 162 Fulham Palace Road, London W6 9ER
Copyright © Peter Berresford Ellis 1990
Reprinted 1991
Paperback edition 1992
Reprinted 1992, 1993, 1996
ISBN 0 09 471350 2
Set in Linotron Sabon 11pt by
Rowland Phototypesetting Limited
Bury St Edmunds, Suffolk
Printed in Great Britain by
St Edmundsbury Press Limited
Bury St Edmunds, Suffolk

A CIP catalogue record for this book
is available from the British Library

Fighting retail, they were beaten wholesale.
Had they been inseparable,
they would have been insuperable.

Publius Cornelius Tacitus on the Celts
(AD 56/57–c.117)
(paraphrased by Harri Webb)

Contents

Illustrations

Preface

THE Celts were the first European people north of the Alps to emerge into recorded history. At one time they dominated the ancient world from Ireland in the west to Turkey in the east, and from Belgium in the north, south to Spain and Italy. They even made their presence felt in the Egypt of the Ptolemy pharaohs, where they attempted, according to one ancient chronicler, a *coup d'état* to gain control of the country. They sacked Rome, invaded Greece and destroyed every army the Greek city states could throw at them. Their sophisticated weapons and sturdy war-chariots devastated all adversaries.

According to Titus Livius (59 BC – AD 17), popularly known as Livy, at the time when Tarquinius Superbus was King of Rome (c.534–508 BC), Ambigatos of the Bituriges ruled over a Celtic empire 'so abounding in men and in the fruits of the earth that it seemed impossible to govern so great a population'. This statement, according to the Celtic scholar Dr Eoin Mac Neill (*Phases of Irish History*, 1919), was the basis on which many nineteenth-century historians wrote about 'a Celtic empire' in ancient Europe.

I have chosen the title *The Celtic Empire* for this history perhaps somewhat mischievously. Any resemblance to empires as we know them, such as the Roman empire or more recent examples, is in fact spurious. There emerges no known sustained series of Celtic emperors having supreme and extensive political dominion over numerous subject peoples. However, I believe there is some justification for my contentious title, as will be demonstrated by this book, in that, during the period of Celtic expansion, Celtic tribes and confederations of tribes spread through the ancient world challenging all who opposed them and settling as the dominant people in the areas they conquered.

I

In this fashion they spread down the Iberian peninsula, into northern Italy and east through what is now Czechoslovakia, along the Danube valley as far as the Black Sea, moving on into Asia Minor, where they established the Galatian state in the third century BC, which state gives us our first information about Celtic political institutions.

The Celtic Empire is not just another work on the linguistic, cultural and social aspects of early Celtic society. In recent years there have been numerous studies from that viewpoint, some good, some bad. There has, however, been a singular lack of an historical survey of the Celtic peoples in the ancient world aimed at a general readership. Most of the peoples of the ancient world have, over the years, become the subject of such general histories – the Greeks, Phoenicians, Etruscans, Carthaginians and Romans. It is time that the Celts were accorded such a record and this volume is an attempt to fill that need.

The Celtic Empire, therefore, is a history for the general reader. It outlines the first millennium of Celtic history, tracing the Celtic peoples from their earliest-known appearance to the start of the Christian era, when they were being crushed by the Roman empire, the time when their civilization began to recede to the north-western seaboard of Europe. Here, today, the inheritors of nearly 3,000 years of unbroken cultural tradition are surviving precariously. Of the populations still regarded as Celtic – the Irish, Scots, Manx, Welsh, Bretons and Cornish – only two millions still speak a Celtic language, the only meaningful hallmark of their Celtic identity. These descendants of the ancient Celtic civilization struggle hard to survive and maintain their individuality in these days of increasing cultural uniformity. Soon, very soon, if the same cultural, economic and political pressures continue to be applied to them, the Celts will disappear from the fabric of Europe. They will go the same way as the Etruscan civilization. And so it is to these survivors, the inheritors of 3,000 years of a cultural continuum and history, that this book is dedicated.

One word of explanation about the spelling of Celtic names in this volume for the linguistically minded: in the recording of some Celtic names by Latin writers, the Latin – us ending was usually used. I have reasserted the Celtic -os ending, following the argument of Henri Hubert, Kenneth Jackson and other leading Celtic scholars. For instance, Professor Jackson used the example of the name of the British King usually recorded by Latin writers as Cunobelinus, the Cymbeline of Shakespeare. Professor Jackson pointed out that in British, the ancestor language of the Brythonic group (Welsh, Breton and Cornish) and close relative to continental Celtic (Gaulish), the name would have been recorded as Cunobelinos (meaning, the 'hound of Belinos'). When used as the subject of the verb, the name would appear as Cunobelinos; when the object, it became Cunobelinon; when 'of Cunobelinos', it became Cunobelini; and when 'to Cunobelinos' it became Cunobelinus. This form of declension is similar to the Latin. Thus the accusative form of the name Virgilius in Virgilium, genitive form Virgilii and dative form Virgilio.

Introduction

CROWDS gathered in the streets of Rome in the year 804 of the foundation of the city (AD 51). Most of the crowds thronged around the foot of the Capitoline Hill, where the Emperor Claudius and his new Empress Agrippina were seated in imperial splendour on viewing platforms set up on the parade ground of the Praetorian Guard. Behind them were platforms bearing the senate of Rome, their ladies and attendants and leading dignitaries of the empire. Rome was in a festive mood for she was celebrating a triumph, a state thanksgiving the like of which had not been seen for many years. Not since the Numidian King Syphax, the ally of the Carthaginian General Hannibal, had been brought in chains to Rome nearly 250 years before, had the Roman crowds anticipated such festivities.

Caratacos, son of Cunobelinos, the British King who had held out against the might of Rome's armies for nine years, had finally been made captive. With his family and retinue he had been brought to Rome to be displayed in chains before her people in imperial triumph. Tacitus, the Roman historian, commented: 'His fame had spread beyond the British Isles, had penetrated the western provinces, and was well known in Italy itself. All were eager to see the man who had so long defied Roman power.'

The victory had not been an entirely military one. The capture of Caratacos had been a rather sordid affair. He had been betrayed by a fellow British Celtic ruler, Cartimandua, Queen of the Brigantes, and handed over to the Roman commander, Publius Ostorius Scapula. However, as Tacitus remarked, the Emperor Claudius was 'willing to magnify the glory of the conquest'. Rome needed celebrations to turn the attention of her citizens away from internal political strife.

The parade of the Celtic prisoners from Britain was guided through

5

the magnificent thoroughfares of the imperial capital. According to Dio Cassius, Caratacos is said to have gazed at the towering marble edifices around him and to have remarked with cynicism to his guards: 'And when you have all this, do you still envy us our hovels in Britain?'

When they reached the foot of the Capitoline, where the Emperor and his senators waited, Tacitus says that the followers of the Celtic King were made to precede him.

> The military accoutrements, the harness and rich collars which he had gained in various battles, were displayed with pomp. The wife of Caratacos, his daughter and his brother, followed next; he himself closed the melancholy train. The rest of the prisoners, struck with terror, descended to mean and abject supplications. Caratacos alone was superior to misfortune.

Well might Caratacos' followers have been apprehensive. It was well known what Rome did to its prisoners displayed in ceremonial triumphs in the city. For 200 years or more Celtic chieftains, those taken prisoner in battle, had been brought to Rome for execution. After the major celebrations they were usually taken to the Tullianum, the underground execution chamber at the foot of the Capitoline Hill where most state prisoners met their end. Had not the great Vercingetorix of Gaul, having surrendered to Julius Caesar, been brought in chains to this spot and eventually executed in 46 BC? Caratacos and his followers must surely have been aware of what fate awaited them.

According to Tacitus, Caratacos marched up to the dais and raised his head to gaze on the mighty Emperor of Rome 'with a countenance still unaltered, not a symptom of fear appearing, no sorrow, no condescension, he behaved with dignity even in ruin.' Was he aware that 400 years before Celts had stood on this very spot as conquerors, when Brennos had stormed and sacked the city? Caratacos asked permission to address the Emperor and his senate. Permission was granted.

'If to the nobility of my birth,' Caratacos began,

> and the splendour of exalted station, I had united the virtues of moderation, Rome had beheld me, not in captivity, but a royal visitor and a friend. The alliance of a prince, descended from an illustrious line of ancestors; a prince, whose sway extended over

many nations, would not have been unworthy of your choice. A reverse of fortune is now the lot of Caratacos. The event to you is glorious, and to me humiliating.

I had arms, men and horses; I had wealth in abundance; can you wonder that I was unwilling to lose them? The ambition of Rome aspires to universal domination; and must the rest of mankind, by consequence, stretch their necks to the yoke?

I held you at bay for years; had I acted otherwise, where, on your part, had been the glory of conquest, and where, on mine, the honour of a brave resistance? I am now in your power. If you are bent on vengeance, execute your purpose. The bloody scene will soon be over and the name of Caratacos will sink into oblivion. But if you preserve my life, then I shall be, to late posterity, a monument of Roman clemency.

Caratacos' speech to his conquerors was audacious and moving. Historically, it told three important facts. First, it indicated that Rome had initially tried to come to terms with him, promising him a client-kingship if he accepted Roman overlordship. Secondly, it demonstrated Caratacos' belief in the cause of liberty and defiance of Roman imperialism. Lastly, it showed that the Celtic chieftain was an astute politician and his plea for clemency was a discerning and clever move.

The Emperor Claudius and his senate took the bait offered them by the Celtic ruler. Caratacos, his family and retinue were granted their lives. There was to be no ceremonial orgy of bloodshed to appease the Roman crowds that day. Caratacos and his family were to remain in permanent exile within the confines of the city of Rome. At their next session, the Roman senate decreed monuments be set up to mark Ostorius's victory over the Celts of Britain.

That year, AD 51, the year Rome established her rule in southern Britain, marked the end of an epoch for the Celtic people. For a millennium they had spread themselves throughout Europe, originating, it is thought, from homelands at the headwaters of the Rhine and Danube. They had spread as far eastwards as the Black Sea and also Asia Minor, west to the British Isles and south-west into the Iberian peninsula as far south as Gades (Cadiz). They had also crossed the Alps and established themselves in the Po Valley of northern Italy. Then, as Rome began to expand from a city state into a mighty empire, the Celtic realms began to fall to the unquenchable Roman thirst for conquest and power. The Celts of Cisalpine Gaul fell first, then the Celts of Iberia, of Transalpine Gaul, of Galatia, of Gaul proper, until finally the Celts of Britain came under the *pax Romana*.

The Celts of northern Britain, known as Caledonia to the Romans, were to keep the Roman armies at bay, fighting for their liberty so fiercely that the Romans had to content themselves with erecting walls (Hadrian's Wall and the Antonine Wall) as the barrier of their northern imperial frontier. Only Ireland and the Isle of Man were entirely to escape invasion by the ruthlessly efficient Roman military machine.

The year AD 51 saw the major part of the Celtic world in bondage to the empire of Rome.

[I]

The Origins of the Celts

T HE Celts were the first European people north of the Alps to
emerge into recorded history. But the first references to them
appear in the sixth and fifth centuries BC when they began to
encounter the peoples of the Mediterranean cultures, for the Celts did
not leave any extensive written testimony in their own languages until
the Christian era. When they emerge in historical record, they are first
called Keltoi, by the Greeks. Polybius also uses the term Galatae,
which had, by his day, become widely used by Greeks. The Romans
referred to them as Galli as well as Celtae. Diodorus Siculus, Julius
Caesar, Strabo and Pausanias all recognize the synonymous use of
these terms. Diodorus Siculus (*c*.60–30 BC) considered that the
term Celt was the proper name for the people he was describing.
Pausanias (AD *c*.160) certainly gives prior antiquity to the name
Celt over the names Gauls or Galatians. And Julius Caesar (100–
44 BC) comments that the Gauls of his day referred to themselves as
Celtae.

There is little doubt that the word Keltoi, or Celts as we will call
them, was a word of Celtic origin. In searching for a meaning of the
name some have pointed to the word meaning hidden – the word
which gives us the Irish form *ceilt*, meaning concealment or secret, and
the word which has given us the English word kilt. Thus some believe
that Keltoi meant the hidden or secret people and that this name
referred to the Celtic prohibition against setting down in written
form their vast store of knowledge. Celtic history, philosophy, law,
genealogy and science were transmitted in oral traditions until the
Christian period. This was not because the Celts were illiterate but
because of a religious prohibition. Caesar comments:

The druids think it unlawful to commit this knowledge of theirs to writing (in secular and in public and private business they use Greek characters). This is a practice which they have, I think, adopted for two reasons. They do not wish that their system should become commonly known or that their pupils, trusting in written documents, should less carefully cultivate their memory; and, indeed, it does generally happen that those who rely on written documents, are less industrious in learning by heart and have a weaker memory.

So it was not until the Greeks and Romans commenced to write their accounts of the Celts, sometimes culturally misconceived and invariably biased, that the Celts emerged into recorded history. Archaeology has to fill the void before recorded history and so we are presented with great difficulties in identifying the Celts and their origins. For example, what is meant by the Celts? The strictest, as well as the easiest, definition is those people who speak or spoke a Celtic language. This is certainly the definition which has been used since recorded history identified the movements of a Celtic-speaking people. But once we go beyond historical record we have to rely on other methods of identification. Historians and archaeologists are agreed that the start of the Iron Age in northern Europe, identified as the Hallstatt Culture, using the town of Hallstatt, in upper Austria, as the centre point of its expansion, 700–500 BC, was a Celtic cultural expansion. They are agreed that another series of Iron Age objects, classified by their centre of distribution, La Tène, 500–100 BC, was also a Celtic cultural expansion. We must therefore ask whether there were Celts in Europe before 700 BC.

The direct answer is – of course! All the ancestors of the peoples of Europe were placed somewhere on the continent at this time. In the nineteenth century it became accepted that most past and present European languages, with the exceptions of Basque, Estonian, Finnish, Hungarian, Lapp and Turkish, were related to one another and were branches of a hypothesized common Indo-European language. When exactly 'common Indo-European' was spoken, and how it broke up into such diverse families as Latin, Slavic, Germanic, Celtic and so forth, is open to intense debate and speculation. And it is merely hypothesis. What we can say is that long before 700 BC there was in northern Europe a people whose language was developing into Celtic.

In more recent years archaeologists have generally accepted that the

Urnfield Folk were Celtic or, as some quaintly phrase it, proto-Celtic, meaning that their language had not quite developed into a form which we would immediately recognize as Celtic today. The Urnfield Culture of northern Europe is roughly dated between 1200 and 700 BC. This people, if we may keep to generalities, were farming folk living in small communities who were also skilled in working bronze and, towards the end of the period, in working iron as well. In many places they lived in hill-forts and they buried their dead in the distinctive manner which gives them their name – urnfields. The cremated ashes and bones of their dead were buried in urns of clay accompanied by small personal items which belonged to the deceased in life.

This culture was identified by a concentration in the Danube basin, around eastern France and western Germany, spreading into eastern Germany and south across the Alps into the Po Valley, south-west to southern France and further south into the Spanish peninsula. It also arrived in the British Isles. This is now accepted as the spread of a Celtic culture. Jacquetta and Christopher Hawkes (*Prehistoric Britain*, 1947) argued that the Celts were emerging in the Middle Bronze Age from a mixture of round-headed Beaker Folk from the south, a solid substratum of Neolithic and ultimately Mesolithic stocks.

We can hypothesize that, at some stage of their historical development, the Celts spoke a Common Celtic language. Celtic scholars have supposed this Common Celtic to have been spoken just before the start of the first millennium BC, and then, soon after, two distinct dialects of Celtic emerged which are identified by their modern names – Goidelic and Brythonic, or the famous Q- and P-Celtic.

The Goidelic group is represented today by Irish, Manx and Scottish Gaelic, the Brythonic by Welsh, Cornish and Breton. Goidelic is said to have been the oldest form of Celtic with the Brythonic (which was of course closely related to continental Celtic, called Gaulish) developing from it at a later stage. This form simplified itself in its case endings and in the loss of the neuter gender and dual number. Differences occurred in the matter of initial mutation and aspiration. Above all, there was the famous substitution of P for Q in the Brythonic group which has led scholars to categorize the groups as P- and Q-Celtic. This is based on the sound in Indo-European which gave *qu* (*kw*). The sound, in Goidelic, later became represented by *c* (always hard), while in Brythonic it was replaced by *p*. For example: the word for son in

Goidelic was *mac*. In the languages representing Brythonic this has altered to (m)*ap* (Welsh), *mab* (Breton) and *map* (Cornish). Another example can be seen with the word for head. In Irish it is *ceann*; in Scottish Gaelic it is also *ceann* while in Manx the sound is represented as *kione*. But in the Brythonic group it becomes *pen* (Welsh), *penn* (Breton) and *pen* (Cornish).

Henri Hubert has asserted that the separation of the Celtic dialects was a fact of great importance, implying a deep division between the Celtic peoples and suggesting the occupation of Britain and Ireland by Goidelic-speaking Celts many centuries before the historical movement of the Brythonic-speaking Celts. So, linguistically, Hubert and other scholars support the archaeological evidence of the Celts being domiciled in Britain, as represented by the Urnfield Culture, before 1000 BC. Similarly, Hubert pointed out that Goidelic-speakers were also settled in Spain and Portugal about the same time, where there are signs of an early Q-Celtic culture which was subsequently submerged by later P-Celtic settlements.

Therefore, separated from their fellow Celts on the continent, among whom the Brythonic form of Celtic was developed, and certainly had developed by the fourth century, the Goidelic Celts continued to develop their dialect, which was to evolve into Irish, Manx and Scottish. Later migrations from the continent of Brythonic-speakers caused the Goidelic-speakers to recede, making the Brythonic language dominant in the southern part of Britain.

We now come to an important question. Where did the Celts begin to develop their distinctive culture? There are two contradictory traditions. One tradition, founded in history, places the point of origin on the north-west coast of Europe by the North Sea. The second tradition places the point of origin around the headwaters of the Danube.

Ammianus Marcellinus (AD c.330–95), quoting Timagenes of Alexandria as his source, claims that when the Celts began their expansion they came from the outermost isles beyond the Rhine, placing them on the coast opposite the North Sea. 'They were', he says, 'driven from their homes by the frequency of wars and violent rising of the sea.' Certainly the concept fits in with people living in the Low Countries. Ephoros of Cyme, one of the most influential Greek historians of the fourth century BC, believed that the Celts came from that area and he is quoted by Strabo (64 BC – AD c.24) but Strabo was somewhat sceptical. Ephoros describes the Celts as remaining obstinately in their lands and losing more lives in floods than in wars until, finally, they were forced to migrate.

When Hecataeus (*c*.500–476 BC) of Miletus and Herodotus (*c*.490 –425 BC) of Halicarnassus first mention the Keltoi they were already spread in an arc from the Iberian peninsula, through France and Belgium, Switzerland, Germany, Austria, northern Italy, and were moving eastwards along the Danube valley towards the Balkans. Herodotus indicates the Celtic homeland as being the upper Danube. If we accept the initial site of Celtic development as being the area around the headwaters of the Danube, the Rhine and the Rhône, we will not be far wrong. Here, Celtic names proliferate. The names of rivers, mountains and towns are Celtic. The Rhine, for example, Renos, means sea; the Danube, from Danuvius, means swift-flowing (cognate with the Irish *dana*) and the Rhur, from Raura, seems to be named after the Celtic tribe, the Raurici. The tributaries and sub-tributaries of the rivers still retain their Celtic origins. Laber (the Labara near Ratisbon) means talking river; the Glan means pure or clean river and so on. There is a strong concentration of Celtic place-names in this area, which weakens as one radiates from its central point. Hubert believes that the place-names indicate that the Celts were living in this region as the aboriginal population. This was the region, therefore, which was the 'cradle' of Celtic civilization and from which the Celts were eventually driven by the arrival of the Germanic people during the first century BC. When Julius Caesar was in Gaul, for example, the Celtic tribes were still moving westward as the Germanic tribes swept in behind them from the north-east to give their name and language to the lands taken from the former inhabitants. The last members of this general exodus were the Helvetii and Boii from Switzerland and Bohemia and the Tigurini from Bavaria. Only place-names and archaeological remains were left behind to mark the birth-place of Celtic civilization.

It is a truism that a conqueror always writes the history and so we have to piece together the early history of the Celts from the hostile viewpoint of the Greeks and Romans. In trying to understand Celtic motivations, their attitudes, philosophies and laws, we are handicapped by the early prohibition of the Celts against committing their knowledge to written record. However, when the insular Celts of Britain and Ireland began to put their knowledge into written form in the Christian era it was not too late to form a perspective, bearing in mind the cultural changes from early times. And we can be wary about taking what the Greeks and Romans say about the Celts as a literal truth.

The Greeks and Romans represent the Celts as a barbaric people; as basically a fierce warrior society, proud, ignorant, illiterate, taking life cheaply, given to childish amusements and often drunk. In other words, Rome and Greece represented civilization while the Celts were depicted as exotic barbarians or noble savages. The image still remains with us. Yet today we realize that 'barbarity' or 'savagery' is just a matter of one's perception. Doubtless to the ancient Celts, the Romans and Greeks were equally as preposterous as the Celts were to the perceptions of the Romans and Greeks.

From the Urnfield Culture, the Celts emerge as an agricultural people – farmers cultivating their lands and living in a tribal society. By the start of the Hallstatt period in the eighth century BC, the development of ironworking enabled the Celtic peoples to make formidable axes, billhooks and other tools with which they could open roadways through previously impenetrable forests, effect extensive clearances and till the land with comparative ease. An old Irish word for road, avenue or pathway, still in use in modern Irish, is *slighe*, from the word *sligim*, I hew. The development of skill in metalworking, particularly in iron, also gave the Celts new armaments of swords and spears which rendered them militarily superior to most of their neighbours and therefore made them more mobile because there were few enemies to be feared.

It was the Celts who were the great road-builders of northern Europe. The ancient roads of Britain, for example, often ascribed to the Romans, had already been laid by the Celts long before the coming of the Romans. This is a fact only now slowly being accepted by scholars in the light of new archaeological finds. Yet Celtic roads were mentioned by Strabo, Caesar and Diodorus Siculus. It is obvious, looking at Caesar's account of his Gallic campaigns, that he was moving his legions rapidly through Gaul because there was an excellent system of roadways in existence. Similarly, when Caesar crossed to Britain, he found a highly mobile army of Celts opposing him in heavy war-chariots, some of them four-wheeled. For the Celts to be able to move in such vehicles with the speed and determination recounted by Caesar it becomes obvious, to the careful historian, that there had to be a well-laid system of roads in existence.

Now archaeology is reinforcing history. For example, in 1985 in Co. Longford, Ireland, 1,000 yards of roadway were uncovered, having been preserved in a bog. The road was dated approximately to 150 BC. It had a foundation of oak beams placed side by side on thin rails of oak, ash and alder. Other such finds of chance survivals demonstrate that the Celts used local materials, the great forests of Europe, with which to build their roads. The Romans simply reinforced these roads with the materials they were used to handling – stone. Thus the Roman roads were preserved over the top of the Celtic roads. There is one fascinating point about the Co. Longford road. In one of the old Irish myths 'The Marriage of Étain', a king named Eochaidh Airemh is said to have imposed the task of building a causeway across the bog of Lemrach on the clans of Tethba, who dwelt in an area covering parts of Longford and Westmeath. The road is where the ancient tale placed it, demonstrating that Irish myth can have a basis in reality.

Incidentally, it is interesting to note that several Latin words connected with transport were in fact borrowed from Celtic into Latin, such as the names of various chariots, carts and wagons: *carpentum* (from which derives our modern car as well as carpenter), *carruca*, *carrus* and *rheda* – all of which were four-wheeled methods of transport used by the Celts – and the *essendum*, the war-chariot used by both Gauls and British Celts which was later adopted by the Romans for their own transportation use.

Archaeology has also shown much evidence of the prosperity of the rich farming communities of the Celts as well as their advances in art, Celtic pottery, jewellery, especially the enamelwork from north Britain and metal jewellery. This artwork found much favour in the ancient Mediterranean world. During the first century BC, before Caesar's invasion of Britain, British woollen goods, especially cloaks (*sagi*), were eagerly sought after in Rome. The ownership of a British woollen cloak was as prestigious in Rome in that period as the possession of a Harris-tweed suit was in the mid-twentieth century.

The Celts generally built their houses and settlements in wood but in some places they used stone, showing great sophistication in the construction of buildings. In Britain the remains of many such stone structures survive from the fourth to second centuries BC. One such structure survives to a height of forty feet, with lintelled entrances and inward-tapering wall, sometimes fifteen feet thick, with chambers, galleries and stairs. Staigue Fort, in Co. Kerry, Ireland, a circular stone fortress built some time during the first millennium BC, still stands with walls thirteen feet high, enclosing a space eighty-eight feet across, with two chambers constructed within the thickness of the walls. Most of these constructions were of drystone. The evidence demonstrates that the Celts were excellent builders.

The basis of their society was tribal. By the time the Celtic law systems were codified, with the Irish Brehon Law system being written down in the early Christian era, the Celtic tribal system was a highly sophisticated one. Comparing the Irish system with that enshrined in the Welsh Laws of Hywel Dda one can observe a common Celtic attitude to law. The good of the community was the basis of the law – in other words, a primitive yet sophisticated communism was prac- tised. Chieftains were elected, as were all officers of the tribe. Women emerge in Celtic society with equality of rights. They could inherit, own property and be elected to office, even to the position of leader in times of war, such as Cartimandua of the Brigantes and her more famous compatriot Boudicca of the Iceni. Tacitus observed, 'There is no rule of distinction to exclude the female line from the throne or the command of the armies.'

The Celtic tribes varied in size. Some were small, others constituted entire nations. The Helvetii, for example, were said to be 390,000 strong when they began their exodus. Of special note was that the Celtic tribes cared for their sick, poor and aged and that, according to Irish records, hospitals, run by the tribes, existed in Ireland around 300 BC, many hundreds of years before St Fabiola founded the first Christian hospital in Rome.

It is not the intention of this book to examine in detail the social life of the early Celts but simply to give some taste of it so that the history might be better understood. The Celtic religion is of importance in the understanding of Celtic attitudes. By the time the Greeks and Romans began to comment on the religion of the Celts, towards the end of the third century BC, it was, in its philosophy, a fairly standard one. It is true that the gods and goddesses were numerous, often appearing in triune form (three-in-one), although a 'father of the gods' is mentioned by many ancient observers. A lot of the gods and goddesses appear as ancestors of the people rather than as their creators – heroes and heroines. Celtic mythology, for example, surviving in Irish and Welsh texts, is an heroic one; for the Celts made their heroes into gods and their gods into heroes. In the lives of these gods and heroes, the lives of the people and the essence of their religious traditions were mirrored. Celtic heroes and heroines were no mere physical beauties with empty heads. They had to have intellectual powers equal to their physical abilities. They were totally human and were subject to all the natural virtues and vices. They practised all seven of the deadly sins. Yet their world was one of rural happiness, a world in which they indulged in all the pleasures of mortal life in an idealized form: love of nature, art, games, feasting, hunting and heroic single-handed combat.

The Celtic religion was one of the first to evolve a doctrine of immortality. It taught that death was but a changing of place and that life went on with all its forms and goods in another world, a world of the dead – the fabulous Otherworld. But when people died in that world, the souls were reborn in this world. Thus a constant exchange of souls took place between the two worlds: death in this world took a soul to the Otherworld; death in that world brought a soul to this world. Thus did Philostratus of Tyana (AD c.170–249) observe that the Celts celebrated birth with mourning and death with joy. Caesar, the cynical general, remarked that this teaching of immortality doubtless accounted for the reckless bravery of the Celts in battle.

The Celtic religion was administered, as was all Celtic learning, law and philosophy, by a group called the druids, first mentioned in the third century BC. To the Greeks and Romans, the druids were described as a priesthood, but they fulfilled political functions as well – indeed many tribal chieftains were also druids, such as Divitiacos and Dumnorix. It took twenty years to learn all the druidical canon, for the druid functioned not only as minister of religion, with its doctrine of immortality and complete moral system, but also as philosopher, teacher, and natural scientist and keeper of the law and its interpretation. Druids were often called upon to take legal, political and even military decisions.

Marcus Tullius Cicero (106–43 BC) reports the druids to have been great natural scientists, with a knowledge of physics and astronomy which they applied in the construction of calendars. The earliest-known surviving Celtic calendar, dated from the first century BC, is the Coligny Calendar, now in the Palais des Arts, Lyons, France. It is far more elaborate than the rudimentary Julian calendar and has a highly sophisticated five-year synchronization of lunation with the solar year. It consists of a huge bronze plate which is engraved with a calendar of sixty-two consecutive lunar months. The language is Gaulish but the lettering and numerals are Latin. Place-names, personal names and inscriptions testify to a certain degree of literacy in the Celtic language. Caesar explains: 'They count periods of time not by the number of days but by the number of nights; and in reckoning birthdays and the new moon and new year, their unit of reckoning is the night followed by the day.'

Bards, poets and minstrels held a high position in Celtic society and were closely associated with the druids. Diodorus Siculus observed: 'They have also lyric poets whom they call bards. They sing to the accompaniment of instruments resembling lyres, sometimes a eulogy and sometimes a satire.' The bards were highly trained, a professional group who were the repositories of Celtic history, legends, folklore and poetry. They were under the patronage of the chieftains. The tradition, as we have noted, was strictly an oral one, the bards having to commit to memory a vast store of knowledge and be word-perfect in their recitations.

As a people, the Celts had a strong natural feeling for learning and intellectual exercise. Greek and Roman writers often remark on this aspect of their temperament, contrasting it with what they considered to be the crudity of their material civilization but praising the refinement and elegance of their use of language and appreciation of linguistic subtlety. Marcus Porcius Cato (234–149 BC) remarked on the sophistication of Celtic eloquence and rhetoric. Poseidonius (c.135–50 BC), quoted by Athenaeus (AD c.200), recorded an incident at a feast in Gaul given by a chieftain named Louernios – whose name means the fox.

A Celtic poet who arrived too late met Louernios and composed a song magnifying his greatness and lamenting his own late arrival. Louernios was very pleased and asked for a bag of gold and threw it to the poet, who ran beside his chariot. The poet picked it up and sang another song saying that the very tracks of Louernios' chariot on the earth gave gold and largesse to mankind.

Both Poseidonius and Diodorus Siculus noted the popularity of music among the Celts and mentioned the variety of instruments which they used. Musical instruments and people dancing can be observed as decorations on Celtic pottery as early as the seventh century BC.

Turning to warfare, Diodorus Siculus observed that the druids had the power to prevent battles between the Celtic tribes:

And it is not only in the needs of peace but also in war that they [the Celts] carefully obey these men and their song-loving poets, and this is true not only of their friends but of their enemies. For oft-times as armies approached each other in line of battle with their swords drawn and their spears raised for the charge, these men come forth between them and stop the conflict as though they had spellbound some kind of wild animals. Thus, even among the most savage barbarians, anger yields to wisdom and Ares does homage to the Muses.

In fact, the Celts preferred to settle warfare by means of single-handed combat between the chieftains or champions of the opposing armies rather than a pitch battle between opposing forces. Diodorus commented: 'And when someone accepts their challenge to battle, they proudly recite the deeds of valour of their ancestors and proclaim their own valorous quality, at the same time abusing and making little of their opponent and generally attempting to rob him beforehand of his fighting spirit.'

In their early conflict with the Celts, some Roman commanders would accept the Celtic form of resolving the battle. But the custom was frowned upon by the Roman senate. Titus Manlius Imperiosus Torquatus (who had received his title Torquatus for taking the hero's torque from the body of a Celt he had slain in single combat) decreed in 340 BC that henceforth no Roman should enter into single combat with a Celt to settle military disputes. One might think that the Celtic method of two men, leaders of the armies, settling the outcome of a military conflict by this means was a little more civilized than the Roman method of total warfare and devastation by large armies.

Yet Celtic society did produce a warrior class, as well as bands of professional soldiers who sold their expertise to whomever would hire their services. Celtic warriors were recruited by Syracuse, Sparta, Carthage, Macedonia, Bythinia, Syria, Egypt and eventually Rome herself. They achieved a reputation for bravery among the peoples of the ancient world, although Aristotle (384–322 BC) wrote somewhat grudgingly:

19

It is not bravery to withstand fearful things through ignorance – for example if through madness one were to withstand the onset of thunderbolts – and again, even if one understands how great the danger is, it is not bravery to withstand it through high-spiritedness as when the Celts take up arms to attack the waves; and in general all the courage of barbarians is compounded with high-spiritedness.

High-spiritedness or not, even Aristotle acknowledged the bravery of Celtic warriors in single-handed combat or acting as a unit in battle. Some of the bands of warriors, such as the Gaesatae (or spearmen) who took part in several Celtic wars and were mistakenly thought to be a tribe by Roman writers, fought naked because of the religious ritual implications. Caesar records that some of the British warriors stained their body with a blue dye to give them a more fearsome appearance in battle. Diodorus Siculus gives a vivid description of the Celts as an army:

Their armour includes man-sized shields decorated in individual fashion. Some of these have projecting bronze animals of fine workmanship which serve for defence as well as decoration. On their heads they wear bronze helmets which possess large projecting figures lending the appearance of enormous stature to the wearer. In some cases horns form one piece with the helmet, while in other cases it is relief figures of the foreparts of birds or quadrupeds.

Their trumpets are again of a peculiar barbaric kind; they blow into them and produce a harsh sound which suits the tumults of war. Some have iron breastplates of chain mail, while others fight naked, and for them the breastplate given by nature suffices. Instead of the short sword they carry long swords held by iron or bronze chains and hanging along their right side. Some wear gold-plated or silver-plated belts round their tunics. The spears which they brandish in battle, and which they call *lanciae*, have iron heads a cubit or more in length and a little less than two palms in breadth; for their swords are as long as the javelins of other people, and their javelins have points longer than swords.

The Romans found the Celtic custom of taking the heads of their slain enemies as trophies somewhat distasteful, but it had a profound religious significance. To the Celts, the soul was contained in the head and not the heart. Diodorus observes:

> They cut off the heads of enemies slain in battle and attach them to the necks of their horses. The bloodstained spoils they hand over to their attendants to carry off as booty, while striking up a paean and singing a song of victory; and they nail up these fruits upon their houses, just as those who lay low wild animals in certain kinds of hunting.
>
> They embalm in cedar oil the heads of the most distinguished enemies, and preserve them carefully in a chest, and display them with pride to strangers, saying that for this head one of their ancestors, or his father or the man himself, refused the offer of a large sum of money. They say that some of them boast that they refused the weight of the head in gold; thus displaying what is only a barbarous kind of magnanimity, for it is not a sign of nobility to refrain from selling the proofs of one's valour.

Diodorus adds: 'It is rather true that it is bestial to continue one's hostility against a slain fellow man.' The Celts, in their turn, regarded as no less barbaric the Roman custom of either slaughtering prisoners wholesale or selling them into slavery rather than ransoming them as hostages back to their own people in accordance with Celtic custom.

What made the Celtic tribes leave their original homelands and spread across Europe? At the start of the first millennium BC the peoples of Europe were in a great state of flux and would remain so until the middle of the first millennium AD. There occurred great movements of peoples across Europe, settling for a while, establishing homelands and then abruptly moving on. Perhaps a drought, several crop failures in consecutive years, would force farming communities to search for new lands and conditions; or perhaps the people would be forced to move on as more aggressive newcomers invaded their lands – this was the cause of the migrations of the Helvetii and Boii in the first century BC.

Even in the Mediterranean world the urge for movement and expansion was dominant. With the collapse of the Hittite empire at the end of the second millennium BC, there was a considerable movement of peoples through the eastern Mediterranean. Then the Phoenicians, from biblical Canaan, began to spread throughout the Mediterranean, settling colonies as far west as Gades (Cadiz) and also in North Africa at Utica and Carthage. The Greeks began a massive expansion in the eighth century BC, establishing colonies which dominated southern Italy and settlements in North Africa, in Spain and – one of their most famous colonies – Massilia (Marseilles). In the fifth century BC, the Phoenician colony of Carthage had become strong enough to develop her own empire. In the next century Macedonia expanded into a major empire in the east under Alexander the Great. Then came the rise of Rome, her conflict with Carthage and victory, which left the way clear for Roman expansion throughout the Mediterranean and beyond. So the expansion of the Celts was merely one of several major movements in the ancient world.

Unfortunately, as we have seen, we do not know anything about the reasons for the Celtic expansion before its collision with the Mediterranean. Latin writers, particularly Livy, record a tradition that the expansions began because the original Celtic homelands had become overpopulated. The Celtic farming communities were looking for new fertile lands to cultivate and settle. This seems an acceptable theory. The Celts, once established in the new territory, did not set up trading colonies like the Phoenicians and Greeks, nor did they impose a military overlordship on the people they conquered, as did the Romans. They simply moved into the new lands, setting up pastoral and agricultural communities, defending them with tribal armies raised from the people. So it is likely that the search for 'living space' was the prime cause of the spread of the 'Celtic empire'.

[2]

The Celts in Italy

T H E Celts were well established in the Po Valley of northern Italy before the beginning of the fourth century BC. If we are to believe Livy, they arrived in the time of Lucius Tarquinius Superbus, who ruled Rome from 534 to 508 BC. Yet some scholars, such as Alexandre Bertrand (in *Archéologie celtique et gauloise*, Paris, 1876), have placed their descent into the Italic peninsula as early as 1000 BC. The earliest clearly identifiable archaeological evidence is an eighth-century BC boundary marker found in 1827 at Zignano, incised with Etruscan characters and depicting a Celtic warrior. The theory that the Celts were in the Po Valley long before the arrival of the group recorded by Livy in the late sixth century BC is not actually contradicted by Livy. The Roman historian states: 'They crossed the Alps by the country of the Taurini and the valley of Dara Baltea, defeated the Etruscans near Ticino, and, hearing that the place in which they halted was called the Plain of Insubres, that is by the very same name as a sub-tribe of the Aedui, regarded this as an omen, which they followed and founded a city there.' If this is true, then the Insubres must already have been settled in the Po Valley before the coming of those tribes mentioned by Livy, which were a confederation of the Bituriges, Arverni, Senones, Aedui, Ambarri, Carnutes and Aulerci. And this would accord with archaeological evidence.

Livy places the homeland of the Celts at this time exactly where it was in his own day – that is, in Gaul proper. He says that the Celts were ruled by a king called Ambicatos.

Gaul was so fertile and populous that the immense multitude threatened to be hard to rule. So the King, being old and wishing to relieve his kingdom of its excess population, declared that he would

23

send his sister's sons, Bellovesos and Sigovesos, who were energetic youths, to whatever country the gods should indicate by omens, and they could take as many men as they wished, so that no people should be able to resist their advance. The omens assigned the Hercynian Forests [central Germany] to Sigovesos, and to the more fortunate Bellovesos, the road to Italy.

Livy was undoubtedly recording a native Celtic tradition which had been transmitted orally until committed to written record in the late first century BC. Hubert accepts that Livy's source was the Celtic writer Cornelius Nepos (c.100−c.25 BC), a native of Cisalpine Gaul. Another source may well have been the Celtic historian Trogus Pompeius, writing in Latin about this time, who compared the Celtic migration into northern Italy to the Roman *ver sacrum* (sacred spring) when, in emergencies, overpopulated communities expelled their members aged twenty years, to go where they pleased and found new communities. Cornelius Nepos says that his Celtic ancestors had been established in the Po Valley long before the capture of Veii (396 BC).

The tradition which Livy records is obviously that accepted by the Celts of Cisalpine Gaul at the time when he was writing. The names he records are certainly Celtic ones. Ambicatos is he who gives battle all round while Sigovesos is he who can conquer. As to Bellovesos, who brought his people across the Alps to settle in the Po Valley, his name means he who can kill. Livy suggests that the Celts crossed the Alps in several bands, all under the general direction of Bellovesos, who went first with the Insubres. Then came a chieftain named Elitovios and his tribe, the Cenomani. Groups called the Libii and Salluvi came next, followed by the Boii and Lingones, who came together through what is now St Gothard's Pass. Finally, the Senones arrived.

Archaeology has identified Celtic cemeteries from the fifth and fourth centuries to the south of the River Po, the oldest being near Bologna. Curiously enough, the oldest-identified Celtic cemetery north of the Po river is only dated to the third century BC. The evidence is that the Celts displaced the original occupants of the Po Valley but there is no indication, either archaeologically or in written record, whether the original occupants were driven out or whether intermarriage occurred. Indeed, were these pre-Bellovesos inhabitants the descendants of an earlier Celtic migration, as suggested by archaeology and tradition? One thing is certain, that when

Bellovesos arrived, the Celts came into immediate conflict with the Etruscans, for the Etruscan empire had exerted control over the Po Valley.

The Etruscans, called Tyrrhenians by the Greeks, came into being as a powerful culture about 700 BC. They were comprised of a loose confederation of city states which were at the height of their power from *c*.620 to 500 BC, controlling an empire from the Po Valley in the north to Campania in the south. When Rome began its rise, Etruria was its main rival. About twenty-five years before the descent of Bellovesos and his Celts into the Po Valley, the Etruscans had taken control of the valley and had established several colonies there. About 474 BC the Celts defeated the Etruscan armies near Ticino. It was, perhaps, in the very same year that Rome destroyed Etruscan naval supremacy in a sea battle off Cumae. Rome had also won a major land battle at Arica, in the Alban Hills, against Etruria, and Etruscan fortunes were clearly on the wane.

Bellovesos and his successors succeeded in driving the Etruscans into the Euganean Hills, overlooking Verona. The Cenomani advanced south on this side of the Italian peninsula. According to Marcus Junianus Justinus, the Roman historian of the second or third century AD, who wrote an abridgement of the history by the Celt Trogus Pompeius, the Cenomani founded the city of Trento (Trent and Tridentum). The name, which also survives in Britain, was applied to a river which was liable to flood. North of Trento is Caverno, which is another survival of a Celtic place-name from the word Cauaros, hero, cognate with the Old Irish *caur*, a giant.

The Celts began to establish thriving agricultural settlements in the fertile Po Valley and the foundation of many cities and towns is ascribed to them, such as Milan, Brescia, Bergamo, Como, Vincenza, Turin, Modena, Lodi and, far south near Ancona, Senigallia. Bologna, which may have already been in existence, was given the Celtic name of Bononia. While some of the older place-names were doubtless kept by the Celts, Celtic names were given to places such as Reno, Benacus, Lake Garda, Treviso and Trebbia. The Celts formed their new country north-east of the Apennines and as far south, according to Livy, as the valley of Chienti beyond Ancona on the eastern coast. This was the land of the Senones, and Celtic tombs have been found as far south in this area as the region of Filottrano and Osimo. Senigallia, just north of Ancona, means the place of the Senones Gauls. Eventually, the

Romans would come to designate the area Cisalpine Gaul, the land of the Gauls south of the Alps.

The Celts of Cisalpine Gaul left behind them funerary inscriptions, graffiti on pottery and manufacturers' marks in surprisingly large numbers, showing that the Celts were not illiterate, as is the popular misconception. We have already discussed their religious prohibition against written records in their own language, but inscriptions from Briona and Brescia record many Celtic names, indicating their literacy. One of the most southerly funerary inscriptions honouring a Celt was found in the valley of the Tiber, at Todi, south of Perugia. This is in Celtic and Latin in commemoration of Ategnatos, son of Druteos. It is unlikely that a Celtic settlement occurred this far south and it may simply be a relic of a Celtic expedition into the area. It could also be the result of an individual migration. By why is it bilingual? Perhaps it is a sign that the Celts and Latins did not ignore one another except in times of savage warfare, as Livy suggests.

The Celts shared the Italic peninsula with several aggressive neighbours to the south. The Etruscans, as we have seen, had been dominant but their power was fading in the fifth century BC. In the region of the southern Apennines were the Samnites, the descendants of the Sabines, whose power had been broken by Rome in the mid-fifth century BC. There was Rome herself, whose year of foundation – *annus urbis conditae* – is given as 753 BC. After a period of kings, the city of Rome had constituted herself a republic in 510 BC, the King being replaced by two magistrates (consuls) elected annually. In times of national crisis, their powers might be temporarily superseded by the appointment of a 'dictator'. During the fifth century BC, Rome was replacing Etruria as the main power on the peninsula. In the south of the Italic peninsula, Greek colonies had been established which were collectively known as Magna Graecia. They were prosperous city states whose independence was to be eroded by Rome in the fourth century BC and ended entirely with Roman victory during the war against Pyrrhus of Epiros.

In 405 BC Rome laid siege to the Etruscan stronghold of Veii, twelve miles north of Rome. After ten years of stalemate, the Roman General Marcus Furius Camillus took charge of the siege and conquered the city by assault in 396 BC. This victory enhanced Rome's prestige and made her the undisputed master of Etruria. Some years later, according to Livy, Arruns of Clusium (Chiusi) became involved in a quarrel with another Etruscan aristocrat called Lucomo. Lucomo had apparently seduced Arruns' wife. Arruns decided to hire some Celtic warriors from north of the Apennines to help him pursue this quarrel. About 390 BC, a Celtic army arrived outside Clusium, led by a chieftain called Brennos. Was Brennos a proper name, or was it merely a title meaning king? The word for king in modern Welsh is still *brenin*. It would seem that Clusium appeared a more attractive proposition for sacking and pillaging than Lucomo's city.

Now Clusium was only three days' march north of Rome, eighty-five miles, and so the city fathers sent to Rome, the new power in the land, to ask for help. Rome sent three envoys, brothers of the noble house of the Fabii, to negotiate with the Celts. Diodorus Siculus says that the Fabii were not ambassadors at all but spies who were to assess the strength of the Celts. Certainly the Fabii brothers, on arriving at Clusium, did not act as negotiators but began to organize the people of the city to attack the Celts. Ambustus Fabius, one of the three, slew one of the Celtic chieftains. Upon this breach of 'international law', says Livy, the Celts demanded the surrender of the Romans. When it was not forthcoming, the Celts began their attack on the city.

Rome now despatched an army some 40,000 strong under the command of one of their consuls, A. Quintus Sulpicius. On hearing that the Romans were marching against them, the Celts, led by Brennos, broke off their attack on Clusium and moved swiftly south to meet them. On 18 July 390 BC (other writers put the date later at 387/386 BC) Brennos and his Celtic army met the Romans for the first time on the banks of the River Allia, about ten to twelve miles north of Rome. The Celts smashed their way through the army of Sulpicius, and the Roman soldiers were seized with panic. Thousands rushed into the river in an attempt to save themselves from the northern warriors by swimming to the opposite bank, and many met their deaths in the water. Sulpicius, with a small body of men, managed to flee back to the safety of Rome. But how safe was Rome?

The city was in total panic. Citizens poured out through the gates, carrying with them their most precious and easily transportable possessions. The sacred objects of the temples were secretly buried, while the vestal virgins carried off the Palladium, the image of the Greek goddess Pallas Athena, said to have been brought to Rome by the Trojan Aeneas after the fall of Troy, as well as the eternal flame. They are said to have escaped in a peasant's wagon along the Janiculus and to have taken refuge in the Etruscan town of Caere.

For long afterwards 18 July was marked as a black day in the Roman calendar. Alliaensis, as it was known, was held to be un-propitious for any public undertaking.

Three days after the battle, Brennos and his victorious Celtic army arrived outside the city of Rome. His scouts reported that Rome stood destitute of defenders. He hesitated before entering the city, fearing some trick which could lead to ambush. But there was no army facing him in the main part of the city. Only the Capitoline Hill, which was the most sacred part of Rome, was barricaded and defended. The rest of the city was open. The Celts advanced along the thoroughfares as far as the Forum, the political, religious and commercial centre of Rome between the Palatine Hill and the Capitoline Hill. It had evolved from the market-place of the city, drained in the sixth century to make way for the building of temples and monuments of civic importance. Here, according to Livy, the Celts found a number of venerable, grey-bearded senators sitting in their robes of office. The Romans believed that by sacrificing their lives to the gods at the hour of defeat, disorder and confusion could be wrought among their enemies; so the aged senators of Rome were determined not to survive the destruction of their city. Livy says that the Celts were amazed at the sight of the old senators, calmly sitting in the Forum, like statues, awaiting death. One Celtic warrior plucked at the beard of a senator called Papyrius, probably to ensure that he was not carved out of marble. The senator immediately struck the Celt a blow on the head. The Celt retaliated and a general massacre of the senators took place.

Brennos turned his attention to the Capitoline Hill. It was one of the seven hills on which Rome was built and had two peaks, the south-west summit being the Capitol, the northern one being known as the Citadel. From earliest times the Capitoline Hill had been used as a religious centre rather than for habitation. On the south-western summit was the temple of Jupiter, and the most sacred part of the city. Its construction had been begun by King Tarquin, but it had not been dedicated until the first year of the republic, 510 BC. At the south-western corner of the Capitol was the Tarpeian Rock, from which criminals sentenced to death were hurled. The rock is said to have been named after Tarpeia, the daughter of the commander of the guard, who offered to betray her father and the garrison to the Sabines in return for gold. According to the historian Plutarch (AD c.26 – c.120), Symlos, whose work has not survived, said that it was to the Celts that

Tarpeia offered to betray the garrison by showing the attackers a secret way up the Capitoline.

The commander of the Romans defending the Capitoline was Marcus Manlius. After a few initial sorties, the Celts realized that the Romans were in a good defensive position which was centred in the temple of Jupiter. While Brennos was feeling out the Roman defences here, other groups of Celts sacked the rest of the city and set it afire. It is said that only a few buildings on the Palatine as well as the Capitoline escaped the conflagration. During this time, a young officer named Pontius Cominius, sent from the Roman garrison at Veii, managed to sneak through the Celtic lines, swim the Tiber and scale the Capitoline by a secret route. He reported to Manlius that the Roman forces at Veii would be coming to his rescue as soon as they found Marcus Furius Camillus, the Roman General who had completed the victory over the Etruscans at Veii. Not long after his victory, the Roman senate had accused Camillus of appropriating booty for his personal use and he had been sent into exile. The Romans now realized that their only hope of repulsing the Celts lay in recalling their general. He was to be offered the position of dictator of Rome.

Cominius was sent back to Veii with the plea for the Roman relief force to come as quickly as possible. According to Livy, Cominius' secret route to the top of the Capitoline Hill had been observed by the Celts. Brennos led his men up in another attempt to take it by storm. The tradition goes that Manlius was awakened by the cackling of the sacred geese in the temple, who gave warning of the Celtic attack, the guard dogs having failed to do so. He summoned his men and they were able to repel Brennos and his men once more. Thereafter the feeding of the sacred geese became the responsibility of the Roman state. In an annual commemoration geese were carried on litters with purple and gold cushions, while dogs were crucified on stakes of elder, a ritual which still existed in Christian times.

Manlius was afterwards accorded the title of Capitolinus, in honour of his defence, but he suffered an unhappy end. A Roman aristocrat, he sided with the poor of Rome, who were forced to pay the costs of the Celtic withdrawal. Manlius, in the political crisis which followed, was accused of trying to overthrow the government and to set himself up as ruler. For this he was cast to his death from the Tarpeian Rock.

In spite of the promise made by Pontius Cominius, that the Capitoline garrison would soon be relieved, the siege dragged on for six months. The Roman garrison were suffering from lack of supplies. Camillus, who had accepted sole command of the Roman forces, did not appear to have sufficient strength to launch an attack on the Celtic army now in and around Rome. He contented himself with ambushes and attacks on Brennos' foraging parties. From the viewpoint of those on the Capitoline, the position was desperate. Manlius decided to open negotiations with Brennos. An agreement was reached that the Celts would withdraw from Rome upon the payment of a sum of 1,000 pounds (weight) in gold. Livy records an incident that when the ransom was being weighed in the Forum, one of the Romans complained that the Celts were using false weights. Brennos is said to have thrown his sword on to the balance and commented: 'Vae victis!' (Woe to the conquered!). In other words, it is the conqueror who states the terms.

It is now that there is a clash of traditions. According to Livy, Camillus and a Roman army suddenly materialized on the spot, declared the agreement null and void and drove the Celts out of the city. He says that on the following day both armies met outside the city and Camillus slew Brennos. But Livy, whose history is fiercely patriotic, is not always to be trusted. Fortunately, Polybius and Diodorus have traces of older sources in their accounts which do not seem to be so falsified. According to Polybius, 'the Celts withdrew unmolested with their booty, having voluntarily and on their own terms restored the city to the Romans.' Diodorus agrees that Brennos and his Celts settled for the ransom and withdrew.

Marcus Furius Camillus, says Livy, became 'the saviour of his country and second founder of Rome', for he steered the city through the civil crisis which followed the Celtic conquest. He put down a revolution of the people, led by Manlius, and reasserted the power of the patricians. But this internal civil strife was to last until 367 BC. During this time, indeed for the next fifty years, the Celts continued to harass Rome. In the year in which the civil strife in Rome ended, the Celts were again at the gates of the city. Yet again, in 361/360 BC, a Celtic army entered the Tiber Valley and came close to Rome. Polybius says that 'on this occasion the Romans did not dare to meet them in battle because the invasion took them by surprise, and they had no time to organize resistance and bring together the forces of their allies.' In 360 BC the Celts descended into Campania and encountered a Roman force. Titus Manlius Imperiosus Torquatus commanded this force and Manlius accepted the challenge of the Celtic chieftain to settle the conflict by single-handed combat. Manlius killed the chieftain and so earned his cognomen Torquatus by taking from the neck of the slain Celt his hero's torc. In 340 BC, when Manlius had become one of the two consuls of Rome, he forbade single combat with enemy chieftains, presumably because Roman commanders were not enjoying a successful record in such encounters.

In 349 BC the Celts were ranging as far south as Apulia. According to Livy, during a campaign against the Celts in 345 BC Marcus Valerius Corvus fought in a single-handed combat against a Celtic chieftain. A crow flew down and pecked the Celt's face and hid the Roman with its wings. This extraordinary episode has been remarked upon by Henri Hubert, who points out that it is entirely unlike anything in Latin tradition but is remarkably similar to an episode in the Irish epic *Táin Bó Chuailgne*, in which the goddess of death and battles, the Mórrígú, attacks Cúchulainn, who has scorned her love, in the form of a crow. The crow, or raven, was the Celtic symbol of the gods and goddesses of death and battle. Valerius Corvus bears, as his cognomen, the Latin designation, crow. Camille Jullian has suggested that the entire history of Livy, which is fabulous and epic, was probably made up of Celtic traditions which Livy knew well, for he was born in Patavium (Padua) in Cisalpine Gaul and did not go to Rome until he was an adult.

It was during this campaign that Rome seems to have recovered from its fear of meeting the Celts in open battle. Polybius says that they 'marched out confidently to meet them, for they were eager to engage and fight a decisive battle'. Presumably, the Romans were also eager to expiate the shame of their previous defeats. It seems, however, that the Celts did not give them that satisfaction and withdrew under cover of darkness without a major battle. 'After this alarm,' says Polybius, 'they kept quiet for thirteen years and then, as they saw that the power of Rome was growing fast, they concluded a formal treaty with them [the Romans] and faithfully observed its terms for thirty years.'

At the start of the third century BC there was another wave of migration from the Celtic tribes living north of the Alps. The new tribes settled in the Po Valley without any conflict. However, about the same time the Etruscans decided to make an attempt to regain their independence from Rome. They formed an alliance with the Celts and a combined army of Celts and Etruscans moved south and plundered

Roman territory. Four years later, in 295 BC, the Celts formed another anti-Roman alliance, this time with the Samnites. The continued growth of Roman power on the Italic peninsula was a considerable source of worry to the other peoples, particularly the Samnites. A series of three wars from 343 to 290 BC brought Roman overlordship to the Samnites. The second of these wars lasted from 321 to 305 BC and ended at Bovianum, where the Samnites sued for peace. In 298 BC Samnium made a last effort to resist Rome and formed alliances with the Celts, the Etruscans and the Lucanians to form a hostile ring around Rome.

The war started auspiciously for the anti-Roman alliances. Two Roman legions under Lucius Scipio were sent to Camerinum, ninety miles north-east of Rome, to hold a pass in the Apennines through which the Celts were expected to advance. A combined army of Celts and Samnites, commanded by a Samnite general, Gellius Equatius, was already in position. The Roman army was badly defeated and one legion annihilated.

In 295 BC Quintus Fabius Maximus was given command of five legions and ordered to the Apennines to take the Samnite town of Sentium (Sassoferrato), about thirty-five miles from the Adriatic coast. Gellius Equatius and his combined Celto-Samnite army were waiting. The war-chariots of the Celts gave the anti-Roman alliance an initial advantage against Maximus' left wing. But on the right wing the Samnites were driven back, enabling Maximus to attack the Celts on the flank. After a savage struggle the centre of the alliance army collapsed. Rome had a complete victory. Gellius Equatius was killed along with 25,000 of his men, and a further 8,000 were captured.

Samnium now accepted Roman terms. Yet the Celts and Etruscans did not surrender. In 284 BC the Senones were besieging Arretium. A Roman army under Lucius Caecilius tried to raise the siege but the Celts defeated his army and Caecilius was killed. The survivors elected Manlius Curius to command them and delegates were sent to negotiate a peace treaty. The Celts were told to beware of the Roman ambassadors. Was this in recollection of the way the Fabii had behaved at Clusium? They slew the ambassadors. Enraged, the Roman survivors under Curius launched an attack so fiercely that the Celts were driven off. In retribution for this, the Romans made a point of invading the territory of the Senones, north of Ancona, and establishing a fortified colony at Senones Gallia (the land of the Senones Celts), present-day Senigallia.

In 283 BC, the year following this event, the combined armies of the Celts and Etruscans were finally defeated. A Roman army commanded by Publius Cornelius Dolabella encountered the Etruscans and Celts near the Vadimonian Lake on the Tiber river, some forty-five miles north of Rome. The Etruscan and Celtic army was in the process of crossing the river and Dolabella fell on them, inflicting severe losses.

For the first time, Rome was confident of her northern boundaries. She now turned her greedy eyes towards the Greek city states of southern Italy – Magna Graeca. The Greeks decided to combine against Roman territorial expansion and they called on Pyrrhus, King of Epiros and former King of Macedonia, to come to their aid. Pyrrhus landed on the coast of Lucania with 25,000 men and twenty elephants. Rome sent P. Laverius Lavinus with an army of 35,000 to meet the Greek King near Heraclea. There Pyrrhus routed the Romans.

Pyrrhus, looking for allies against Rome, marched north to Apulia, where he was joined by Celts. At Asculum (Ascoli Satriano) Pyrrhus encountered a Roman army of equal force commanded by Sulpicius Saverrio. Both sides fought furiously and then the Romans began to fall back. Roman losses were 6,000 compared with 3,500 men of Pyrrhus' army. Nevertheless, Pyrrhus is said to have commented, 'Another such victory and we are lost' – hence the phrase, pyrrhic victory.

Pyrrhus suddenly abandoned his campaign on the Italian peninsula and sailed to the aid of the Greek city states in Sicily. After four years' campaigning, he returned to Italy and raised an army of Samnites, Lucanians, Bruttians, Greeks and Celts. At the Samnium town of Beneventum, 130 miles south-east of Rome, they encountered the Roman army of Manlius Curius Dentatus. The Roman victory here ended Pyrrhus' attempt to curb the power of Rome. He returned to Greece leaving the Greek city states of southern Italy at the mercy of Rome. By 270 BC Rome had completed her conquest of the south. The republic now stood master of all Italy as far north as where the Rubicon (Fiumicino) emptied into the Adriatic. It was the Rubicon which marked the boundary between Italy and Cisalpine Gaul until 42 BC.

Polybius tells us that there was a period of peace between Rome and the Celts of the Po Valley for the next forty-five years.

As time went on, and those who had actually witnessed these terrible battles passed away, they were replaced by a younger generation, men who were filled with an unreflecting desire to fight and who were completely without experience of suffering or of national peril, and their impulse, not surprisingly, was to destroy the equilibrium which had been imposed by the treaty. They interpreted the slightest action of the Romans as a provocation. . . .

The provocation was that Rome was continuing to colonize the lands of the Senones and was evicting these Celts. Refugees from the country of the Senones were arriving among the Boii and the Insubres to the north. Once more, the territorial expansion of the 'old enemy', Rome, was worrying the Celts of the Po Valley. In 243 BC, the chieftains Atis of the Boii and Galatos of the Insubres, having discussed the situation, sent north of the Alps to their fellow Celtic tribes for aid. Polybius and Appian of Alexandria (AD c.160) both record that bands of warriors arrived from the north and met the Po Valley Celts at Ariminum (Rimini). The Celts of Cisalpine Gaul became suspicious about the objectives of their northern kinsmen. Even the intentions of Atis and Galatos were questioned. There was an uprising in which Atis and Galatos were killed and the Transalpine Celts were driven out of the Po Valley. Meanwhile, Rome had despatched a legion to the northern border but it was able to return having witnessed the result of the inter-Celtic warfare.

In 237 BC, when Marcus Aemilius Lepidus was one of the two Roman consuls, the Roman senate decided to take over the Celtic territory of Picenum and colonize it. Polybius says: 'This policy of colonization was a demagogic measure introduced by Gaius Flaminius, which may be said to have marked the first step in the demoralization of the Roman people, as well as precipitating the war with the Celts which followed.' Gaius Flaminius' scheme was designed to give the Roman proletariat a stake in the land, a move strongly opposed by the patrician senators, who had profited from the occupation of land acquired by conquest in the past. Gaius Flaminius eventually carried his measure as a tribune in the popular assembly against the wishes of the patrician party. Polybius' assertion that it demoralized the Roman people is a comment on his attitude towards this new phase of democratic assertiveness in Roman life.

Hearing of the plan to dispossess part of their people of their lands, the Celts of the Po Valley sent envoys to their fellow Celts north of the Alps. Polybius says they contacted a tribe who dwelt near the River Rhône called the Gaesatae, 'because they serve as mercenaries'. Indeed, the Gaesatae was not a tribal name at all but the name given to a band of professional warriors who sold their services. They could be likened to the Fianna of the ancient Irish tradition. The name drived from the Celtic word for spear, *gae* (still found in modern Irish and in Welsh, as *gwayw*). Thus they were called 'spearmen'. So the Celts of the Po Valley now recruited in their defence a professional band of warriors. It is the first time we hear of 'professionals' defending the Celts rather than the tribal armies.

In 225 BC the Celtic army had gathered in the Po Valley commanded by two chieftains – Concolitanos and Aneroestos. According to Polybius, still regarding the Gaesatae as a tribe:

> The Gaesatae, then, having mobilized a strong and lavishly equipped army, crossed the Alps, and in the eighth year [225 BC] after the distribution of the lands of Picenum, they descended into the valley of the Po. The Insubres and the Boii stood loyally by the pledge they had given their allies, but a Roman delegation succeeded in persuading the Veneti and the Cenomani to their side; and so the Celtic chiefs were obliged to detach part of their forces to guard their territory against an attack by these tribes.

So already the Romans had seen the wisdom of *divide et impera*, divide and rule, by splitting the Celts of the Po Valley against each other. One of the Roman consuls, Lucius Aemilius Paullus, was despatched to Ariminium with an army. An unnamed praetor, combining the office of a chief magistrate and military commander, was sent to Etruria. The second Consul, Gaius Atilius Regulus, son of a hero of Rome's first war against Carthage, was occupied in Sardinia. Messages were sent to advise him to return with his army.

Polybius remarks that the Romans, having provoked the Celts into war, reacted with panic:

> Meanwhile in Rome itself the people were filled with dread; the danger that threatened them was, they believed, both great and imminent, and these feelings were natural enough, since the age-old terror inspired by the Celts had never been altogether dispelled [a reference to the sack of Rome by Brennos], their thoughts always

returning to this possibility, and the authorities were continuously occupied with calling up and enrolling the legions, and summoning those of their allies who were liable for service to hold themselves ready. All Roman subjects in general were required to provide lists of men of military age, since the authorities were anxious to know the total strength that was available to them, and meanwhile stocks of corn, of missiles and of other warlike stores had been collected on a scale which exceeded any such preparations within living memory.

Polybius estimates that the Celtic army of Concolitanos and Anero-estos numbered 50,000 infantry and 20,000 cavalry. Rome had recruited in her defence an astonishing 700,000 infantry and 23,000 cavalry. Polybius is surely unique among historians in not exaggerating the numbers of the enemy to enhance the standing of the Romans.

The Celts made the first move by crossing out of the Po Valley and over the Apennines in a descent on Etruria. There was little opposition until they reached Clusium, the city where Brennos had first encountered the Romans. It was here that the Roman Praetor and his army had taken up positions. According to Polybius:

> At sunset the two armies were almost in contact, and they encamped for the night with only a short distance separating them. When it was dark, the Celts lit their camp fires. They left their cavalry there with orders that they should wait for daybreak, and then as soon as they became visible to the enemy they were to follow the route which the infantry had taken. In the meantime, the Celts withdrew their main body under cover of darkness towards a town named Faesulae [Fiesoli] and took up their positions. Their plan was to wait for the cavalry, and at the same time to disconcert any attack by the enemy with an unforeseen situation.

As Fiesoli is eighty miles from Chiusi (Clusium), Polybius was clearly saying that the Celts did not actually reach the town but only marched 'towards it' before they encamped. They were still, therefore, within the vicinity of Clusium. Here we have evidence of just how professional the Celtic commanders were. We have none of the massed tribal armies of the Celts, waiting until daybreak and then throwing themselves on their enemies. Here are signs of experience and well-thought-out strategy. It was a strategy which certainly fooled the Romans. Polybius says:

When the Romans sighted the cavalry at daybreak and saw them unsupported, they concluded that the main body of the Celts had fled, and so pursued the cavalry along the line of the enemy's supposed retreat. Then, as the Romans approached, the main body of the Celts sprang forward from their positions and charged them. A fierce battle followed which was stubbornly contested on both sides.

Rome lost 6,000 men in this battle and the rest fled. A large number reached a hill where they established a strong defensive position. Part of the Celtic army, pursuing them, tried to take it but, exhausted by their night march, decided to rest for the following day and attempt it on the next morning.

The Roman Consul, Lucius Aemilius Paullus, having received word at Ariminium that the Celts had crossed the Apennines to the west rather than turning east to meet his army, had been hurrying across country. The Celtic commanders now heard from their scouts that Paullus' army was not far away.

A council of war was held among the Celtic chieftains. Aneroestos felt that the army should not give battle again so soon. Paullus' army was only one day's march away. He argued that as soon as the warriors had rested, they should make a strategic withdrawal back into the Po Valley. The other chieftains agreed. The Celts began to move south-west towards the Etrurian coast. Paullus arrived in time to rescue the survivors of the Praetor's army and unite them with his force. He followed the Celts at a safe distance, not risking a pitched battle for fear that his army might be decimated, as the Praetor's army had been, which would leave Rome wide open without any means of defence.

However, Rome's second Consul, Gaius Atilius Regulus, had already crossed from Sardinia with his legions, landing at Pisae (Pisa), and was marching south to Rome. Unbeknown to them, his army was marching directly towards the Celts, who were now moving north. The Celts were caught between two Roman armies of tremendous strength.

Regulus was the first to appreciate the position, having caught some forward scouts of the Celtic army and interrogated them. His army was stationed across the main highway near Cape Telamon and he immediately deployed his men so that they would be on the high ground which dominated the road along which the Celts had to pass. The Celtic commanders were still unaware of the arrival of Regulus and when they encountered the forward positions of the Roman army they thought that Paullus had simply outflanked them. But they soon discovered that they now had two Roman armies to face, both armies of superior strength to their own.

Polybius tells us that the Celtic commanders placed the Gaesatae, backed by the Insubres, against Paullus while the Boii and the Taurisci (from Turin) faced the army of Regulus. We now have an interesting piece of cultural misinterpretation by Polybius:

> The Insubres and the Boii wore their trousers and light cloaks, but the Gaesatae had been moved by their thirst for glory and their defiant spirit to throw away these garments, and so they took up their positions in front of the whole army naked and wearing nothing but their arms. They believed that they would be better equipped for action in this state . . .

This was not the case. The Gaesatae, the professional band of warriors, fought naked for religious reasons, believing in the oneness of nature and the communion of all things. To fight naked was to increase their *karma*, their unity with nature and harmony with living things. To the Romans, however, the nakedness of the Celtic warriors bore no religious symbolism: 'the movements of the naked warriors in the front ranks made a terrifying spectacle. They were all men of splendid physique and in the prime of life, and those in the leading companies were richly adorned with gold necklaces and bracelets. The mere sight of them was enough to arouse fear among the Romans.' The gold necklaces Polybius refers to were of course the gold heroes' torques which denoted a warrior.

The battle opened. Once more Polybius impresses upon his readers how the Romans 'were terrified by the fine order of the Celtic army and the dreadful din – for there were innumerable horn-blowers and trumpeters and, as the whole army were shouting their war cries at the same time, there was such a tumult as if not only the soldiers but all the country around had got a voice and caught up the cry.' In the opening moments of the battle the Consul Atilius Regulus was killed. He was decapitated in Celtic fashion and his head brought to one of the Celtic chieftains. But the Romans stood firm and began to discharge their javelins. Polybius says that the shields used by the Celts in this battle, unlike subsequent battles, did not cover the whole body and the tall stature of the naked warriors made the missiles more likely to find a mark. The Gaesatae made a wild charge on the Roman lines. The Romans countered and many Celtic lives were thrown away. The Romans, having blocked the charge, moved forward, pressing the Gaesatae back. On the other front, the Boii and Taurisci met a fierce Roman charge but held their ground. Countless hand-to-hand encounters were taking place.

'The end came', writes Polybius, 'when the Celts were attacked by the Roman cavalry, who delivered a furious charge from the high ground on the flank; the Celtic cavalry turned and fled, and their infantry were cut down where they stood.' Concolitanos was captured and eventually taken to Rome for a triumph and execution. Aneroestos and a group of companions managed to escape capture and leave the battlefield but, again according to Polybius, he and his entire retinue took their own lives rather than fall into Roman hands. The figures provided by Polybius show that the battle of Telamon was a major Celtic defeat, with 40,000 Celtic warriors slain in battle and 10,000 taken prisoner.

Even then the surviving Roman Consul, Paullus, was thirsting for revenge. Having united the two Roman armies, he marched a section of them across the Apennines and into the country of the Boii. 'There he allowed his troops to take their fill of plunder,' says Polybius, attacking the rich farming settlements and townships of the Boii. He returned to Rome in the autumn of 225 BC bearing the standards and gold necklaces worn by the Celtic warriors, with other booty, to decorate the Capitol.

This was how the most formidable of the Celtic invasions, which had placed all the Italians and above all the Romans in mortal danger, was finally destroyed. The victory encouraged the Romans to hope that they could clear the Celts from the entire valley of the Po, and so in the following year [224 BC] they sent out both the consuls, Quintus Fulvius and Titus Manlius, with a strong well-equipped force. Their attack took the Boii by surprise and frightened them into making submission to Rome. But the rest of the campaign produced no practical results; this was partly owing to the onset of heavy rains, and partly to the outbreak of an epidemic in the army.

Thus from Polybius we see that the intention was to drive out the Celts of the Po Valley and colonize it from Rome.

In 223 BC the consuls Publius Furius and Gaius Flaminius led another invasion of the Celtic territory. This time they marched into the country of the Anamari, in the area of Placentia (Piacenza). The Romans agreed a treaty with the Anamari and then moved into the territory of the Insubres. Against the Insubres the Romans suffered heavy losses and were forced to withdraw. The Roman commanders then tried a different tactic by marching in a circular route, crossing the River Clusius, moving through the territory of the Cenomani and descending on the Insubres again. The Insubres retired to Milan, where they gathered an army of 50,000 men and brought from their temples certain gold standards which were to put strength into their people in their fight against the Romans. The Romans managed to persuade the Anamari and Cenomari to help them. In the ensuing battle the Romans were able to manoeuvre the Celts so that they were hemmed in by the Roman lines.

> The Romans closed with them and rendered them helpless by leaving them no room to raise their arms to slash; this is the stroke which is peculiar to the Celts, and the only one they can make, as their swords have no points. The Romans, on the other hand, made no attempt to slash and used only the thrust, kept their swords straight and relied on their sharp points, which were very effective.

The Romans gained another victory over the Insubres but withdrew to Rome having collected enough plunder to pay for the season's campaign.

Before the start of the 'campaigning season', in the spring of 222 BC, the Celtic tribes of the Po Valley sent a united delegation to Rome to ask for terms of peace. The new consuls, Marcus Claudius Marcellus and Gnaeus Cornelius, refused to discuss any such terms. Peace was not to be granted to the Celts of the Po Valley. Rome was intent on driving them from the valley or exterminating them. Hearing this, the Celts once more sent across the Alps to their northern kinsmen and raised a force of another 30,000 Gaesatae, professional warriors commanded by a chieftain called Viridomar, who called himself a 'son of the Rhine'.

Marcus Claudius Marcellus and Gnaeus Cornelius marched the Roman armies north and immediately made for the land of the Insubres once again. They laid siege to Acerrae, a Celtic township between the Po river and the Alps. The Celts, in an attempt to force the Romans to raise the siege, detached a part of their army and crossed to the south of the Po, entering the territory of the Anamari, one of the Celtic tribes who had shortsightedly entered an alliance with Rome. The Celtic army was led by Viridomar, who promptly laid siege to Clastidium (Casteggio), which was the chief town of the Anamari. When news of this action reached Marcus Claudius Marcellus he set off with a body of infantry and cavalry to relieve Clastidium. The ruse had worked and Viridomar turned his army to face the Romans in open battle.

The battle opened with a furious charge of the Roman cavalry. The Celts held their ground and fierce fighting began. Slowly the Romans began to encircle the Celtic positions. Here we find a surprising development. It appears that Viridomar offered a challenge, in the traditional Celtic fashion, to the Roman General, Marcus Claudius Marcellus, to settle the issue by single combat to the death. Surprisingly, the Roman General accepted. He succeeded in slaying Viridomar and the Celtic army crumbled before a renewed Roman charge. The battle of Clastidium became a major Roman victory, of equal significance to Telamon.

Clastidium also becomes important as the point at which the Germanic peoples, the ancestors of the English, French, Germans and so on, first emerge into recorded history. The Roman *Acta Triumphalia* says that Marcus Claudius Marcellus gained the *spolia opima*, spoils of honour, for slaying Viridomar and triumphing 'over the Insubrian Celts and the Germans'. Now the Germans at Clastidium were not there as invaders, nor were they fighting for their own lands. Indeed, they were fighting under a Celtic commander with a Celtic army. We are faced with the conclusion that the first appearance of the Germanic peoples in history, fighting for the Celts of the Po Valley against Rome, was either as hired troops or as forces levied on a subject territory. Professor Eoin Mac Neill regards the presence of the Germanic people at Clastidium as indicating that they, or some portion of them, were under Celtic political dominance.

Professor Mac Neill points out that this interpretation is supported by philological evidence and that a number of words of Celtic origin are found spread through the whole group of Germanic languages. A number of these words are connected with political organization and, says Mac Neill, this is indicative of Celtic political dominance at the time of their adoption into Germanic speech. For example, the German *reich*, meaning state, originally realm or royal dominion, is traced to the Celtic *rigion*. From the Celtic word *ambactus*, used by Caesar in the sense of client or dependant, indicating one of the retainers of a Celtic chieftain, but originally meaning one who is sent about or an envoy, comes the German word *amt*, meaning office, charge, employment. *Ambactus*, incidentally, provides the Romance languages (and English via Norman French) with the words embassy and ambassador. The Celtic word *dunon*, a fortified place, found in the *dun* place-names, made its way through the Germanic languages and arrived in English as the word town.

With the defeat at Clastidium the remnants of the Celtic army reached Mediolanum (Milan), which was the chief city of the Insubres. Acerrae fell to the Romans. Gnaeus Cornelius was in charge of besieging Mediolanum. The Celts made a spirited attempt at defence and launched a raid against his siege lines in which the Romans, taken by surprise, broke and many of them were killed. However, Gnaeus Cornelius organized a counter-attack and checked the Celtic gains. Mediolanum was taken by storm and the Insubres were forced to make unconditional surrender to Rome. Polybius records: 'So ended the war against the Celts. If we consider it in terms of the audacity and the desperate courage displayed by those taking part and of the number who fought and died in the battles, this conflict is unsurpassed by any other war in history . . .'

The Romans moved quickly to consolidate their victory. They established permanent garrisons at Placentia among the Boii and at Cremona and Milan among the Insubres. Colonists were encouraged to come from Rome, to Romanize areas and to settle on lands seized from the Celts. Another garrison was established at Mutina. Roman garrisons now controlled a conquered, sullen and resentful population. And so the seeds were sown for the Celts of the Po Valley to organize secretly and prepare themselves for yet another war against Rome – and this time, they realized, it would be a war for their very survival.

[3]

The Iberian Peninsula

ONE of the founding fathers of prehistoric archaeology in Spain, Louis Siret (*Questions de chronologie et d'ethnographie ibérique*, Paris, 1913) was the first scholar to assert that the Celts arrived in the Iberian peninsula during the Bronze Age and, indeed, that it was the Celts who introduced the working of bronze into the region. This wave of settlers were Goidelic-speakers. If we accept the Irish traditions it was from Spain that the Gaels (the Goidelic-speakers) invaded and colonized Ireland.

The story is recounted in the *Leabhar Gabhála*, The Book of Invasions, the earliest fragment of which survives in *Leabhar na Nuachonghbála*, known as the *Book of Leinster*, compiled about AD 1150 by Fionn Mac Gorman. The Irish tradition has it that a warrior named Golamh of Spain took service with a king of Scythia and married his daughter. Golamh became known under the Latin form of his name, Milesius, given in Irish as Míle Easpain (the Spanish soldier). After Milesius' wife, Seang, died, the Scythian King grew fearful of Milesius and plotted to kill him. Discovering the plot, Milesius fled to Egypt with his sons Donn and Airioch Feabhruadh and his followers and took service with the Pharaoh Nectanebus. He was successful in conducting a war for the Pharaoh against the Ethiopians. There were, in fact, two pharaohs of the Thirtieth Dynasty named Nectanebus but their dates are 380–363 BC and 360–343 BC – too late for the accepted date of the Goidelic Celtic colonization of Ireland and too early to associate the tradition with known Celtic service in the army of the Egyptian pharaohs. Irish traditions has it that Milesius married Scota, the daughter of the Pharaoh, and two sons Eber and Amairgen were born in Egypt. A third son, Ir, was born on the island of Irena near Thrace after Milesius and his followers left Egypt. A fourth son,

Colpa, was born on the island of Gotia. Milesius eventually returned to Spain. Here he learned of the death of Ith, given as his nephew, in Ireland – slain by Mac Cécht, Mac Cuill and Mac Gréine, the three sons of Ogma, the Irish god of eloquence and learning – and he decided to take revenge by conquering Ireland. But he did not reach Ireland, although his wife Scota did. She was killed fighting the Dé Danaan and was buried in Kerry. It was Milesius' sons who carried out the conquest and became the ancestors of the Gaelic people of Ireland. Although the story is classified as mythology, frequently mythology is based on fact and the native origin-myth of the Irish has enough correlation with historical fact to make it a case for fascinating speculation.

The Goidelic settlers in Iberia were replaced in the middle of the first millennium AD by a new wave of Gaulish (or Brythonic) speakers. By the time the Greek mariners began establishing their trading posts and settlements on the Iberian peninsula during the seventh and fifth centuries BC, the Celtic population had switched languages. Furthermore, the Celtic peoples were well established throughout the land. Herodotus (c.490–425 BC), the Greek historian who was the first to give a detailed account of the people of the Iberian peninsula, says that the Pyrenees were 'in the Celtic country' and that 'the Celts are outside the Pillars of Heracles [Gibraltar] and marched with the Cynesii, who are the westernmost people of Europe.'

Aristotle (384–322 BC) gives the name Celtica to the entire mountain mass of the Iberian peninsula. One of the most influential Greek historians of the fourth century BC, Ephoros of Cyme, writing about 350 BC, states that the Celtic realms reached as far as Gades (Cadiz), a colony founded by Phoenicians from Tyre at the start of the first millennium BC and for a long time the westernmost point of the known world. Other writers named specific Celtic tribal areas from Gades in the south northward to the Pyrenees. Pytheas, in the second half of the fourth century BC, a Greek explorer from Massilia (Marseilles) who made a famous voyage through the Straits of Gibraltar, north along the Spanish coast and as far as the British Isles, spoke of Iberian rivers flowing into the Atlantic as passing through the land of the Celts.

Herodotus writes of the Tartessus river, which is the modern Guadalquivir, in whose valley stand the cities of Cordoba and Seville. The Tartessus valley was famed, even in Herodotus' time, for its silver mines. Greeks from Phocaea began to form trading settlements there about 600 BC and made a treaty with the local King, who helped them build their settlements. His name was Arganthonios. The name obviously comes from the Celtic word for silver, *arganto*. Arganthonios' name became proverbial for longevity. Herodotus says he lived 120 years, of which he reigned as King some 80 years. Arganthonios is referred to as having died some time before 564 BC.

The Celtic place-names of the peninsula have enabled scholars to determine fairly accurately most of the territory occupied by the Celts. Names ending in -briga, such as Segobriga (Sergorbe) and Lacobriga (Lagos), were widespread in the Celtic world. Names of fortified townships ending in the Celtic -dunon are also widespread, such as Caladunum (Calahorra), near Mount Alegro in Catalonia, Arialdunum, the site of which is now uncertain, and Virodunum (Verdum), in the province of Heusca and Verdu. Some argue that, while the Celts were widely dispersed throughout the peninsula, they only established isolated settlements and did not constitute the mass of the population. This is open to debate. It was Eratosthenes, writing about 230 BC, who gave the name Iberia to the peninsula. Timaeos of Tauromenium in Sicily, originally an Athenian (*c.*356–260 BC), is thought to have been the first to use the term Celtiberian. There is a school of thought which maintains that the name Celtiberian had a precise value as opposed to Celt, for some ancient writers make a distinction between them. One generally accepted notion is that the Celtiberians were a 'mixed race', Celts intermixed with the native population of Iberia. The ancient chroniclers also make the distinction between the Celtiberia *citeriores*, those close to the coast, and Celtiberia *ulteriores*, those furthest from the coast.

It emerges quite clearly that, during the wars of independence against the Roman empire, all the named leaders bear Celtic names – Rhetogenes, Caraunios, Caros, Ambon, Leukon, Megaravicos and Auaros. And although some writers distinguish the Lusitani as an Iberian tribe, their leader in the war against Rome, Viriathos, has a Celtic name. So were the Lusitani a Celtic people or did the Celts manage to establish a dynastic rule over an Iberian people? Gaius Plinius Secundus (Pliny the Elder), AD 23/4–79, states categorically that the Lusitani were Celts and spoke Celtic. But Henri Hubert supposes that some Celtic families were accepted into the native tribes and achieved power, perhaps assimilating while continuing to use Celtic names. For example, James Callaghan (Prime Minister of the

United Kingdom, 1976–9) bore an Irish surname but was certainly not Irish.

It can be accepted, however, that by the time Iberia began to be conquered, first by the Carthaginian empire and then by the Roman empire, the Celts constituted the major population and held political predominance in the peninsula. Some historians, like Rufius Festus Avienus, writing in the fourth century AD, describe the Celts of the Iberian plateau as pastoral herdsmen leading a hard and penurious life. Yet, at the time of Ephoros of Cyme, gold, silver, copper and tin were being worked and exported and there is much evidence of a thriving trade with the Greek world.

The end of the independence of Celtic Iberia had its origins in the conflict between Carthage and Rome. The city of Carthage, occupying a strong strategic position on the Tunisian coast of North Africa, had been established by Phoenician colonists traditionally in 814 BC. During the sixth century BC it grew as a strong trading power and its interests began to conflict with Greek settlements throughout the Mediterranean. Forming an alliance with the Etruscans, the Carthaginians were able to drive the Greeks from Corsica and gain control of Sardinia, Sicily and several coastal towns on the Iberian peninsula, such as Gades. By 264 BC Carthage was the centre of a major empire.

Rome was now emerging as a dominant power and, at first, Carthage was content to establish commercial treaties with her. But it became inevitable that, as Rome rose in power and influence, a military conflict would occur. The first war, known as the First Punic War, broke out in 264 BC and lasted until 241 BC. The Romans managed to defeat the Carthaginians, eventually gaining dominance of the seas. Carthage was forced to pay indemnity to Rome and to evacuate many of her colonies. During the war, Carthage found that her colonies on the southern coast of Iberia had come under attack from the natives. The Carthaginian parliament, the Suffete, decided that the city must regain control of them as a first attempt to recover her prestige. Iberia was not yet in the Roman sphere of interest and Carthage could extend her empire in this direction. A Carthaginian general named Hamilcar Barca was sent with an army to reassert Carthaginian power in Iberia. Hamilcar Barca had fought in the war against Rome with some distinction and had been one of those who had negotiated the terms of peace in 241 BC. He arrived at Gades in

237 BC and began a systematic reduction of the south-western coast before pushing forward to the south-eastern side of the peninsula and moving along the Mediterranean coastline northwards towards the Greek colonies. In 229 BC, during the siege of Helice, one of the Greek colonies, he accidentally drowned while crossing a river.

Hamilcar Barca's son-in-law, Hasdrubal, son of Gisgo, was appointed Carthaginian commander in Spain and continued the campaign. The Greek colonies by this time had signed an alliance with Rome and the Carthaginians were forced to give an undertaking that they would confine their campaigning to south of the River Ebro. Meanwhile, Hasdrubal was bringing the Celtiberian and Iberian tribes in the area firmly under Carthaginian rule. During these campaigns, three of the sons of Hamilcar Barca, Hannibal, Hasdrubal and Mago, were distinguishing themselves as military leaders. In 221 BC, among the slaves taken from a defeated Celtic tribe, was one unnamed Celt who managed to get close enough to the Carthaginian commander, Hasdrubal, to assassinate him.

With Hasdrubal's death, Hannibal (247–182 BC) became commander. He was twenty-six years old. For two years he consolidated his position and then, in 219 BC, despite the agreement with Rome, he launched an attack over the Ebro against Saguntum (Sagunto), one of the rich Greek city states in alliance with Rome. As he fully realized, his attack precipitated war with Rome – the Second Punic War. Saguntum took eight months to fall, during which Rome tried to assert her authority by diplomatic means while the Carthaginian parliament procrastinated. Hannibal had planned an audacious invasion of the Italian peninsula which he intended to carry out before Rome was fully prepared.

In addition to his Carthaginians, he recruited levies from the Celtiberians and Iberians. Soon he had ready an army of 100,000 men with thirty-seven war-trained elephants. Knowing that Roman fleets dominated the seas, Hannibal chose to move his army by an overland route, a march of 1,500 miles across two of the greatest European mountain barriers – the Pyrenees and the Alps. It was obvious that the young Carthaginian commander had a good knowledge of events in Italy and that he knew of the recent defeats of the Celts of the Po Valley by Rome. Furthermore, he knew that the Celts, while recently conquered, were unsubdued. He despatched ambassadors to the Celts of northern Italy and an alliance was made. Food, supplies and men were promised to Hannibal once he crossed the Alps into Italy. Polybius comments: 'He knew that the only means of carrying the war against the Romans in Italy was, after surmounting, if possible, the difficulties of the route, to reach the above country and employ the Celts as allies and confederates in his enterprise.'

Soon all was ready. The command of the Carthaginian army in Spain was given to Hannibal's brother Hasdrubal. His invasion force gathered at New Carthage (Carthago Nova), Cartegna, and marched in May 218 BC. They kept to the Mediterranean coast, moving along the eastern side of the Pyrenees and into Gaul. It was, of course, necessary either to win over or to subdue the Celtic tribes in this area and a younger brother Hanno was left with 10,000 infantry and 1,000 cavalry to keep the Celtic tribes of the Pyrenees in check and guard the passages.

Moving along the southern coast of Gaul, Hannibal seems to have developed good relations with the Celtic chieftains in that area. Livy mentions that the chieftains 'came without reluctance to the Carthaginian, being won by his presents, and suffered his army to pass through their territories . . . without molestation'.

Hannibal's first battle occurred when he neared the Greek colony of Massilia (Marseilles), which was in alliance with Rome. A Roman army had already landed there under the command of Publius Cornelius Scipio. However, most of the Roman soldiers were incapacitated by sea-sickness and fever. Scipio sent out some Massiliot guides and some local Celtic mercenaries to explore the country for Hannibal's army. They found Hannibal crossing the Rhône about four days' march north of Massilia. Scipio had been able to persuade a Celtic tribe, the Volcae Tectosages, whose capital was at Tolosa (Toulouse), to ally themselves with Rome. He now asked them to dispute Hannibal's crossing of the Rhône and engage the Carthaginian until his own Roman troops were recovered. The Tectosages took up positions on the eastern bank, but Hannibal outflanked them with his Numidian cavalry, which had crossed on their left flank. The Tectosages, wedged between the Numidians and the frontal assault of the Carthaginians, broke in disorder.

Hannibal pressed on immediately to the Alps, where he received ambassadors from the Celts of the Po Valley. These appear to have been members of the Boii. Hannibal took the opportunity to lecture his army, instructing them to discount the popular notion that the Alps were insurmountable. He introduced the Po Valley Celts to them and said:

> These very ambassadors whom you see before you have crossed the Alps. They didn't fly over them on wings. What, in reality, is impervious or insurmountable . . . ? Are you going to let it be said that the Celts gained possession of a country which the Carthaginians were afraid even to approach? Take your choice. Either submit that the Celts are better men than you, or else follow me; and look forward at the end of your journey to that rich plain which spreads between the Tiber and the walls of Rome.

And so Hannibal, with his army, with its Celtiberian and also Gaulish auxiliaries, passed through the Alps to their destiny on the Italian peninsula and nearly seventeen years of continuous warfare there. We will follow their story in Chapter 4. But, in the meantime, we will return to events in Iberia.

Gnaeus Cornelius Scipio, the brother of the Consul Publius Cornelius Scipio who had missed encountering Hannibal's army north of Massilia, had been sent to Iberia to liberate the Greek colonies from Carthaginian control. He was joined a short time later by his brother, who had been decisively defeated by Hannibal in the Po Valley. The Scipio brothers won some successes, managing to retake the area as far south as Saguntum. In 212 BC Hannibal's brothers, Hasdrubal and Mago, launched a counter-offensive and in a series of successes both the Scipio brothers were killed. In 210 BC, however, Publius Cornelius Scipio's son, then twenty-seven years old and bearing the same name, though later taking the title Africanus, landed with a new Roman army.

In 209 BC Scipio Africanus force-marched his army down the east coast to New Carthage. In seven hours his legions had stormed the city. The tide was turning against Carthage on the Iberian peninsula. Three years later, the Carthaginians were driven out of the peninsula altogether and Rome now exerted her control over the country.

In 197 BC, with the Second Punic War ending in Rome's favour, the Iberian peninsula was divided into two colonial provinces by Rome. 'Hither Spain' centred on the Ebro basin, while 'Further Spain' was the area around Gibraltar across to the valley of the Guadalquivir. Rome sent officials and fixed annual taxes for the area. This resulted in the first of the general insurrections of the Celtiberians against their new imperial masters. The Turdetani rose in 196 BC and were defeated at Turta. In 195 BC the Consul Marcus Porcius Cato was sent to deal with the rebellious tribes. He was an austere military man and his severity was proverbial. He is famous for uttering the cry: 'Carthago delenda est!' (Carthage must be destroyed!).

Cato's wars of pacification lasted for several years. He did not make any significant headway against the Celtiberians but seems to have made unsuccessful attempts to capture the Celtic towns of Siguenza and Numantia. He managed to seize control of the silver mines in 195 BC in what is now Catalonia. The Lusitani also rebelled and defeated a Roman general, Aemilius Paullus, in 190 BC. However, Paullus managed to regroup his legions and win another battle later in the year.

Insurrection continued. In 179 BC Tiberius Sempronius Gracchus (d. 154 BC) was sent to Hither Spain to pacify it. Polybius says he destroyed 300 Celtic towns, while Poseidonius corrects the word 'towns' to 'fortresses'. His subsequent measures of pacification won him some fame for he revised the treaties with the Celtic tribes, placed the system of land tenure and taxation on a more equitable basis and established several Roman towns in the interior of the country. He also encouraged Celtiberian enlistment into the Roman army and even persuaded some of the Celtic chieftains to accept posts of command within the Roman army. He believed that this would keep the 'wilder spirits' among the Celtic population under control. The result was a period of twenty years' comparative peace.

In 154 BC, however, Roman control was disturbed by the incursions of the Lusitani from what is now modern Portugal. The Lusitani began raiding Roman garrisons and towns and persuaded other Celtiberian tribes to join them. In 153 BC the Romans decided to besiege the formidable Celtic hill-fort of Numantia, situated on the upper Douro in north-central Spain, thought to be the site of modern Soria. It was a stronghold of Celtic resistance to Rome, surrounded by impenetrable forests, with two rivers cutting deep ravines on either side. In their attempt to reduce the hill-fort, the Romans brought up elephants. The defenders dropped rocks on them. One elephant, sent mad with fury, turned and trampled the Romans, causing them to panic and flee. The Celts were able to set off in pursuit, and severely mauled the Roman army. The fighting went on until 151 BC, when M. Atilius, the Roman commander, agreed terms. These terms, however, were rejected by the new commander, a praetor named Servius Sulpicius Galba. He succeeded in defeating the Lusitani and, when they had surrendered, proceeded to massacre them and enslave the survivors. Even in Rome this incident was strongly criticized and the former commander in Spain, Marcus Porcius Cato, then an old man, came forward to prosecute Galba for this 'crime' before the senate. However, most senators in Rome approved of what Galba had done. Iberia was proving a troublesome acquisition and Galba obtained an acquittal.

Among the survivors of Galba's massacre was a young man named Viriathos. He became chieftain of the Lusitani survivors and began to lead his people in guerilla war against Rome which lasted for eight years. In 148 BC the Roman Governor and his army were defeated and the Governor killed. In 141 BC one of the Roman consuls, sent to crush the Lusitani, found himself surrounded and was forced to conclude a treaty with Viriathos. The Roman senate was compelled to ratify it. However, in 140 BC Servius Caepio was sent to Spain and he immediately reneged on the treaty and while pretending to open new negotiations with Viriathos he bribed some Lusitanian traitors to murder the Celtic leader while he slept. It was characteristic of Rome that this blood money was never paid and presumably the murderers were slain in turn. It is recorded that during the funeral rites for Viriathos some 200 pairs of warriors fought in mock single-handed combat as a tribute.

The loss of Viriathos weakened Celtiberian resistance, although it continued until 138 BC when one of the Roman consuls, Decimus Junius Brutus, who organized a fleet to attack the Lusitani strongholds on the Atlantic coast, managed to wear them down. He established garrison settlements at Lisbon on the Tagas and at Valentia.

The war against other Celtiberian tribes was continuing. Under the settlement of Gracchus, the Celtiberians had been given permission by Rome to continue to fortify their townships. Galba, however, had revoked this right and subsequent Roman commanders had made punitive expeditions against Celtic fortified towns. This warfare continued until 132 BC, when the Celtiberians began to redouble their efforts against Rome. Polybius writes: 'This war between the Romans and Celtiberians is called "The Fiery War", for while wars in Greece or Asia are settled with one or two pitched battles, the battles there drag on, only brought to a temporary end by the darkness of night. Both sides refused to let their courage flag or bodies tire.'

In 136 BC during the siege of a Celtiberian hill-fort at Pallantia, the Roman commander, Mancinus, allowed his supplies to run out and decided to evacuate his positions at night. He left his sick and wounded behind. The Celtiberians emerged from their hill-fort and the retreat turned into a rout, the Romans being slaughtered. Some 20,000 Romans surrendered to the Celts. Mancinus was stripped of his command by the outraged senate.

In 134 BC a new commander was sent to the troublesome provinces. This was the grandson of Scipio Africanus – Publius Cornelius Scipio (c.185–129 BC). He was, in fact, adopted and his real father had been L. Aemilius Paullus, regarded as the conqueror of Macedonia. Scipio had fought in this war under his father's command. During the Third Punic War between Rome and Carthage (149–146 BC), Scipio had broken into Carthage itself and destroyed the city. He was now elected one of Rome's two consuls and given command in Spain. On arrival he found the Roman troops there demoralized by their long war against the Celtiberians. Discipline was almost non-existent and he had to set to work to revitalize them and retrain them. Only when he was satisfied with the quality of his troops did he examine the position of his enemy.

Once more, as in 153 BC, it seemed that the hill-fort of Numantia was the centre of Celtiberian resistance to the Roman conquest. Here, under the chieftain Avaros, the Celtiberians were in an impregnable position. If Numantia fell, the Celtiberians throughout the province would be demoralized. Scipio moved his legions through the surrounding countryside, looting and burning, although they were constantly harassed by the Celtiberian guerillas. Looking at Numantia for the first time, Scipio realized just how formidable the hill-fort was. He decided to erect seven fortresses around the town and link them with ditches and palisades. *Ballistae* and *catapulta*, Roman artillery for throwing rocks and missiles, were set up. The Numantians were still able to receive provisions at this stage from across the neighbouring rivers but Scipio slowly cut off all routes of supply. He was able to make alliances with a few surrounding Celtiberian tribes who, shortsightedly, saw the reduction of Numantia simply as the end of a powerful rival.

The Numantians made several forays against the Romans, fighting hand to hand and using the *falcata*, a heavy cleaver-like weapon. According to Livy, the weapon could sever heads or cut off arms with one blow. In their night attacks on the Roman positions the Celts used javelins tied with rags which had been soaked in pitch and ignited. But as time progressed it became obvious to Avaros, the Celtiberian chieftain, that the Roman siegeworks were just as impregnable as the walls of his hill-fort. But there was one difference – the Romans had access to supplies and he had not.

A chieftain named Rhetogenes was chosen, with a few comrades, to attempt to break through the Roman lines and raise the surrounding Celtiberians tribes against the Romans. Carrying a scaling ladder, the Celtiberians left Numantia during darkness and managed to scramble unseen over the Roman siegeworks. They silenced the guards, seized horses and rode off into the night. Rhetogenes made for the hill-fort of the neighbouring Arevaci and entreated them to come to the aid of Numantia. But the Arevaci had made an alliance with Rome and refused. Rhetogenes went on to Lutia. There he found young Celtiberian warriors willing to join him. However, word was sent to Scipio that the young men of Lutia were preparing to fight against him. He reacted immediately. He withdrew one of his legions, surrounded Lutia and demanded that the young warriors be paraded before the town or his legion would destroy it, men, women and children. The young men were lined up. Scipio had 400 of them seized and had their right hands cut off.

Rhetogenes' attempts to persuade the surrounding Celtiberians to help Numantia failed. As the weeks passed, starvation forced Avaros to send envoys to Scipio to ask for terms of surrender. Scipio demanded unconditional surrender. Perhaps through a Roman *agent provocateur* it was rumoured that Avaros and his family had secured terms for themselves from Rome and had agreed to sell out the rest of the Numantians. The people, desperate and starving, assassinated Avaros. Many also took their own lives. Famine and disease had broken their spirit. Appian, the historian of the event, seems moved by the suppression of 8,000 Celtiberians by 60,000 Romans in such a drawn-out siege. As the Numantians opened the gates of their town and came out to surrender, Appian records: 'Their bodies were foul, their hair and nails long, and they were smeared with dirt. In their eyes there was a fearful expression; an expression of anger, pain, weariness and the awareness of having eaten human flesh.' It was reported that the starving Numantians had resorted to cannibalism in their extremity.

Scipio selected fifty leading warriors to be sent to Rome for his ceremonial triumph. The rest of the population were sold into slavery while the town was put to the torch. Scipio was astute enough to divide the territory among those tribes with whom he had formed an alliance, as a bribe. Although the heartland of Celtiberian resistance had been devastated, and Celtiberian independence smothered, Celtiberian chieftains continued to rule their tribal areas under the suzerain power of Rome.

When, in 105 BC, the Cimbri and Teutones, having destroyed three Roman armies, crossed the Pyrenees into the Iberian peninsula, it was the Celtiberians who confronted them and, after two years of struggle, forced them back across the Pyrenees. The Celtiberian tribes were not entirely subservient to the *pax Romana* and several minor insurrections occurred. It appeared that many of these insurrections were deliberately provoked by Roman governors in order to secure an easy victory and earn prestige in Rome. In 93 BC Titus Didius was one such military governor who provoked the Celtiberians and then suppressed them with a savageness which shocked even Roman susceptibilities. Having reduced the Arevaci to starvation and then effected a surrender on the condition that he would give them new lands on which they could resettle, Didius had them disarmed and promptly proceeded systematically to massacre men, women and children. Appian of Alexandria, writing AD *c.*160, disapprovingly comments: 'For this Didius was actually honoured with a triumph!'

These uprisings of the Celtiberians were no more than brief episodes in the political history of the new Roman province.

In 83 BC Quintus Sertorius arrived to govern the Roman province. He was a distinguished Roman soldier who firmly believed in the Roman republic, joining Cinna's march on Rome against those who wanted to established an emperor as ruler. In 80 BC the Lusitani persuaded him to lead them in revolt against Rome. Lucius Cornellius Sulla (*c.*138–78 BC), whose vindictive cruelty was long remembered in Rome, had finally seized the city in 82 BC after a ruthless civil war and had been made dictator. Sulla was the leader of the *optimates* (best class), the Roman upper classes who sought to rule as an oligarchy against the *populares*, those on the side of the people. Sertorius, who had been a leader of the *populares*, learned that Sulla was now busy compiling lists of people who might be killed without trial and their property confiscated. Although Sulla died in 78 BC, his supporters, such as Gnaeus Pompeius Magnus (Pompey the Great, 106–48 BC), continued to dominate in the senate. Sertorius therefore placed himself at the head of the Lusitani insurrection and was joined by many Roman colonists and numerous political exiles arriving from Rome to escape Sulla's purges.

From 81 to 73 BC Sertorius was in firm control of all Spain and was successful in holding the province against attacks from several Roman armies, including one led by Pompey himself in 77 BC. But gradually he lost ground to Pompey and Metellus and his popularity waned. He was assassinated in 73 BC by his lieutenant Perpenna. Spain was once more under Roman control and Julius Caesar, the rising star of Rome, went there as Governor in 68 BC. He fought a campaign against the Celtiberians and captured the hill-fort of Brigantium. Pompey became Governor in Spain in 55 BC while Caesar was busy in Gaul and during the ensuing civil war, in 49 BC, Caesar managed to defeat the army of Pompey's lieutenants, M. Terentius Varro and Marcus Petreius, having formed alliances with the Celtiberians.

By the time of the Emperor Augustus (63 BC – AD 14) Latin was widespread across the Spanish province. Towns, agricultural settlements and trading prosperity created stable and peaceful conditions. The remnants of the old Celtic civilization seemed to vanish very quickly before the Romanization. Muncipal self-government was widely granted and the standard of prosperity in Spain became unique among the provinces of the Roman empire.

During the governorship of Sertorius, schools had been established for the children of Celtiberian chieftains. Soon the Celtiberians themselves were contributing to Latin literature. Among the most famous was Marcus Valerius Martialis, or Martial (AD c.40–103/4), born in Biblis, who made a frank assertion of his Celtic identity. The poet Egnatius was a Celtiberian whose work was ridiculed at Rome for its 'provincialness'. Marcus Fabius Quintilanus (b. AD 35) was a Celtiberian from Calagurris who became a famous teacher of rhetoric at Rome. Roman writers had long extolled the Celtic mastery of rhetoric. Quintilian, as he is known, became the first rhetorician to receive an official salary from the state treasury, under the Emperor Vespasian. His most famous work became *Institutio oratoria* (Education of an Orator). By a curious twist of fate the Florentine humanist Poggio Bracciolini (1380–1459) discovered the only complete manuscript of the work in the Abbey of St Gallen (St Gall) in Switzerland in 1416.

Curious because St Gallen, near the Lake of Constance, had been founded in the early seventh century AD by an Irish monk, Gall, who was one of Columbanus' disciples.

There were many other writers from Spain, such as Lucius Annaeus Seneca the Elder (c.55 BC – AD c.37/41), born in Cordoba as was his son Seneca the Younger (4 BC – AD 65) and his grandson Marcus Annaeus Lucanus, Lucan (AD 39–65). But it is hard to establish whether they were Romanized Celtiberians or the children of Roman colonists in Spain. Pomponius Mela (AD c.43) was from Tingentera, and his work on the Celts, especially on the druids, preserves information not found elsewhere. Was he using lost written sources or was his information from personal knowledge as a Celtiberian? However, there is no distinct Celtic note in the works of such writers as Canius Rufius of Gades, Decianus of Emeritia, Maternus of Biblis or Valerius Licinius, all of whom added to the treasury of Latin literature in the years following Rome's conquest of Celtiberia.

We know that a Celtic language was still spoken in many parts of Spain during the first century AD. Publius Tacitus (AD 56/57 – c.117) records this fact. But there are no mentions of Celtic survivals afterwards. We can only assume that by the following century Celtiberia had become merely a geographical label and that the Celtic language and civilization was lost in that area.

It is worth departing from our period for a word of explanation about a popular myth which has sprung up concerning the continued presence on the Iberian peninsula of a Celtic people, particularly in Galicia and Asturias, in the north-west of Spain. It is true that there are some identifiable signs of the remnants of Celtic culture there and several words of Celtic origin have survived in the Galician language, which is now spoken by 80 per cent of the population of Galicia and is being reintroduced into schools after nearly fifty years of ruthless persecution by Franco's Fascist state. Galician is a Romance language, deriving from the same Hispanic dialect as Portuguese; Portuguese crystallized into a literary language distinct from Spanish in the sixteenth century.

Because of these remnants there has been a tendency to believe that the Galicians are a survival of the original Celtic inhabitants of the Iberian peninsula. This is not so. During the fifth century AD, as the ancestors of the English began to push into Britain, driving the original Celtic inhabitants westward, many Celtic tribes decided that migration was the only way to escape the pagan hordes flooding into their once prosperous homelands. The major migrations to the Armorican peninsula, later to take its name of Brittany (little Britain) from the new settlers, is well known. However, other Celtic tribes from southern Britain arrived on the northern seaboard of Spain, mainly in Asturias, between Lugo and Oviedo. Their settlements were recognized at the Council of Lugo in AD 567 as constituting the Christian see of Bretoña, whose bishop, Mahiloc, signed the *acta* of the Second Council of Braga in AD 572. The settlements spread and the settlers bequeathed a name to the new country – Galicia, which, it is argued, comes from the same root as Galatia. But the British Celtic settlements in Galicia and Asturias were quickly absorbed and even the Celtic Church's influence, which had been imported with them, ceased when Roman orthodoxy was accepted at the Council of Toledo in AD 633. The see of Bretoña (see of the Britons) existed until at least AD 830, when it was ravaged by the Moors; perhaps it existed as late as the Council of Oviedo in AD 900. It was finally merged with the see of Oviedo and Mondonedo. Any Celtic remnants in this area of the country derived from the small British Celtic settlement of the fifth century and not from the pre-Roman-conquest period of Celtic occupation.

[4]

Cisalpine Gaul

THE Celts of the Po Valley of northern Italy, decisively defeated at Telamon in 225 BC and subsequently in Roman incursions into their country culminating with the defeat at Clastidium in 222 BC, were now subjected to the establishment of Roman military garrisons in their territory and to an aggressive Roman colonization policy. It was in the early spring of 218 BC that secret envoys arrived from Hannibal, the Carthaginian commander in Iberia, seeking an alliance against Rome. It would seem that Hannibal's envoys went to the chieftains of the Boii, for it was envoys of this tribe who went to meet Hannibal and his army and led them through the passes of the Alpine ranges.

Hannibal and his army had made his famous march from New Carthage in Iberia to Cisalpine Gaul in six months. He arrived with some 20,000 infantry and 6,000 cavalry and a few elephants. The army consisted not only of his Carthaginian soldiers but also of Numidian cavalry, Celtiberians and some Gaulish Celts who had joined him en route. During his march he had lost some 15,000 to 20,000 men from his army: most of these casualties were during his astonishing November crossing of the Alps. The role of the Celtic guides from the Boii of Cisalpine Gaul in that crossing has never been properly acknowledged by historians. But without the Celts' knowledge of the mountain passes Hannibal could not have journeyed successfully over the Alps in winter.

When the news came that Hannibal was through the Alps and nearing their territory, the Boii and their Insubrean neighbours rose up, as prearranged, and pinned down the Roman military garrisons in their fortifications. The first garrison to be attacked was one which the Romans had placed at Taurini (Turin), the chief city of the Taurini tribe. However, Publius Cornelius Scipio, one of Rome's two consuls for that year, 218 BC, who had failed to intercept Hannibal north of Massilia, had already sent a warning to Rome. An army under a praetor was despatched north to check Hannibal before he could break out of the confinement of the mountain passes into the fertile valley of the Po, where he would have complete manoeuvrability. The Boii, who must have been able to field a considerable tribal army, moved south to meet the Romans and were able to check the progress of the Praetor's army, allowing the Carthaginians time to pass into the valley in safety.

Scipio and his army had returned with all haste from Massilia, landing at Pisa, and began an immediate advance into the valley of the Po. Meanwhile, Rome's second Consul, Tiberius Sempronius Longus, then in Sicily, was ordered to return and move his troops to Ariminium (Rimini) to support Scipio. In December 218 BC, on the Tincino river, the northern tributary of the Po where the Celts had defeated an Etruscan army two centuries before, Scipio and Hannibal clashed. The Romans were routed and Scipio wounded. The Romans fled south of the Po. Tiberius Sempronius Longus, having marched from Sicily in a record forty days, crossed the Trebbia, a southern tributary of the Po, with an army of 40,000 men to launch a surprise attack on Hannibal during a snowstorm. Hannibal had been warned by the Celtic population. His cavalry struck hard at the advancing flanks of the Roman army, bending them back. From a concealed gully, Mago, one of Hannibal's younger brothers, led a fierce charge against the enemy's rear. The encircled Romans fought desperately. By the end of the day only half of their original force were able to fight their way to Placentia. The rest were fugitive, captured or dead in the drifting snow. The Carthaginian victories put heart into the Celts of the Po Valley. In two brief encounters, Cisalpine Gaul was free of Rome. Thousands of Po Valley Celts now flocked to join Hannibal's army.

During the rest of the winter, Hannibal rested his army near Bononia (Bologna), the Boii tribal capital. In the early spring of 217 BC he began marching south towards Rome, crossing the Apennines on the western side of the Italic peninsula. Rome had now changed her consuls. Scipio had been sent off to Iberia to join his brother Gnaeus Cornelius Scipio in seeking to drive the Carthaginians out.* Gaius

*See Chapter 3.

Flaminius, the veteran of the war against the Cisalpine Celts, and Servilius Geminus had been given command of the armies. Flaminius was sent to Aretium (Arezzo) while Geminus was sent to Ariminium (Rimini). Flaminius' plan was to attempt to get Hannibal's army between his army and that of Geminus, as had happened to the Celts at Telamon. He allowed Hannibal's army to pass by his position then, sending messages to Geminus, set off in pursuit. Hannibal's scouts were well informed. Reaching Lake Trasimeno, the Carthaginian commander placed his 35,000 men in wooded hills overlooking its waters. On the mist-shrouded morning of 21 June, the unsuspecting Flaminius and his 40,000 legionaries were suddenly assaulted by Celts, Celtiberians, Carthaginians and Numidians as they were strung out in marching formation. It was one of the bloodiest ambushes of history. The entire Roman army was destroyed, its soldiers either killed or taken captive. Among the dead was Flaminius. On Hannibal's side there were only 2,500 casualties, mostly Celts, demonstrating the leading part played by them in the attack. Hannibal always placed his Celtic allies in his centre-front ranks during battle.

Now Geminus' army, hastening up, was also attacked and destroyed. Rome was in turmoil. The senate appointed Quintus Fabius Maximus Verrucosis as dictator. The dictator soon became unpopular for he avoided any open conflict with Hannibal and limited his attacks to harrying actions. However, Quintus Fabius had a reason for this. It gave him time to raise and organize a new army. Perhaps Hannibal's greatest military mistake was not proceeding directly to Rome after Lake Trasimeno. Without an army, the city would surely have fallen swiftly. But Hannibal believed that Rome would be defended and that he did not possess enough trained troops and equipment to conduct a siege. Instead, he marched into the country of the Samnites and then south-east into the rich plains near the Adriatic coast. He halted in Apulia and made his headquarters at Geronium.

Quintus Fabius had built up an army of 150,000 men, a force double the size of Hannibal's. This army was now given over to the two new consuls, Gaius Terentius Varro and Lucius Aemilius Paullus, another veteran of the war against the Cisalpine Celts. Varro was commander-in-chief. They marched to engage Hannibal, arriving in Apulia in June 216 BC. After some minor skirmishes, they offered battle to Hannibal near the city of Cannae (Cannosa), near modern

Barletta, overlooking the low flat lands beside the River Aufidus (Ofanto).

Varro placed in the field the largest Roman army ever assembled. He drew it up in the traditional manner with his infantry in the centre and cavalry on either wing, his lightly armed troops placed before his heavily armed legions. Hannibal positioned his Celtic and Celtiberian troops in the front ranks of his centre army; behind them were his Carthaginians, while on his left flank he placed Celtic cavalry and on his right Numidian cavalry. He had 40,000 infantry and 10,000 horse facing 80,000 Roman infantry and 6,000 horse.

On 3 August 216 BC, the Roman army opened the battle with an attack on the centre of Hannibal's army. The Celts and Celtiberians moved out to meet the attack and then, in a prearranged plan, began to fall back as if being forced by the Romans. Varro, thinking the centre was weakening, pushed his troops into the bulge, securing a large salient. However, as this was happening, Hanno, son of Vomilcar, led the Celtic cavalry around the right flank of the Roman lines and launched an attack on both flanks of Roman cavalry, while Maharbal led his Numidian cavalry from the left flank. The Roman cavalry was routed and the encirclement of the Roman army was complete. Hannibal pressed on the Roman infantry. They were assailed on all sides and cut to pieces. Accounts give Roman deaths at Cannae as 50,000, with 4,500 taken captive.

Livy tells a story of a military tribune, Gnaeus Lentulus, who recognized the Consul Lucius Aemilius Paullus wandering on the battlefield covered in blood. Lentulus urged the Consul to take his horse and escape. Paullus refused and told him to escape to Rome himself and tell the senate to fortify the city. Lentulus escaped and the Consul was never seen alive again. The commander-in-chief, the Consul Varro, had already fled from the field and rallied a few thousand survivors at Canusium. Among the officers killed were the former consuls Servilius, Atilius and Minucius. Out of thirty-three military tribunes, twenty-nine were killed, and eighty Roman senators were also slain. It was Rome's greatest defeat. Hannibal had lost 5,700 men killed in the battle, of whom 4,000 were Celts, 1,500 Celtiberians and Numidians.

The Carthaginian commander had destroyed all Rome's fighting forces. The entire Italian peninsula was his. Yet once more he refused to attack Rome herself. In his defence it is said that he lacked troops knowledgeable in siege warfare and the necessary siege equipment. Once more he gave Rome time to rebuild her shattered forces. In Rome every house had lost sons and fathers. The dictator, Quintus Fabius, was not associated with Varro's defeat and was in firm charge of the defences. Hannibal sent an envoy, Carthalo, to Rome to demand her surrender. Rome refused. Hannibal was content to make Capua his headquarters.

Most of the cities of southern Italy, the former Greek colonies of Magna Graeca, were happy to be liberated from Roman control. They joined Hannibal, and Capua became the capital of a powerful alliance supporting the Carthaginian. The fortunes of the Cisalpine Celts, the Celts of the Po Valley, were also in the ascendant.

Rome was beaten but she refused to submit. Quintus Fabius started to raise a new army and, because Hannibal refused to lay siege to Rome, the Carthaginian forces had to be content with taking secondary objectives.

Among the various heroic actions which took place was the escape of a young Roman military tribune named Publius Sempronius Tuditanus with 600 men from behind Carthaginian lines. Sempronius Tuditanus later wrote an historical account of the rise of Rome in which he maintained that the Etruscans were, in fact, a Celtic people; and this gave rise to a myth which has existed to this day. (See Epilogue.)

From Capua Hannibal marched to Naples, hoping to take the city, which was still holding out in alliance with Rome. He wanted to establish a seaport through which to bring in reinforcements from Carthage. However, at Nola, sixteen miles north-east of Naples, Marcus Claudius Marcellus, the victor of Clastidium, had established a strong defensive position. Hannibal was forced to attack it and was repulsed. Quintus Fabius was raiding the countryside around Capua in an attempt to carry off corn and supplies. This war of skirmishing went on until 214 BC. Then Syracuse, in Sicily, taken from Carthage as part of the settlement of the First Punic War, rose in revolt against Rome. Marcellus was sent to bring it back under Roman rule. He laid siege to it with 25,000 men. It was a siege which lasted two years, ending when the Romans forced their way in during a festival. The gates were opened, letting the Roman army flood into the city, where Marcellus allowed them to massacre many of the inhabitants. One of the most famous people to be killed in this slaughter was Archimedes (*c*.287–212 BC), perhaps the greatest mathematician of the age, an astronomer, physicist and inventor, who lived at the court of Hieron II of Syracuse.

During 212/211 BC a Roman army laid siege to Hannibal's capital at Capua. Hannibal tried to relieve the pressure on it by marching south and seizing Tarentum (Taranto) on the southern coast, hoping to draw the Roman army after him. However, although he captured the town he was unable to reduce the Roman fortress which guarded the entrance to the harbour mouth. This prevented the use of the harbour by the Carthaginian fleet. Hannibal's ruse had failed, for the Roman army besieging Capua was not lured after him. The city was eventually forced into surrender and, as a reprisal for its support of Hannibal, some fifty-three of its senators were executed while other officials were sold into slavery.

Roman morale was boosted by the successes in Iberia. But the war became a slow chess game, with Hannibal throughout 210–209 BC managing to take some important pieces in the form of strategic towns. In 209 BC Hannibal was able to maul severely the Roman army of Marcellus, now returned to the Italian peninsula. However, the Romans managed to recapture Tarentum.

In 207 BC Hannibal received news that his brother Hasdrubal was following his route through Gaul and across the Alps with a new Carthaginian army, its composition much like Hannibal's, with Numidians, Celtiberians and Celts as well as Carthaginians. Hasdrubal had also recruited Ligurians, a people living west of the Po Valley and straddling the Alps between Cisalpine Gaul and Gaul itself. There is confusion over whether the Ligurians were Celts or constituted a separate people. Hasdrubal arrived with his army in the spring of 207 BC and was able to recruit a great many Celts of the Po Valley. He sent a message to his brother Hannibal, urging him to join him at the Metaurus river near Ancona for a united attack on Rome. The message never reached Hannibal – it was intercepted by the Romans.

Rome now sent one of its consuls, Marcus Livius Salinator, to face Hasdrubal's army, while the second Consul, Gaius Claudius Nero, was sent to blockade Hannibal and prevent him moving north to join his brother. However, when Nero realized that Hannibal had not received his brother's message, he made a decision which altered the course of the war. He took 7,000 men from his army and marched to reinforce Livius Salinator in the north.

Hasdrubal's informants told him that the Roman armies had united and so he began to pull back to the Metaurus river before they could launch an attack. But he was too late. Nero, commanding the right flank, launched an attack on the Celts holding Hasdrubal's left flank. The Romans were quickly checked by the skill of the Celtic troops. It was then that Nero made a second decisive decision. Withdrawing his men he force-marched them around the back of Livius Salinator's main army to the left flank and launched an attack on the Numidian positions. The Numidians crumbled before his attack before Hasdrubal knew what was happening. In this flanking attack some 10,000 of Hasdrubal's army were slain, including Hasdrubal himself. Only 2,000 Romans were killed. The first Hannibal knew of his brother's defeat and death was when a Roman threw Hasdrubal's severed head into Hannibal's camp.

Although Hannibal remained in Italy for a further four years, the Carthaginian commander never regained the impetus or success against Rome that the early years had given him. In 205 BC his brother, Mago, landed at Genoa with another army, but it was pinned down there by Roman forces for two years before Mago re-embarked for Carthage. In the winter of 203 BC Carthage, under pressure from a Roman army which had landed in Africa under Scipio Africanus, called Hannibal and his army back to protect the city.* By the following year, with Hannibal's defeat at Zama, the Second Punic War had been brought to a close and once more Rome emerged as the victor.

Rome now turned her gaze on Cisalpine Gaul, on the Celts of the Po Valley, which had been the door through which Hannibal had gained entrance to the Italic peninsula. They had been Hannibal's unswerving allies against Rome. On the grounds that Carthage was still inciting the Celts of the Po Valley to insurrection against Rome, the Roman senate authorized the conquest of the area. Roman armies marched north across the Apennines. In 199/198 and 197/196 BC it is recorded that the Insubres alone lost 75,000 fighting men in battles with Rome. By 197 BC the Cenomani had surrendered. In 196 BC the Insubres were granted surprisingly good terms of surrender. In 192 BC the Boii decided to ask for terms. A chieftain of the Boii and his family arrived at the camp of the Proconsul, T. Quinctius Flamininus, and sur-

* See Chapter 7.

rendered. The Proconsul murdered the chieftain and his family, apparently, says Livy, to entertain a sulky boyfriend. Flamininus was taken off the senate poll in 182 BC for this and other acts considered unworthy of a Roman senator. From the Celtic viewpoint, Roman justice was a trifle tardy.

However, in 187 BC, Cisalpine Gaul was still far from conquered. Even those tribes which had already surrendered were a source of concern to Rome. That year the Roman General commanding the area decided to disarm the Cenomani, who immediately objected that this was against the treaty they had made with Rome in 197 BC. They took their case to the Roman senate and one of the consuls, M. Aemilius Lepidus, reversed the decision of the Roman commander and allowed them to keep their arms.

In 186 BC a Celtic tribe called the Carni crossed the Alps with 17,000 fighting men, and tried to settle in the Po Valley. This seems to indicate that the Celtic population of the Po Valley was never static and that the tribes were continually moving. A Roman army commanded by a praetor was sent against them but it was not until 183 BC that they were driven back across the Alps. A similar thing happened in 178 BC when a smaller group of 3,000 Celts appeared. They were named the Stratielli and they built a town in the district of Aquileia. A Roman army under Marcus Claudius Marcellus destroyed it. It was not until 173 BC that the Stratielli finally surrendered to M. Popilius Laenas, who promptly sold the entire tribe into slavery and auctioned their property. There were protests in the Roman senate but Laenas had sufficient political backing for his actions.

The gradual displacement of the Celtic population of Cisalpine Gaul by war and conquest gave Rome an excellent opportunity to carry on a programme of colonization. Ex-soldiers of the Roman army, as well as other settlers, were encouraged to take over the farmsteads of the Celts as well as the towns. Those Celts who were not driven out of the Po Valley were to be Romanized. The Alps were now to be considered the boundary of the Roman/Celtic world and the Roman senate issued a proclamation forbidding the Celts to enter the territory. Cisalpine Gaul became Gallia Togata, the land of the Celts who wear the toga, that is Romanized Celts.

Polybius (c.200 – c.118 BC), the Greek historian from Megalopolis in Arcadia who became pro-Roman, visited Cisalpine Gaul during these early years of Roman colonization and at a time when Celtic civilization there still thrived. 'Words fail to describe the fertility of the country,' he says,

> . . . travellers stopping at the inns do not make terms over each item separately, but ask what the rate is per head; as a rule the innkeeper undertakes to give them all they want for a quarter of an *obol* [about half-a-penny in modern currency] and this price is seldom exceeded. Need I speak of the enormous population of the country, of the stature and good looks of the people, and of their warlike spirit?

The description of the inns, or hostels, given by Polybius reminds one of the descriptions of the inns and hostels in ancient Ireland as described in native tradition, and of the native laws pertaining to the way such inns and hostels should be run. The Celtic system of hospitality, the network of inns and hostels, had already become a by-word in the ancient world. Clearly the system lasted long after Rome's conquest of Cisalpine Gaul. Excavations at Ornavasso and in the neighbourhood of Como show that the Celts, and in particular the Insubres, remained as distinctive civilizations in the Po Valley down to imperial times.

In 90/89 BC, one hundred years after the conquest, the senate granted automatic Roman citizenship to all the inhabitants of Roman settlements and this was extended in 49 BC to cover all the inhabitants of Cisalpine Gaul. In 82 BC the Roman dictator, Lucius Cornelius Sulla, designated Cisalpine Gaul a Roman province. In 42 BC Cisalpine Gaul was part of Italy, Rome having achieved the conquest and absorption of all the peoples of the Italian peninsula. Cisalpine Gaul had ceased to exist and even the Celtic tribes in the southern foothills of the Alps were conquered by the Emperor Augustus just before the start of the Christian era.

Only once more were the Celts of Cisalpine Gaul able to offer a threat to Rome, when many joined the slave army of Spartacus. In 73 BC Spartacus, a Thracian who had been brought to Capua, in Italy, to serve as a gladiator, broke out of captivity and established himself as a guerilla leader on the slopes of Mount Vesuvius. After a year all attempts to capture him had been beaten off and he gathered a large rebel army which defeated two Roman armies. Thrace had ceased to be a Celtic kingdom only a hundred years before this time* and one can speculate whether Spartacus himself was a Thracian Celt. What is certain is that a large part of his army was Celtic. The Celtic custom of single-handed combat rendered most Celtic captives liable to recruitment as gladiators. And, indeed, Spartacus' two generals, Crixos and Cenomaros, were Celts bearing Celtic names. When Crixos was killed in 72 BC, Spartacus slew 300 Roman prisoners in retaliation. He defeated three more Roman armies and reached Cisalpine Gaul, where he drew large numbers of recruits from the Celts of the Po Valley.

In 71 BC Marcus Licinius Crassus finally cornered Spartacus in southern Italy and defeated him. Spartacus appears to have been killed in the battle. Gnaeus Pompeius Magnus (Pompey the Great) had just returned from Spain in time to annihilate the remnants of Spartacus' army and take credit for ending the war. Crassus celebrated his victory by crucifying 6,000 prisoners along the Appian Way from Capua to the gates of Rome. Spartacus has become a legend not only for his daring successes but for his reputation for personal bravery and his qualities of strength and humanity.

By the start of the period of the Roman empire, which began when Augustus (Gaius Octavius Caesar) accepted tribunician power for life in 23 BC and turned the republican government into an hereditary system of emperors, the Celtic civilization of the Po Valley was disappearing rapidly. It seems to have disappeared altogether by the end of the first century of the Roman empire. The loss to the Celtic world, however, was certainly Rome's gain, for a great deal of literary talent from Cisalpine Gaul gave a new impetus to Latin literature.

The Celts of the ancient world, like their descendants, were rich in literary talent, from poets and storytellers to historians. Prior to the Christian era, however, the Celts were constrained by their culture which, as we have seen, prohibited the writing down of their knowledge. Therefore only a few texts in continental Celtic (Gaulish) survive. The famous Coligny Calendar of the first century BC, and the recently discovered Larzac inscription on a lead tablet, give us our longest-known Gaulish texts to date. The only other written remains appear on funerary inscriptions, manufacturer's markings on pottery and other goods and the occasional names and words recorded by

* See Chapter 5.

Greek and Latin writers. The Celtic literary tradition was an oral one, highly sophisticated and relying on the power of mental cultivation. Caesar observed that it could take a druid up to twenty years of training before he was sufficiently knowledgeable in law, philosophy, history and genealogy. It was from this oral tradition that the Irish Brehon Law system was first committed to writing in the Christian era and, soon after, the Welsh law system known as the Laws of Hywel Dda. But, as we have seen, the Celts of the ancient world certainly knew how to write, not only using the alphabets of the Greeks and Romans but adopting them to their own sound systems in order to write their names. Following the Romanization of Cisalpine Gaul, many Celts achieved enough fluency in Latin to give literary expression through it, and soon these Celts gained literary reputations.

These writers tend to be classified simply as 'Latin writers', just as in modern times there is a tendency to claim many Irish, Scots, Welsh, Manx and Cornish writers as 'English' or Breton writers as 'French', largely because they write in the English or French language. For example, unfortunately typical is an entry in *The Reader's Encyclopaedia** which states: 'Stoker (Abraham) Bram. (1847–1912). English writer. Stoker is best known for *Dracula* (1987) . . .' Stoker was, of course, an Irishman, born in Dublin and educated at Trinity College. He was thirty-one years old before he first went to England. A close reading of his works shows his Irish origins but, because he wrote in English and not Irish, he is classed as English. In the same way many regard Jonathan Swift, Oliver Goldsmith, Richard Brinsley Sheridan, Oscar Wilde, G. B. Shaw, Peter Cheyney – the list is endless – as English writers. As it is in modern times, so it was in the period before the start of the Christian era. The Celts who wrote in Latin have become Latin writers, just as Martial, a Celtiberian, is now generally regarded as a Roman.

However, during the first century BC, Rome recognized a 'school' of Celtic poets emanating from Cisalpine Gaul. One of the leading figures of this 'school' was Gaius Valerius Catullus (*c*.85–54 BC), whose body of poetry has survived. He came from Verona, which was not then a Roman colony, and his name derives from the Celtic word *catos* – clever. Catullus' patron appears to be Metellus Celer, Governor of Cisalpine Gaul about 62 BC. Among other members of the 'school' was

* Harper & Row, 1988, third edition.

Helvius Cinna, who was from Brixia, one of the chief towns of the Cenomani. Catullus mentions that he wrote a long and complex poem entitled 'Zmyrna', based on mythological concepts. Cinna's poems are fascinating in that he introduces into Latin a number of Celtic words mainly connected with equestrian matters. Furius Bibaculus (c.103–25 BC) was from Cremona. His only surviving work is epigrams in which he mentions a fellow Cisalpine Gaul, a poet named Valerius Cato. Cato was originally a supporter of Julius Caesar during the civil-war period but later turned against him. Tacitus mentions that he wrote satires about Caesar. Another writer, usually associated with this Cisalpine Celtic 'school', is M. Terentius Varro (b. 82 BC), who was in fact from Transalpine Gaul. He contributed satires, love elegies and a war epic, *Bellum Sequanicum*, which is thought to have been an account of the conquest of his own people, the Sequani, by Julius Caesar. Unfortunately, of the few lines of this which survive, little can be deduced about its subject.

It is difficult to say how long the Celts of the Po Valley were contributing to Latin literature. As early as 179 BC, actually during the conquest and colonization of Cisalpine Gaul, we find Caecilius Statius (or Statius Caecilius) of Mediolanum (Milan), which Strabo says was the chief town of the Insubres. Quintus Horatius Flaccus (65–8 BC), the famous Horace, is on record as praising Caecilius, who is said to have combined lyrical quality with Aristophanic humour.

Around 90/89 BC we find Lucius Pomponius of Bononia (Bologna), who becomes the first Celt to satirize his fellow countrymen. Among the many farces attributed to him is one called *Galli Transalpini*. Doubtless, Pomponius would be presenting his fellow Celts to the Roman world in much the same way as certain Irish playwrights of the nineteenth century developed the 'stage Irishman' for English consumption. While the Celtic writers made an impression on Rome, Roman writers were generally dismissive of their work, just as the English and French in modern times, when speaking of their Celtic neighbours, make their 'Celticness' a matter of denigration. Cicero disliked the Celts, for example, although he had a number of Celtic friends. He particularly disliked the Celts' accent when they spoke Latin. He scorned Lucius Calpurnius Piso Caesonius, who became one of the two Roman consuls in 58 BC, because he was actually the grandson of an Insubrean Celt! Piso's daughter, Calpurnia, married Julius Caesar. There is some irony there – that the first Roman emperors were descended from Celts. Quintilian (AD *c*.35–96), himself a Celtiberian, was quite dismissive of the Celtic writers from the Po Valley, although he did allow himself to offer qualified admiration for an Insubrean writer on Epicurean philosophy, T. Catius.

Better known, however, was Cornelius Nepos (*c*.100–*c*.25 BC), another Insubrean Celt who, it is said, was a protégé of T. Catius, from Ticinum. Catullus dedicated his book of poems to Nepos, who was a friend of Cicero and of Atticus. His writings included a universal history, *Chronica*, love poems, anecdotes and biographical works. According to Professor H. D. Rankin: 'He was a respected senior Celtic intellectual of his time, and perhaps, to some degree, the patron of Catullus and others from his native country.' How Nepos managed to be on friendly terms with Cicero probably reflects on Nepos' attitude to his Celtic background. Cicero, for example, felt the Celts to be unrefined, barbaric and lacking in manners. He once launched an attack on the 'arrogance' of the Celts coming to Rome and walking about in their alien dress in 'uncouth fashion' through the Forum. One conjures up a picture of Nepos as being similar to certain modern Irish media personalities, making their way in the English world by denigrating the habits and attitudes of their fellow countrymen. Perhaps one does Nepos an injustice.

Yet another respected Celtic historian was Trogus Pompeius, writing in the time of the Emperor Augustus (*c*.27 BC–AD *c*.14). He was a native of Transalpine Gaul and Justin says he was a member of the Vocontii tribe. The Celtic philologist, Professor Horst Schmidt, in a work on Gaulish personal names, quotes a number of Gaulish names beginning with *trog-* and connects them with the Irish *tróg/truag* meaning 'miserable', cognate with the Welsh *tru*. Trogus wrote a universal history in forty-four books entitled *Historiae Philippicae*, but only an epitome of it survives, written by Justin.

More contentiously, Publius Vergilius Maro, the famous Virgil (70–19 BC), is claimed as a Celtic writer. He was certainly from Cisalpine Gaul, born in Andes, near Mantua, and educated at Cremona and Milan before going to Rome to study rhetoric and philosophy. Most general works agree on his Celtic origin although some believe his family were Etruscan settlers in the area. Professor Rankin says: 'We need not deny Celtic influences in the background of Virgil's life.' His poems are certainly rooted in the life among the Po Valley Celts. The *Eclogues* deal with the problems of land expropriation – a subject which Celtic poets were dealing with 2,000 years later. Virgil's epic poem the *Aeneid* has secured him a place in the history of literature and, according to Professor Rankin, 'a Celtic flavour has been perceived in it.' The work became the supreme epic of the Roman world.

Before leaving the Celtic influence on Latin writing at this time we must mention Titus Livius, the historian Livy (57 BC – AD 17), who is something of an enigma. He was a native of Patavium (Padua) in Cisalpine Gaul. He can scarcely be claimed as an admirer of anything Celtic and makes it clear that he considers the Celts' culture to be inferior and claims they have a lack of stamina and instability of temperament. And yet his writing shows a style which differentiates itself from his fellow Latin writers. Can it be that he speaks of the Celts simply as a Latin who is proud not to be one – a Latin colonial, having to grow up in a Celtic territory, perhaps in much the same way that Rudyard Kipling grew up in Bombay despising Indians? Or, more significantly, does Livy write as a Celt who is ashamed of being one and is at pains to conceal the fact – a figure all too familiar in the history of the Celtic peoples?

Livy's history of Rome from its founding, written in 142 books of which only 35 survive, has been described as imaginative and epic rather than scholarly. Camille Jullian has suggested that Livy's work was probably based on the imaginative Celtic epics interwoven in the Roman historical tradition. Episodes from Livy's history compare fascinatingly with episodes from native Celtic tradition. We have already mentioned the story of Valerius Corvus* and his single-handed combat: the episode of the crow which seems more at home in the *Táin Bó Chuailgne* than in a Latin history. The Roman historian, literary patron and statesman Gaius Asinius Pollio (76 BC – AD 4) criticized Livy for his provincial manner of expression, and clearly Livy was associated with the 'barbaric' lifestyle, speech and habits of the Celts of the Po Valley.

By the time of the Roman emperors, the Celts of the Po Valley, becoming more and more Romanized, were also playing their part in building the empire, just as the Irish, Scots, Welsh, Manx and Cornish gave individual contributions to the creation of England's empire. But they did so as Latins. From Celtic speech, the Celts of the Po Valley had

---

* See Chapter 2.

passed through a period of bilingualism, which, according to Professor Rankin, had given the impetus for the Celtic 'school' of writing during the first century BC. Referring to the Cisalpine Celtic poets' use of onomatopoeia and wordplay, he comments that this 'could easily be stimulated by the linguistic and cultural influence of a Celtic substrate'. All too soon, bilingualism gave way to monolingualism in the language of the conqueror and the Celts of the Po Valley became merged in the new Italian nation created by Rome.

[5]

The Sack of Delphi

L IVY informs us that at the same time that Bellovesos led the Celtic tribes into northern Italy his brother, Sigovesos, took other tribes eastwards in Europe. Livy says they settled in the Hercynian Forests of Central Europe. Archaeology indicates an eastward movement along the course of the Danube. Justin, writing his abridgement of the *Historiae Philippicae* by the Romanized Celtic historian Trogus Pompeius, says the Celtic tribes made for Illyria, guided there by birds, 'for the Celts are pre-eminent in the augur's art'. Illyria was an area of modern Yugoslavia, east of the Adriatic and bordering on the kingdoms of Macedonia and Epiros. Justin also records that some of the Celts settled in Pannonia (modern Hungary) and 'had various wars with their neighbours which lasted for a long time, and at last reached Greece and Macedonia, overthrowing everything before them'.

Unfortunately, we know little of the eastward movement until the Celts came into conflict with the Greeks and their arrival emerges in the written record. Trogus, via Justin, confirms the presence of Celtic tribes in the Carpathians around 358 BC. Archaeological evidence confirms that during the fifth and fourth centuries BC the Celts had started to settle at the start of the Balkan peninsula. Theopompos of Chios (*c.*376 – after 323 BC), an able Greek historian and friend of Philip II of Macedonia and later of Alexander the Great, wrote numerous books, including a continuation of Thucydides' history of Greece. In this later work he recounts the collision of the Celts with the Illyrian tribes on the Dalmatian coast opposite Pharos (Lesina) and Corcyra Nigra (Curzola) somewhere near the mouth of the Naron (Narenta). The predominant people of Illyria at this time were the Antariatae, whose lands extended into Bulgaria. According to the

Periplus of Scylax of Caryanda (521–486 BC), often quoted by Hecateus and other authors, they were a large, powerful people at the height of their military powers when the Celts arrived there. The Antariatae had exerted their authority over Macedonia and forced Amyntas II, the father of Philip II, to pay tribute to them in 393 BC. In 359 BC Bardulis, King of the Antariatae, defeated the army of Perdiccas III of Macedonia, brother of Philip II, and killed him. It was thus that Philip became King and he was eventually successful in driving back the Antariatae.

It has been suggested that Philip of Macedonia might have formed some alliance with the Celtic tribes settling in Illyria as a means of subduing the power of the Antariatae, for many of his coins have appeared among the Celtic archaeological finds in the Danube Valley. Similarly, it has been suggested that it was the Celts who kept the Antariatae occupied while Alexander of Macedonia was subduing the Thracians just after he came to the throne.

One of the most influential Celtic tribes of the area was the Scordistae, who built their tribal capital at Singidunum, near present-day Belgrade. Dr Jan Filip, the Czech Celtic scholar, is of the opinion that in some areas of the east the Celts settled as a ruling class only, but we lack reliable information. What we do know is that the Celtic move eastward covered a very wide area. Celtic cemeteries dating from this period and hill-forts have been found as far north as Wroclaw (Breslau) in Poland and as eastward as Krakow (Cracow) and even further along the Tisza river, beyond Košice into the Ukraine. These settlements are, however, sparse. The concentration of such hill-forts and cemeteries, showing a density of Celtic occupation, occurs in Czechoslovakia and Hungary. And we know that the Celtic Boii gave their name to part of this area – Bohemia. Unfortunately, it is only when the Celts entered the Greek world that they emerge into recorded history.

The Greeks had recognized the quality of Celtic warriors in the fourth century and had started to recruit them as mercenaries into their armies. Yet the recruitment was made, not from the Celts on their northern borders, but from the Celts of Cisalpine Gaul. Xenophon (c.428–354 BC), the historian and disciple of Socrates, records that Dionysius of Syracuse, the Greek colony in Sicily (430–367 BC), had recruited 2,000 Celts from Cisalpine Gaul in 366 BC and sent them to Sparta. Sparta was then engaged in a war against the rising power of

Thebes. Xenophon had great praise for the Celtic prowess as cavalry. He knew what he was talking about for he had served in the Spartan cavalry. Describing an encounter between the Celts and the Thebans near Corinth, Xenophon says:

> Few though they were, they were scattered here and there. They charged towards the Thebans, threw their javelins, and then dashed away as the enemy moved towards them, often turning around and throwing more javelins. While pursuing these tactics, they some-times dismounted for a rest. But if anyone charged upon them while they were resting, they would easily leap on to their horses and retreat. If enemy warriors pursued them far from the Theban army, these horsemen would then turn around and wrack them with their javelins. Thus they manipulated the entire Theban army, compelling it to advance or fall back at their will.

When Epaminondas of Thebes invaded Sparta, the Spartans used their Celtic cavalry to good effect. Sparta's dominant role had been weakened by the loss of Messenia, which had been re-formed in 370/369 BC into an independent state after 300 years' servitude to Sparta. Thebes had had a hand in this, and the formation of a league of Arcadian states against Sparta was also the work of Thebes. The war between Thebes and Sparta ended in 362 BC at the battle of Maninea, in which the Celtic cavalry played an important role. While Maninea was nominally a Theban victory, Thebes suffered the death of her king Epaminondas and so a peace was made.

It was about this time that Ephoros of Cyme named the Celts as one of the three great peoples on the circumference of the world and assigned north-west Europe as their homeland. But the Celtic peoples were already nearing the northern borders of the Greek states.

In 336 BC Philip II of Macedonia was killed by one of his bodyguard, coincidentally with a Celtic sword. When the sword was removed it was described as a short, broad-bladed Celtic sword with an ivory handle carved with the image of a chariot. The Macedonians saw this as a fulfilment of a prophecy which had warned Philip to beware of chariots. Philip's son Alexander (356–323 BC) became King of Macedonia. Soon he exerted his authority as overlord of all the Greek states and then turned to consolidate his northern frontiers. Having brought Thrace under his rule he moved to the banks of the Danube, and the peoples of the surrounding area came to his camp to form alliances and settle treaties with him.

Among the peoples who sent envoys to his camp were the Celtic tribes who now dwelt on the Adriatic coast of Illyria. Arrian, who is quoting Ptolemy, son of Lagus, who was one of Alexander's generals, says that Alexander received the Celts amicably. He gave a feast for them. They were, says Arrian, 'men of haughty demeanour and tall in proportion'. During the feast Alexander asked the Celts what they feared most, expecting them to answer 'You, my lord.' However, their reply was startling to the would-be conqueror of the world: 'We fear only that the sky will fall on our heads.' Strabo also describes the scene, again attributing it to Ptolemy's account. The Celtic envoys added, however, that they also 'put above everything else the friendship of such a man as he'. Alexander, perhaps somewhat abashed, made a treaty of friendship with them. Later, records Arrian, Alexander commented that for barbarians the Celts had a ludicrously high opinion of themselves.

Alexander and his historians seem to misunderstand the main thrust of the Celtic statement. While certainly declaring that they had no fear of Alexander, they were using a ritual formula to emphasize their good intentions and a desire for a treaty of equals. Their words were, in fact, a form of oath which was still to be found in Irish law tracts a millennium later, committing the individual's corporeal integrity to keep a bargain but also invoking natural elements: 'We will keep faith unless the sky fall and crush us or the earth open and swallow us or the sea rise and overwhelm us.'

This meeting of Alexander the Great and the Celts on the banks of the Danube in 334 BC was a significant one. It was the first meeting of Celts and Macedonians on an equal basis and the treaty of friendship seems to have lasted during the rest of Alexander's reign, while he left his northern frontiers undefended and took his army into Asia Minor to carve his famous empire. Again quoting Ptolemy, Arrian says that in 323 BC a group of Celtic envoys made the journey to Babylon to meet with Alexander, at that time engaged in plans to open a sea route from the mouth of the Euphrates to Egypt. Not long after this, Alexander suddenly fell ill at a drinking party, perhaps through fever or poison, and, after ten days, died.

In order to understand the subsequent history of the Celts in the Hellenic world, we must understand the turmoil into which that world was plunged following the death of Alexander. He was only thirty-three years old when he died and no provision had been made for a successor. Unlike the Celtic system, where chieftains were elected, and unlike the system then pertaining in the Roman republic where two consuls were elected annually, the system among the Greek states was that kings inherited titles under the law of primogeniture, under which the eldest-surviving legitimate son inherited. Alexander had been survived by an illegitimate son, Heracles, a boy of ten years of age. But he had left his wife Roxana pregnant. The Macedonian empire fell into chaos as Alexander's generals formed factions and these rival factions went to war. The Wars of the Hellenistic Monarchies, as they became known, lasted for a couple of centuries until the Roman republic eventually established its rule over the kingdoms.

Following a battle at Ipsus in 301 BC, Alexander's empire split into four major spheres of power – the kingdoms of Macedonia, Thrace, Egypt and Syria. In Macedonia Antipater became Regent, ostensibly for Alexander's legitimate heir, a son born of Roxana after his death. But Antipater established his own dynasty, which lasted until 294 BC, when a series of usurpers seized power for varying periods. The last of these was Ptolemy Ceraunnos (281–279 BC), who led the Macedonian army out to confront the Celtic army of Brennos and Acichoros, only to meet defeat and death.

In Egypt at the time of Alexander's death, Ptolemy son of Lagus was Military Governor. He decided to hang on to Egypt, ruling it until in 306 BC he adopted the title of pharaoh, becoming Ptolemy I Lagi, the founder of the Ptolemy dynasty, which survived three centuries until the death of Cleopatra, the last Ptolemy ruler.

Another general, Seleucos, a close friend and comrade of Alexander, had been his deputy in Syria. Seleucos now established himself as Seleucos I (312–280 BC) with his capital at Babylon. He then built a new city, Seleucia, on the Tigris, which he used before finally making his capital at Antioch (modern Hataz Antakya). Like all the former generals squabbling over Alexander's empire, Seleucos had an ambition to rule the entire empire. Lysimachos, another general, had seized the Macedonian throne and the two former comrades met at Corupedion in 281 BC. Both men were now octogenarians. They decided to settle their differences by fighting in single combat; Seleucos slew Lysimachos and put the Macedonian army to flight. Seleucos then crossed into Macedonia in 280 BC to claim the throne. However,

Ptolemy Ceraunnos, another former general of Alexander, had mean-while seized the throne. He was able to slay Seleucos and drive his Syrian army back into Asia Minor. Seleucos' son, Antiochus, called Soter or saviour, became King of Syria.

In the meantime, the Celts were still expanding on the northern borders of the Greek states. Greek chroniclers noticed that in 310 BC their old enemies the Antariatae of Illyria, the former great military power of the area, began to flee south in panic. The event was so extraordinary that it caused ructions in the Macedonian world. The Antariatae attempted to cross into Macedonia in strength. Cassander (c.358–297 BC), who was son of Antipater and ruler of Macedonia at this time, managed to contain them and allowed 20,000 of them to settle on his border. What had happened was that a great Celtic army led by a chieftain named Molistomos had moved into Antariatae territory, causing them to flee before them. It was the first indication that the Celts, who had remained quiet and settled since their treaty with Alexander, were now beginning to move down the Balkan peninsula towards the Greek states.

By 300 BC they were spreading eastward as well and had reached the valley of Morava, from where they became a threat to Thrace. In 298 BC a Celtic army advanced into the territory of modern Bulgaria where the Macedonian King Cassander opposed them. Cassander and his Macedonians managed to defeat the Celts on the slopes of Haemos. The following year Cassander died and once more the Celts were on the move. A Celtic army entered Thrace, led by Cambaules (which name perhaps means crooked hand). Thrace was bounded by the River Danube (called the Ister) to the north, the Black Sea and Bosporus in the east and Hellespont, Macedonia and Propontis in the south. An Indo-European people, the Thracians were considered primitive and barbaric by the Greeks, who had colonized the country extensively. Under Philip II of Macedonia Thrace had become a Macedonian protectorate. Now Thrace fell to Cambaules and re-mained under Celtic dominance for a hundred years. The last King of Thrace to bear a distinct Celtic name is recorded in 193 BC.

In 281/280 BC the Celts took further advantage of the rivalries between Alexander's successors. Three separate Celtic armies gathered on the northern borders and began an invasion of the Greek heartland. The main source of the history of these events would appear to be Hieronymus of Cardia, regarded as the most trustworthy historian of the period between the death of Alexander and the death of Pyrrhus of Epiros (323–272 BC). Hieronymus lived during the period he was describing and therefore his knowledge is first hand. While his original history is now lost, he is quoted extensively in the works of Diodorus and Arrian.

An eastern army of Celts, commanded by Cerethrios – the name could mean the rock – attacked from Bulgaria, coming out of Thrace on the eastern side of the peninsula. From Illyria, another army led by Bolgios – the name could mean glutton, although Hubert prefers thunderbolt – came to Epiros and Macedonia. Bolgios entered Macedonia near Monastir (Bitola). He sent envoys to the King, Ptolemy Ceraunnos, who, having killed Seleucos of Syria, was consolidating his position in order to take over Alexander's empire. Ptolemy Ceraunnos was not perturbed by the arrival of the Celts; after all, they were merely outlandish barbarians with, as Alexander had said, a ludicrously high opinion of themselves. He promptly killed the Celtic envoys who arrived at his court.

When Bolgios and the Celtic army appeared on the plains of Macedonia seeking vengeance, Ptolemy realized his mistake. The Macedonian army, which had fought and conquered under Alexander as far as India and Egypt, was scattered like chaff. Ptolemy Ceraunnos himself was slain in the battle and his head was placed on the point of a spear. The Celts moved through Macedonia pillaging and burning. A Macedonian officer named Sosthenes managed to regroup remnants of the army and conduct a small-scale guerilla war which kept Bolgios pinned down in Macedonia.

However, in 279 BC, the main Celtic thrust against Greece came with the appearance of a central army commanded by Brennos and Acichorius. Brennos, like his namesake who had sacked Rome, could be a proper name or simply a title, *brennin* – king. It has been suggested that Brennos and Acichorius might have been one and the same person. Most historians, however, identify them as separate individuals. Diodorus refers to Acichorius as Cichorius. The name could mean his sister's dog.

This central army had been fighting the hill tribes of Haemos through Paepnoa. When it descended into Macedonia it was reckoned, by Greek historians, to consist of 150,000 infantry and between 15,000 and 20,000 cavalry. Each horseman was accompanied by two mounted companions, the body of three being called a *trimarkisia*.

The figures were undoubtedly boosted by Greek historians to allow them a dignified position in the events which followed.

In Macedonia, Sosthenes, a soldier of modest origins we are told, had managed to keep Bolgios from entirely swamping the kingdom. But with the arrival of Brennos and Acichorius the Celtic army became overwhelming and soon passed on towards the other Greek states, leaving troops to prevent Macedonia from rising behind them. The Celtic army swept southwards.

The Greeks decided to confront the Celts at Thermopylae, the narrow pass linking Greece with the north between Thessaly and Locris. The Phocians had built a wall there to check the southerly raids of the Thessalians. In 480 BC the Persian invaders found a mountain pass at Thermopylae and managed to outflank the Spartan defenders and annihilate them there. That tragic piece of Greek history could not have escaped the memory of the armies that gathered at Thermopylae to defend the pass against the Celts. The army was predominantly an Athenian army, commanded by Callippus, son of Moerocles. Callippus decided to prevent the Celts from reaching the pass and sent a detachment of horsemen to the River Spercheius, north of the pass, to break down all the bridges over the fast-running waters.

Brennos and Acichorius reached the Spercheius and found the bridges down and the Greek army encamped on the opposite bank. Brennos sent a detachment of men to ford the river higher up in calmer water. The Celtic warriors are said to have swum across using their long shields as rafts. The next morning they created a few diversionary raids, causing Callippus to believe that the main Celtic army had crossed. He withdrew his army back to the pass at Thermopylae.

With the opposition gone, Brennos and Acichorius were able to cross the river at leisure. They commenced the rebuilding of the bridges, using the local population as forced labour. The Celtic army raided the surrounding countryside for provisions but they did not launch an attack on the city of Heracleia, whose citizens had shut their gates. Instead of engaging in a prolonged siege, the Celts seemed anxious to meet the Greek army and defeat it. Each day, Callippus' army was being reinforced with contingents from other Greek states.

Brennos and Acichorius reached the pass at Thermopylae within a few days. It was Callippus who began the battle, advancing on the Celtic lines at sunrise, quietly and in good order. The rough terrain and steep slopes of the mountains rendered use of the Celtic cavalry and chariots impossible. The fighting had to be done by the footsoldiers. Pausanias (AD *c.*160) says the Celts fought impressively, some reportedly pulling out Greek javelins from their bodies and casting them back at their enemies. As the battle for the pass raged, Callippus ordered an Athenian contingent to row down the coast and land to attack the flank of the Celtic army, using arrows and slingshots. The Celts were hard-pressed and many, trying to face the new attack from the seaward flank, encountered a coastal marshland, caused by the silting of the coast, which bogged them down in its mud. Casualties were heavy. Fighting lasted all day and both sides finally withdrew to their respective lines at nightfall.

For an entire week the two armies kept their positions. Brennos is said to have devised a plan to split the Greek ranks. Obviously well informed about Greek politics and knowing that the union of the Greek city states was a temporary phenomenon, he detached his cavalry, which had been useless for fighting at Thermopylae, to enter the neighbouring region of Aetolia. They sacked the town of Callion and although the Oatians sent an army to the Aetolians' aid they were completely defeated. Greek propaganda went overboard in recounting the sack of Callion. Here the Celts were said to have eaten the flesh of infants and drunk their blood, while the women of the town ran themselves on to the Celts' swords rather than be taken alive. The Celtic warriors are said not to have abstained from intercourse with the dead and dying women. The list of atrocities is remarkably similar to Herodotus' account of the Persian invasion. The Celts certainly plundered Aetolia and the news reached the ears of the Aetolians serving in Callippus' army, as the Celtic commanders knew it would. The Aetolians immediately left their comrades to hasten to defend their homeland. Brennos and Acichorius had succeeded in splitting the Greek army.

Brennos now persuaded some of the local people to show him a mountain pass across Mount Oeta which would outflank Callippus' position in the main pass of Thermopylae. On Mount Oeta was a temple of Athena which Callippus had garrisoned in case the way was discovered. Telesarchos was the Greek commander of this garrison and despite an assault by the Celts he managed to hold out. Finally, however, the Celts bypassed the temple and moved round the flank and rear of Callippus' army. Their descent behind the Greeks was hidden in a morning mist. Fighting was fierce but the Celts held the advantage. Callippus managed to save the majority of his Athenian contingent by evacuating them to their ships and so prevented the disaster which had overwhelmed Leonidas and his Spartans when they tried to hold the pass against the Persians in 480 BC. The Greek accounts praise the bravery of a young Athenian named Cydias, who was fighting his first and last battle. When he fell his shield was taken to Athens and dedicated in the temple of Zeus Eleuthrios. Centuries later it was stolen by the Roman dictator Sulla when he campaigned in Greece between 86 and 84 BC.

The Greek army had been beaten. The pass at Thermopylae lay open, the road to the rich Greek city states was unimpeded. All Greece lay undefended before the Celts.

Leaving Acichorius at Heracleia to keep the Aetolians and Phocians at bay, Brennos turned his army and came by way of the gorges of Parnassos to Delphi in Phocis. Delphi was situated on the southern slopes of Mount Parnassos, the site of the most famous oracle of Apollo, and the most sacred site of the Hellenic world. It had been continuously occupied since Mycenaean times (c.1400 BC). This was the residence of the oracle, the Pythia (python), a female who had to be fifty years of age before her appointment and thereafter lived a life of seclusion making pronouncements to those who consulted her. Kings, emperors and dictators throughout the Hellenic world, and later Rome, came to seek her judgements. Terracotta figures of the priestess dating back to the twelfth century BC have been found, although worship of Apollo as an oracle god of prophecy is said to have commenced only in the eighth century BC. The temple of Delphi had been destroyed in 373 BC in an earthquake but had been rebuilt. It was not until AD 391 that the Emperor Theodosius finally closed it in the name of Christianity.

Brennos and his Celts made their way to the temple complex. The Greek historians claim storms and earthquakes marked their coming, causing panic among the Celtic warriors. The ghosts of Greek heroes were said to have risen up to defend the sacred site. Although the Greek historians had the gods on their side, they were unable to change history. The Celts raided Delphi and slew the Pythia, making off with the fabulous treasures which had been collected at the site over the centuries. An army of Aetolians and Phocians came racing up to defend their gods and treasures but were unable to prevent the Celts making an orderly withdrawal, with the treasure, to rejoin Acichorius near Heracleia. However, Brennos was said to have been wounded in the attacks.

The Romanized Celtic historian Trogus Pompeius, quoted by Justin, recorded that within the Celtic army were warriors from a tribe called the Tectosages. The Tectosages are later named as one of the founding tribes of Galatia. However, they also appear in Gaul, where their tribal capital was Tolosa (Toulouse). Whether the three geographically disparate people were one tribe, or whether they were different tribes using a similar name, or – again – whether they were different branches of one tribe, is unclear. Trogus says that part of the great treasure of Delphi passed into their keeping. When the Romans captured Tolosa in 106 BC, the Consul Quintilius Servilius Caepio found treasure in a sacred Celtic lake nearby. Strabo claimed it was part of the Delphic treasure. Caepio took charge of it and was ordered to transport it to Rome. However, it vanished en route with its guards. Caepio was said to have been ordered into exile for complicity in the affair and a new phrase entered the Latin language – *aurum Tolosanum*, 'Toulouse gold', meaning ill-gotten goods.

What happened to Brennos, Acichorius and the Celtic army is somewhat confused. The Greek historians, enraged by the sack of Delphi, now draw a picture of a broken and accursed Brennos. For his act of sacrilege at Delphi, it is said that Apollo wounded him three times with his own hand. Then they say that Brennos, realizing his profanity, took his own life. A small bronze statue in the Naples museum, a replica of the original, is said to represent his suicide. The Celts are then reported to have moved northwards out of Greece, leaving it in disarray. Accepting the suicide of Brennos as true, or his death by some other means, such as from his wounds in battle, it is obvious that the Celtic army did not leave Greece in confusion. They withdrew in an orderly manner taking their loot with them. No Greek army was strong enough to attack them. In fact, the city states were in such turmoil that the famous celebration of the Panathenaea had to be suspended for the year 278 BC. Soon afterwards a festival to celebrate the deliverance of the Greeks by the puzzling withdrawal of the Celts, called the Soteria or Salvation Festival, was instituted by the Amphictiones, the religious assembly of the Greek states.

The Greeks were clearly shocked by what had happened. The event had an effect on the Greek literary world, and for a long time poetic epics about the Celtic invasion were composed and these works were collectively known as *Galatika*. Unfortunately, none has survived. The Celtic invasion was also commemorated by other artforms. Pausanius says that the battle at Thermopylae between Brennos and Callippus was depicted in a great wall painting in the council chamber of Athens. Other such paintings were to be found in the temples of Apollo in both Greece and Italy; many also showed the sack of Delphi. Propertius (*c*.50 BC – after 16 BC) records that at Delos and even in Rome there were commemorations. In Rome, on the ivory doors of the temple of the Palatine, were carvings of the Celts sacking Delphi. Minor artworks, pendants, as well as paintings, have emerged in various parts of the Hellenic world. A medallion found in Capua shows a Celtic warrior with his foot on the severed head of the Pythia while on the bottom of a goblet, produced in Cales, Celtic warriors are seen against a background of the burning colonnades of Delphi.

In 277 BC a Celtic army was still in northern Greece. Antigonus Gonatas, the grandson of one of Alexander's generals who had been killed at Ipsus in 301 BC, had arrived in Macedonia. Since the Celts had slain Ptolemy Ceraunnos, Macedonia had been without a king. Antigonus Gonatas had made an alliance with Antiochus I of Syria and with his blessing was able to claim the Macedonian throne. His father Demetrios had ruled Macedonia from 294 to 287 BC, and on that fact he had based his claim. Antigonus Gonatas found that he had one obstacle in his path. The Celts were still in Macedonia. According to Trogus, quoted by Justin, he despatched envoys to the Celts, asking them to send ambassadors to meet with him. The ambassadors duly went to see him and returned to their chieftains with enthusiastic accounts of Antigonus Gonatas' wealth and simplicity of character. It would appear that Antigonus had crossed from Asia Minor into Macedonia, for the Celts believed they could overwhelm his camp by a surprise night attack and loot his treasures. They gathered their army on the Gallipoli peninsula and made their attack. It was an ambush. The camp was deserted and suddenly the Celts found Antigonus attacking them in the rear.

Having defeated the Celts, Antigonus Gonatas came to an agreement with them. He was obviously not yet sufficiently secure in his position as King of Macedonia simply to attempt to drive them out of the country. He therefore recruited a large force into his army under the leadership of their chieftain Ceredrios. When Pyrrhus of Epiros returned to Greece in 275 BC, following his campaigns in Italy, the

Celts served Antigonus Gonatas against him. Pyrrhus, who had reigned as King of Macedonia for a brief year in 287 BC, wanted to re-establish himself as king there. He defeated Antigonus Gonatas and, according to Pausanius, especially rejoiced that he had been able to vanquish the Celtic mercenaries in the Macedonian army. He recruited them into his own army and allowed them to sack the rich tombs of the ancient Macedonian kings at Aegae. In an attempt to reassert Macedonian authority he marched against Sparta in 272 BC with a strong Celtic contingent and then turned against Argos, in the north-east Peloponnese, where he was killed.

Antigonus Gonatas returned to the throne of Macedonia, which he was able to keep for thirty-two years, from 271 to 239 BC. He continued to use Celtic warriors as mercenaries in his army and Justin recounts that down to the end of the Macedonian Wars of Succession the Celts left their dead scattered about the battlefields of Greece, martyrs to the cause of every Greek party and faction.

In 265 BC a contingent of Celts were stationed in the city of Megara and mutinied because of irregular and poor pay. Megara, a Dorian city at the eastern end of the isthmus of Corinth, was where Eucleides of Megara (c.390 BC) founded his school of philosophy. The mutiny was suppressed and all the Celts were put to the sword.

Celtic warriors were still serving in the Macedonian army when Perseus, the last of the Antigonidae kings, ascended the throne in 179 BC. He devoted his energies to consolidating Macedonian power in Greece, supposedly independent but, in reality, subject to the will of Rome. In 171 BC Perseus actually felt strong enough to challenge Rome's will and the Third Macedonian War began. At Larissa, in eastern Thessaly, Perseus, using a large force of Celtic warriors, repulsed the Roman army. In 168 BC Lucius Aemilius Paullus led a Roman army into Macedonia where, on 22 June, he encountered Perseus. Perseus attacked the Romans at Pydna on the western shore of the Gulf of Salonika. Rome triumphed and some 20,000 members of the Macedonian army were killed and 11,000 were taken prisoner. Perseus himself was captured and he ended his days in exile in Rome in 166 BC. The mighty empire of Alexander the Great was now a province of Rome. However, Andriscos, a claimant to the Macedonian throne, attempted an uprising in 149 BC, causing the Fourth Macedonian War. The uprising was crushed, Andriscos was executed and the tradition of Celtic mercenaries serving in the Macedonian army was finally brought to an end.

Returning to the year 277 BC, when Antigonus Gonatas defeated the last independent Celtic army in Greece and recruited them not only for Macedonia but, as we shall see in subsequent chapters, for the armies of other Hellenistic kings, there is a question to be asked. The dispersal of the Celtic armies could not have been achieved simply by their recruitment as mercenaries, that is if we are to believe the Greek estimates of their size. It would seem that the bulk of them moved north again, having found no room in populated Greece to settle.

The Celts discovered more space on the northern plains of Morava, Maritza and along the Danube Valley, where towns sprang up bearing Celtic names such as Bonia (Vidin), Ratiaria (Artcher), Durostorum (Silistria) and Noviodunum (Isakcha). Cambaules' original conquest of Thrace still held firm but according to Polybius and Trogus, as quoted by Justin, the Celts of Thrace eventually became Hellenized and disappeared as a distinct culture, leaving few remnants of their civilization. They struck coins, some bearing Celtic names like Cauros, the last King of Thrace to bear a distinctive Celtic name in 193 BC. According to Polybius, Cauros was a very successful political leader who acted as an arbiter between Byzantium and the King of Bithynia. He is recorded as a diplomat and a just man who had a kingly nature and greatness of soul. He is also said to have kept good order in his dominions. Polybius, writing in praise of Cauros, sounds as if he knew Cauros personally and this is certainly possible.

In addition to the Celtic kingdom of Thrace there were other Celtic regions established in the aftermath of the Celtic exodus from Greece. A Celtic tribe led by a chieftain named Comantorios settled on the slopes of Haemos. The Scordisci had also established a fairly prosperous and strong kingdom around modern Belgrade. There emerges an entire region of Celtic place-names and sites, albeit thinly sown, running northwards along the Black Sea. Pausanias speaks of a Celtic people, the Cabari, remarkable for their great stature, living far to the north 'on the edge of the frozen desert'. Certainly Celtic objects dating from this period have been found in the southern Ukraine, along the Dnieper, while on the Dniester was a town with the Celtic name of Camodunum (Zaleszcyki). Plutarch, the Greek historian (AD c.46–120), fixed the eastward limit of the Celtic world as far as the Sea of Azos (Maeotis).

The Boii, a tribe found in northern Italy, are also frequently mentioned as inhabitants of the area which is now Czechoslovakia and, in fact, gave their name as Boiohaemum, or Bohemia, to the area. Celtic graves exist here which date back to the fifth century BC and burials continued on the sites regularly until the third century BC. It would seem that there were at least two branches of the Boii, or two tribes with the same name, as with the Tectosages, who were found at the same time in Asia Minor and in Gaul. Some historians have tried to make the Boii into one tribe with one leader and have ascribed their appearance in Czechoslovakia to their alleged expulsion by the Romans from northern Italy about 190 BC. This would not fit in with archaeological evidence, which places the Celtic occupation of the area long before 190 BC. However, the first confirmation that the Celts in the area were called the Boii does not occur until 113 BC, when they repulsed the eruption of the Cimbri. Following this, archaeologists have pointed to a fall-off in the number of Celtic burials, which seems to indicate that the Celts were generally losing their population and power in this area.

We have also seen that by the fourth century BC the Celts had settled along the valleys of Mures, Somes and Cris in Transylvania and also in Moldavia among the Geto-Dacian population. They seemed to have been absorbed by the second century BC, their knowledge of metal-working contributing to an acceleration of the development of Dacian culture. By the second century BC, according to Trogus, Oroles, the Dacian King, had built up Dacia as a powerful kingdom. When Rome made her first intervention in the Balkans, M. Minucius Rufus attempted an attack on Dacia, which made an alliance with the Celtic Scordisci in the Danube Valley. But by the first century BC, Rome was gradually gaining control of the territories which bordered Dacia. Yet the Dacians were able to keep the Romans at bay and go through a high point of cultural development. From 70 to 44 BC Burebista was King and centralized the state. According to Strabo:

Having become the leader of his people, exhausted by frequent wars, the Getic Burebista raised them so much through drilling, abstention from wine and obedience to orders, that he achieved a powerful state within a few years and subjected to the Getae the major part of the neighbouring populations, coming to be feared by the Romans themselves.

In 60 BC Burebista launched an offensive against the Celtic peoples, the Boii and Taurisci, in Pannonia and in Slovakia, in order to expand the frontiers of his Dacian state. He also extended his rule to the Greek colonies in the area. It was after their defeat by Burebista that the Celts began to leave Bohemia. According to Greek lists some 32,000 men, women and children of the Boii moved from Bohemia and went to Noricum (Austria), where they besieged Noreja (Neumarkt) without success. They then moved into Switzerland to join the Celtic Helvetii in their westward migration into Gaul, where they were checked and defeated by Julius Caesar. The survivors of the Boii were allowed to settle in the country of the Aedui and remain there permanently as farmers. Burebista, who had caused their migration, offered an alliance to Pompey against Caesar during the Roman civil war. The alliance did not materialize as Pompey was killed in Egypt. Caesar considered an expedition against Burebista, 'the first and most powerful among all the kings who had ever reigned in Thrace, ruling over the entire area, beyond the great river'. A few months after Caesar's own assassination, Burebista was killed, the victim of a plot, and his kingdom was divided. Soon the Emperor Augustus extended Roman influence to the area.

The clash of the Greek and Celtic worlds led to an exchange between the cultures. There was certainly a Hellenization of those Celts who settled within the world of Hellenic influence. There was also a Celtic input into the Hellenic world, even to the extent of some loan-words entering the Greek language from Celtic. The Celts also take their place in literary tradition, not only in the *Galatika* epic poetry, previously mentioned, but in the work of Theocritus, writing in the first half of the third century BC, in which he introduces Galatea, the sea-nymph daughter of Nereus and Doris. Galatea is, of course, the synonym for Galatian, Gaul or Celt, and is said to mean, significantly, milk-white. The Greeks often praised the beauty of the fair, 'milk-white' skin of the Celts. Theocritus tells the story of Galatea being wooed by the ugly Polyphemus, the Cyclops. Galatea becomes the eponymous ancestor of the Celts (the Galatians). From echoes by Virgil and Ovid, the story was set down by the English poet John Gay and this provided the libretto for Handel's *Acis and Galatea*.

One of the most intriguing mysteries of the contact between the Greek and Celtic worlds was the suggestion by the Alexandrian school of Greek writers that the Greeks accepted 'much of their philosophy' from the Celts. The Celts were among the first to develop a doctrine on the immortality of the soul. This doctrine was passed from the Celts to the Greeks, so it is claimed by Sotion of Alexandria (*c*.200–170 BC). Alexander Cornelius (Polyhistor) (*c*.105 BC) quotes a text by Aristotle in support of this idea. Some scholars have said that the Aristotle of Polyhistor was not the famous Aristotle (384–322 BC) who taught Alexander the Great. Many later Greek writers mention the claim, some using sources that have become lost to us. How valid are their arguments?

It is generally accepted that the doctrine of immortality was a teaching of Pythagoras, a Greek polymath, philosopher and mystic, of the late sixth century BC. Yet it was said that Pythagoras did not write anything down and within a few years of his death (*c*.500 BC), owing to the contradictions in the traditions of his life and teaching, he had become a figure of mystery and legend. His teachings were spread by disciples and, when they became a highly political organization, they were suppressed about 450 BC. Therefore, one has to bear in mind that there is no definite evidence of what Pythagoras taught.

Yet the most celebrated claim to fame was that he taught a doctrine of the immortality of the soul, which was more a doctrine of reincarnation or transmigration of the soul. It has been said that he claimed to have been, in a previous reincarnation, the Trojan Euphorbus, who had been slain at Troy. Xenophanes of Colophon (*c*.570 BC), and therefore a contemporary of Pythagoras, is reported to have been shocked by this idea.

Now the superficial similarity of this doctrine and that of the druidic teaching has been remarked upon by many writers of the ancient world. The druids taught that death was only a changing of place and that life went on with all its forms and goods in another world, a world of the death which gave up living souls. Therefore, a constant exchange of souls takes place between the two worlds – this world and the famous Otherworld of the pre-Christian Celtic religion. Death in this world took a soul to the Otherworld; death in the Otherworld brought a soul to this world. So Philostratus of Tyana (AD *c*.170–249) observed that the Celts celebrated birth with mourning and death with joy.

The cynical soldier in Julius Caesar could remark, 'The druid's chief doctrine is that the soul of a man does not perish but passes after death from one person to another. They hold that this is the best of all incitements to courage as banishing the fear of death.' This was how Caesar accounted for the reckless courage of the Celts in battle.

Sotion, writing in the second century BC, is the earliest-surviving reference to the idea that the Greeks took the doctrine of immortality from the Celts. The earliest-known contact between the Greek and Celtic worlds was in the fourth century and if Pythagoras taught the idea in the late sixth century surely its adoption by the Greeks predates the coming of the Celts? But did the Celts have earlier contacts with the Greeks? Hecataeus of Miletus (c.520 – c.476 BC) was a contemporary of Pythagoras and he certainly knew of the Celts. This would make feasible the claim of Aristotle, as quoted by Polyhistor, that the doctrine came from the Celts and, moreover, that it was a Celt who taught Pythagoras the idea. Polyhistor, quoting Aristotle, says that Pythagoras learned the doctrine from a slave named Zalmoxis. Zalmoxis is identified as Pythagoras' slave by Herodotus. Clement of Alexandria (AD c.150–211/6), a theologian with a thorough knowledge of Greek literature and Stoic philosophy, reiterates that Zalmoxis taught Pythagoras and that Zalmoxis must have been a Celt.

Sotion, who wrote accounts of the philosophers of different schools, became a main source of Diogenes Laertius (writing in the third century AD), who says, 'the study of this philosophy had its beginning among the barbarians.' Indeed, Celsus (AD c.178–80), quoted by Origen (AD c.186–256), points out that the Celts were a 'very wise and ancient nation'.

There is, however, a contrary tradition. Diodorus Siculus (d. c.21 BC) was the first to reverse the claims, saying that the Celts had developed their philosophy from that of Pythagoras. 'The Pythagorean doctrine prevailed among the Celts, teaching that the souls of men are immortal, and after a fixed number of years they will enter into another body.' He continues: 'The druids, who were of a loftier intellect, and bound by the rules of brotherhood as decreed by Pythagoras' authority, were exalted by investigation of deep and serious study, and despising human affairs, declared souls to be immortal.'

Hippolytus (AD c.170–236), obviously using Diodorus as his source, makes the same claim, but goes even further, clearly aware of the suggestion that Zalmoxis was Pythagoras' teacher. He states that, at the death of Pythagoras, Zalmoxis returned to Thrace, where he taught the Celts. Hippolytus was under the impression that Thrace had been a Celtic country longer than it had, for, as we have seen, Cambaules and his Celts did not conquer Thrace until 300 BC, 200 years after Pythagoras' death. Hippolytus, in his *Philosophumena*, writes:

> The druids among the Celts having profoundly examined the Pythagorean philosophy, Zalmoxis, a Thracian by race, the slave of Pythagoras, became for them the founder of this discipline. After the death of Pythagoras, he made his way there, and became the founder of this philosophy, for them. The Celts honour them [the druids] as prophets and prognosticators because they foretell matters by ciphers and numbers according to the Pythagorean skill . . .

While the Alexandrian school, arguing that the Greeks took the doctrine from the Celts, is certainly older than those writers arguing that the Celts took it from the Greeks, there is a third possibility to consider – perhaps the doctrine was simply a case of parallel development. And, if one considers very carefully, there is yet a fourth possibility – perhaps the similarity is so superficial that it does not really exist. After all, the Pythagorean belief was in the transmigration of the souls through all living things, according to those who wrote it down centuries after Pythagoras' death; whereas the Celtic belief was in the rebirth of the soul in human bodies from one world to another. It could therefore be argued that the Celtic and Pythagorean doctrines were mutually exclusive.

[6]

Galatia

'WHAT we know of the Galatian state gives us our first example of the organization of a Celtic state,' says Henri Hubert in *The Greatness and Decline of the Celts* (1934). Galatia was established by the Celts in Asia Minor during the third century BC and a Celtic language was still spoken there in the fourth century AD. The Galatians had become one of the first peoples to accept the new religion of Christianity and are now best known through Paul of Tarsus' famous Epistle to the Galatians written about AD 55.

Galatia had been established through the disunity of the petty kingdoms of Asia Minor, once united under Alexander the Great's empire. Antiochus I's Syrian empire claimed the territory of Asia Minor, or modern Turkey. In reality, however, there were many subdivisions. After the battle of Ipsus in 312 BC, Armenia, which had been part of the Syrian empire, revolted and two kingdoms emerged – Armenia Major and Armenia Minor. It is not until 190 BC that the first-known kings of these territories find record.

Bithynia was a kingdom still claiming independence, stretching from the Bosporus along the coast of the Black Sea. When Alexander invaded Asia Minor, Bithynia had been a semi-independent kingdom within the Persian empire, ruled by Bas (334–326 BC). Bas had managed to retain his kingdom in spite of quarrels with Alexander's successors. On his death his son Zipoetes (326–278 BC) continued his father's policies, enjoying a reign of forty-eight years. When he died his two sons, Nicomedes and Zipoetes, argued over the kingdom but Nicomedes emerged as the next king, reigning from 278 to 250 BC. Nicomedes was to play an important part in the settlement of the Celts in Galatia.

In north-east Asia Minor (Turkey), there was another semi-independent kingdom, that of Pontus, founded by Arionarzanes in 363 BC. The monarchy he founded survived Alexander's conquests and the quarrels of his generals, with the Pontic kings retaining their independence until Pharnaces II submitted to Julius Caesar at Zela in 47 BC. Near to Pontus was the smaller kingdom of Paphlagonia, which had become part of the Pontus kingdom at the dissolution of the Persian empire, but seems to have retained a series of petty kings. To the south-east lay another semi-independent kingdom – that of Cappadocia, founded by Ariarathese I (331–322 BC). It was taken over as the personal fiefdom of Alexander's friend Perdiccas but reasserted its independence in 315 BC and managed to retain it until AD 15. To the south-west, on the coastline of the Aegean, a new kingdom was founded by Philetaerus (281–263 BC) in the turmoil of the conflict between Syria and Macedonia – this was the kingdom of Pergamas or, more popularly, Pergamum.

Into the turmoil of the rivalries and wars of these kingdoms, in the wake of the dissolution of Alexander's empire, came the Celts.

Antigonus Gonatas, having defeated the last remaining Celtic army in Greece, had recruited a section of them, under their chieftain Ciderios, into the Macedonian army. At the same time Antigonus Gonatas recruited many thousands of Celtic warriors for service in the army of Ptolemy of Egypt. Nicomedes of Bithynia saw an opportunity to use the Celts in his own war of survival, first against his quarrelsome brother Zapoetes and secondly against the claims of Antiochus I of Syria. He asked the Macedonian King, Antigonus Gonatas, to recruit a force of Celtic mercenaries. In response to the request, the Macedonian King recruited some 20,000 Celts, of whom 10,000 were under arms. The pay was a gold piece per warrior. The Celts consisted of three tribes – the Tolistoboii, the Tectosages and the Trocmi. According to Poseidonius (c.135–50 BC) these tribes had already detached themselves from the Celtic army before the sack of Delphi. They were led by their chieftains Leonnorios and Lutarios. They crossed at the Hellespont (Dardanelles) into Asia Minor, taking their women and children with them.

With such troops, Nicomedes of Bithynia was able to reach a prompt and successful conclusion with his brother and end his ambition to become king. But Leonnorios and Lutarios soon became aware of the warring Greek factions within Asia Minor and realized that they could take personal advantage of this situation. They left the service of Nicomedes and began demanding tribute from the Greek city states of Troy, Ephesos and Miletos on the Aegean coastline. Tradition has it that the vestal virgins of Miletos killed themselves when the Celts sacked the city. Livy says that the Celtic tribes divided Asia Minor between them as far east as Taurus. This seems an exaggeration. However, within a few years the Celts had certainly formed settlements in the area which was to be named after them – Galatia.

It was Hieronymos of Cardia who is credited with the first-known use of the term Galatia, the land of the Gauls, Galli or Celts. The area was in the northern zone of the central plateau of Asia Minor, a region rising to 2,000–4,000 feet above sea level. It was a country of few trees, bare hills but small and fertile plains during the rainy season. It was frequently affected by droughts and consequent famine. The area had once been the centre of the Phrygian kingdom, famed for King Midas and Gordius of the famed Gordian knot. Phrygia had lost its independence in the sixth century BC. In the *Iliad* the Phrygians were represented as an heroic warrior people. It is generally thought that they were part of an early movement from Greece and therefore spoke a form of Greek.

When the Celts settled in the area they lived side by side with the native population and did not, in general, occupy the cities, preferring to build their traditional hill-forts and farming settlements. Deiotaros I of Galatia was known to have ruled from a *dun*, although Pessinus, once the main religious centre of the Phrygians, was said to be the chief town of the Celts. Eventually the remnants of the Phrygian civilization were assimilated into Celtic culture and not, as some have maintained, the reverse. The three Celtic tribes settled in separate enclaves. The Tolistoboii settled the upper valley of the Sangarios (Sakarya), by whose winding path the tombs of long-dead Phrygian kings lay. Pessinus was claimed to be their centre. In this territory stood the famous city of Gordium (now Polatli), which had been the capital of ancient Phrygia where, in the acropolis of the temple of Zeus Basileus, there stood a pole around which was tied an intricate knot. Legend had it that Gordius, father of King Midas, had tied this knot and a prophecy was handed down that he who unravelled it would become lord of all Asia. In 333 BC Alexander had rested in the city and, on examining the knot, simply hacked it to pieces with his sword, claiming the prophecy to be fulfilled. And into many languages has come the phrase 'to cut the Gordian knot', meaning to overcome a difficulty by violent measures.

Further east the Tectosages claimed the territory around Tavium, which was their centre. And again, eastward, the Trocmi settled along the banks of the River Halys (Kizilirmak), with Ancyra (Ankara) as their chief settlement. Strabo referred to Ancyra as a Celtic *phrourion*, a stronghold. So perhaps Ancyra was originally a hill-fort. Strabo assures us that all three Celtic tribes spoke the same language (*homoglotti*). He says that each tribe was divided into four septs and actually names some of them. The Tolistoboii, for example, contained the Voturi, Ambitui and Tosiopes while the Tectosages had a sept called the Teutobodiaci. Each sept was ruled by a chieftain and two sub-chieftains, with a judge. Was this judge, in reality, a druid? Strabo goes on to say that the twelve septs sent a total of 300 elected representatives to an assembly at the main centre of Drunemeton. Unfortunately the exact site of Drunemeton is not clear. Perhaps, if Pessinus was the chief city of the Celts, they are one and the same place. The name is typically Celtic, the sanctuary of oaks. *Nemeton* as the word for sanctuary occurs in many Celtic names. Nemetodurum was the early name for Nanterre. Nemetobrigia occurs as a place-name in Spanish Galicia. Vernemeton is mentioned by Fortunatus as a Celtic centre in Nottinghamshire, while Medionemeton was situated in southern Scotland.

The form of government described by Strabo as existing among the Celts of Galatia is paralleled by the assembly of Gaul, which met at Lugdunum (Lyons). The Greeks referred to the state as Koinon Galaton, the Commonwealth of Galatians, and it is true that the name of no particular overall leader emerges for a long time. This form of government accords with everything we know of later social and political structures among the Celts, with the electoral system ensuring that no despot could exert supreme sovereignty. It is certain that the Celts took their druids and religion with them into Asia Minor. Diogenes Laertius, writing in the third century AD, says that they had seers called *druidae* and *semnotheoi*. Even earlier writers such as Clement of Alexandria (AD *c*.150–216) says the Galatians had a druid class. This has been echoed by Cyril of Alexandria (*c*. fifth century AD) and Stephanus of Byzantium (*c*. seventh century AD), who cited earlier sources now lost.

The Celts of Galatia issued their own coinage. However, not many clearly identifiable Celtic archaeological remains have been uncovered in the area. Certainly there have been many brooches of the second century BC, identified as Celtic La Tène C types. In a chambered tomb at Mal Tepe, at Mezek, the third-century BC remains of a Celtic chariot with bronze fittings have been found. Like their fellow Celts in Europe, the Galatians did not bequeath any documentation in their own language. The few inscriptions that survive were written in Greek. According to Henri Hubert: 'Their Greek is so correct . . .' He maintains: 'Greek was the language of the Gallic troops . . . Greek was likewise the official language of the Gauls of Asia Minor. They have not left a single inscription in Celtic.' However, Professor Rankin propounds the theory that the Galatians were, in fact, anti-Greek and did not become Hellenized to any large degree and, when the area fell under Roman conquest, actually adopted Roman forms in preference to Greek. There could be some truth in both arguments. The Galatians certainly used Greek and later Latin in their commerce with the surrounding Graeco-Latin world. But the truth is that they maintained their own Celtic language until a surprisingly late period.

According to Strabo the Galatians spoke Celtic in his day (c.63 BC–AD 21), and Lucan (AD c.39–65) supports this. He refers to a soothsayer from Paphlagonia, bordering on Galatia, who spoke Celtic. And then we have the famous evidence of St Jerome (Eusebius Hieronymous) in the fourth century AD. St Jerome spent some time in Trèves, in Gaul, and when he stayed in Ancyra for a while he was able to state categorically not only that the Galatians still spoke Celtic but that the language was very close to that spoken by the Gauls of Trèves, the Treveri. So we may safely say that Celtic was spoken in the central plain of what is modern Turkey for at least seven centuries. How long it existed after the end of the fourth century is unknown. It would be fairly safe to say that it must have lasted a few centuries more in the area.

The state of Galatia had not come about by conquest but rather by agreement with the surrounding Hellenistic kings, who were anxious to resolve the 'Celtic problem' which threatened their security. Nicomedes of Bithynia, having invited the Celtic tribes into Asia Minor, had been unable to control them or check their ravages against the Greek city states of the western coast. The term *Galatika* (Gaulgeld) or 'Celtic tribute' had entered into the Greek vocabulary, for the

Celts roamed the area demanding tribute from the Greek kings; it was a highly organized 'protection racket' on a grand scale.

In 275 BC Antiochus I of Syria defeated the Celts, crushing them with his elephants, against which they had no experience. In the wake of this defeat, and seemingly with the approval of Antiochus and surrounding monarchs, the Celts were allowed to settle in Galatia. Like other Celtic communities, they turned to farming. But not long afterwards they began to raid outside their agreed territorial borders. In 265 BC they met with the Syrian King Antiochus once again and in a battle near Ephesus they defeated and slew him. They seemed to take no advantage of the defeat of the Syrians and Antiochus Theus, Antiochus II, was allowed to succeed his father, becoming a rather weak and profligate ruler. During his reign two more territories in the north-east, Bactria and Parthia, broke off from Syria and established themselves as independent kingdoms. Antiochus tried to impose his rule on the Celts at Ancyra but was unsuccessful. He was finally murdered by his wife Laodice and was succeeded by Seleucos II (246–226 BC), who lost most of the Syrian kingdom beyond the Euphrates. A civil war raged between him and his brother Antiochus Hierax, who hired the Celts of Galatia to do most of his fighting. Seleucos was therefore anxious to drive the Celts out of Asia Minor. He fought a major battle against them at Ancyra but was defeated. Thereafter the Celtic raids on the surrounding population were frequent and destructive, ranging from eastern Asia Minor as far south as Apameia and Themisonium. From this time on the newly emerged kingdom of Pergamum was forced to pay the Celts an annual tribute.

In 241 BC Attalos I succeeded to the Pergamum throne and he seems to have been a stronger king than his predecessors. When the Celts arrived to collect their tribute in 240 BC Attalos met them near the source of the Caice and defeated them in battle. Pergamum now began its rise under Attalos as one of the most powerful Hellenistic kingdoms. In 232 BC the Tolistoboii, making a bold raid into Pergamum territory, were defeated once more by Attalos near the shrine of Aphrodite, close by the city of Pergamum itself. It was a decisive battle for, by the defeat of the Celts, Pergamum also emerged as a dominant state. The defeat marked the end of Celtic raids against Pergamum, as well as against Bithynia and Pontus. In return, Attalos of Pergamum and the other Hellenistic monarchs recognized Galatia as a distinct state.

The Greek states of Asia Minor undoubtedly saw the victory over the Celts as a noteworthy achievement. Attalos and his successor Eumenes II (197–159 BC) set up numerous monuments which, says Henri Hubert, must have formed a single scheme. Pergamene statues were erected in bronze – copies were made in marble, such as 'The Dying Gaul' of the Capitoline Museum and the Ludovisi group showing a Celt stabbing himself with his own sword having killed his female companion, in the National Roman Museum. The Celts in these remarkable works are recognizable by the detail of their costume, ornaments, weapons and features. According to Pliny, Epigonos created a masterpiece depicting a dead Celtic mother being caressed by her child. Statues of Celts were set up at the Acropolis of Athens, while frescoes at Pergamum, and even as far afield as Naples, depicted Attalos' victory over the Celts. Medallions from Capua also commemorated the event.

Seleucos II of Syria had died from a fall from his horse in 226 BC and had been succeeded by Seleucos III Ceraunnos (225 – 223 BC), who determined to reconquer the whole of Asia Minor for Syria. Before he could move his army he was assassinated by one of his mercenary soldiers – interestingly recorded as a Celt named Apotouros. Polybius writes that the Syrian army had a large number of Celtic mercenaries, recruited from Europe rather than neighbouring Galatia. Seleucos was succeeded by Antiochus III (223–187 BC), called 'the Great', who set about restoring the pre-eminence of Syria.

Meanwhile Attalos I of Pergamum, whose reign was to last forty-four years, was busy recruiting Celtic mercenary troops from Europe for his own armies. He settled a tribe called the Trocnades in a portion of the Pergamum kingdom. Whether there was any intercourse between them and the Galatians is not recorded. In 218 BC Attalos invited another Celtic tribe called the Aegosages from Europe. He used these Celts to make a series of raids into Aeolis and across Lydia into northern Phrygia – presumably against their fellow Celts of Galatia. He rewarded the Aegosages with lands around the Hellespont. After a while the Aegosages rose in revolt against Attalos and started to plunder the surrounding countryside and besiege Ilium (Troy). The Aegosages do not appear to have made any attempt to unite with the Galatians. Their siege of Ilium was lifted by a force from Alexandria Troas commanded by the Pergamum General Themistes. The Aegosages withdrew from Pergamum into Bithynia. The Bithynian King,

Prusias I (228–180 BC), was worried by the arrival of the Celts in his lands and managed to corner them at Arisba where, in 217 BC, he massacred all of them, including, observes Polybius, their women and children.

Attalos of Pergamum and Antiochus the Great formed an alliance. Within a short time Antiochus had recovered most of the Syrian empire and was moving westward. Attalos extended his rule over most of the northern part of Asia Minor and forced Prusias of Bithynia to accept him as suzerain during a campaign in 207/206 BC. The ambitious Syrian ruler Antiochus observed that a Roman victory over the Macedonians at Cynoscephalae, in 197 BC, had left the Greek states powerless. Would Rome follow up the advantage and take Greece or could he make a grab for Greece first? Antiochus, with the help of the Aetolians, took his army to Greece in 191 BC. Rome's reaction was swift. She landed an army in Epiros and drove the Syrians back to Thermopylae. Here, where Brennos and his Celts had smashed the Greek army a century before, 40,000 Romans under Manpius Acilius Glabrio and Marcus Porcius Cato turned back the Syrian outposts and inflicted a disastrous defeat on Antiochus. The Syrian King fled with only 500 survivors from his army.

Antiochus was a confirmed enemy of Rome and, when the Carthaginian Hannibal asked him for sanctuary, Antiochus agreed. Hannibal, who had been defeated at the battle of Zama in 202 BC by Scipio (see Chapter 7), had lived for seven years under Roman rule but realized that Rome still considered him a threat and plotted his death. Rome now had another excuse to land her armies in Asia Minor: to do battle with Antiochus of Syria. The result was that Asia Minor was to be absorbed into the fast-growing empire of Rome.

The Celts of Galatia had a choice in the matter. Attalos of Pergamum had died in 197 BC to be succeeded by Eumenes II (197–159 BC). Eumenes was pro-Roman. Arguing against Professor Rankin's theory that the Celts were also pro-Roman, we find that the Galatians started to raid Pergamum again and demand tribute from the city of Lampsacos. There now occurs one of the earliest examples of the recognition of a solidarity between the Celtic peoples, even when of differing tribes and at great distances from one another. The city of Lampsacos had sent envoys to Massilia (Marseilles) in southern Gaul. The Massilots were pro-Roman. The senate of Massilia sent a letter to the Tolistoboii of Galatia via the envoys from Lampsacos, attempting to persuade them not to fight for Antiochus III against Rome. They pointed out that the surrounding Celtic tribes enjoyed good relations with them and the Romans. This fact shows that the Greeks of both Massilia and Lampsacos knew of a sense of common identity among the Celtic peoples even when living far from each other. Some years earlier, for example, they had – when demonstrating a pro-Carthaginian line – sent envoys to the Volcae Tectosages with a request for them to be neutral when Hannibal passed through their country.

The Tolistoboii ignored the entreaty and the Galatians joined forces with Antiochus against Rome. In 190 BC the Roman navy defeated the Syrian navy off Crete and Rome was able to launch its land invasion of Asia Minor with 40,000 legionaries commanded by Lucius Cornelius Scipio and his famous brother Publius Cornelius Scipio, called Africanus. The Roman forces landed near Magnesia. Eumenes II of Pergamum immediately allied himself with the Romans.

At Magnesia Antiochus III gathered 80,000 troops, including his Galatian allies. The Syrians began the battle by striking at the Roman left flank while Eumenes II struck at the Syrian left. The Syrians were driven back and the elephant corps stampeded and smashed into Antiochus' main phalanx in the centre. The troops of the Scipio brothers followed up the advantage. Roman chroniclers claim that 40,000 Syrians and their allies were killed compared with 300 Romans. Magnesia was a disaster for Syria and those who had supported her.

Antiochus accepted the Roman peace terms and paid a large indemnity to Rome, promising to give up his navy and accept Roman overlordship of his empire. Armenia and Bactria became independent again. Hannibal, now no longer safe under Antiochus' protection, fled to the court of Prusias of Bithynia. He was traced by Roman agents and, realizing that he was trapped, is recorded as saying: 'Let us now put an end to the life which has caused the Romans so much anxiety.' He took poison. The victor of Trebbia, Trasimene, Cannae and many other battles was sixty-five years old. He had crossed the Alps and for sixteen years held his Carthaginian army together undefeated. Four centuries after Hannibal's death, when Roman mothers wished to quieten their rebellious children, they would whisper: 'Hannibal ad portas!' Hannibal is at the gates!

The Scipio brothers were now concerned about the pacification and annexation of Asia Minor. They decided that the Celts of Galatia presented the most immediate problem. Gnaeus Manlius Volso was given command of a punitive expedition against Galatia in 189 BC. According to Livy, Volso gave his Roman troops a pep-talk before they had their first encounter with the Galatian army. He wanted to make sure that his men knew the type of warriors they were up against. Volso said:

> They sing as they advance into battle; they yell and leap in the air, clashing their weapons against their shields. The Greeks and Phrygians are scared of this display, but the Romans are used to such wildness. We have learned that if you can bear up to their first onslaught – that initial charge of blind passion – then their limbs will grow weary with the effort and when their passion subsides they are overcome by sun, dust and thirst. And anyway, these Celts we face are of a mixed blood, part Greek. Not the Celts our forefathers fought.

Volso defeated the Tolistoboii and the Trocmi at the battle of Olympus, near the city of Pessinus. According to Livy, this was done with great slaughter and some 40,000 Galatians, including women and children, were subsequently sold into slavery. Volso then went on to Ancyra and defeated the Tectosages in a battle at a hill called Magaba. In the wake of this 'pacification', the Romans made Galatia a vassal territory of the Pergamum kingdom. Livy actually suggests a reason why the Romans used extreme severity in their conquest of Galatia. He says that they had inherited a fear of the Celts. By smashing the power of Galatia the Romans had secured the eastern world from potential Celtic conquest and dominance.

Volso's conquest did not have a lasting effect. Soon afterwards the Galatians formed an alliance with Prusias of Bithynia and Pharnaces of Pontus against their Roman-imposed overlord Eumenes of Pergamum. Trogus Pompeius points out, and perhaps with some pride as a Celt himself, that the Galatians were still a formidable people in spite of Volso's conquest.

There now emerges a leader of the Galatians with some vision. Ortagion of the Tolistoboii, according to Polybius, realized that there was only one path available to the Galatians if they were to stand against conquest. The loose confederation of the Celtic tribes must be united and under one leader. In other words, the Commonwealth of Galatia should become a centralized state in order to secure the Celts'

freedom from the surrounding kingdoms and from the overall author-
ity of Rome. Polybius recounts that he interviewed Ortagion's wife,
Chiomara, in Sardis and learned first hand of her husband's plans.
Plutarch mentions this reference in a lost book of Polybius', from
which it appears that Polybius might also have met Ortagion. The
Celtic chieftain is described as full of charm and highly intelligent.
However, it seems that Ortagion's attempts to unite the Celts of
Galatia met with little success. There survives from 181 BC a list of the
chieftains of the Celtic septs who refused to depart from adherence to
the traditional Celtic tribal form of government. Ortagion vanishes
from historical record. It may be conjectured from Polybius' interview
with Chiomara, and perhaps Ortagion, in Sardis that they were in exile
there.

The Celts of Galatia continued their various factions and alliances
and soon Pharnaces I of Pontus (c.190–160 BC) had taken advantage
of their divisions to establish Pontus' supremacy over Galatia. The
Galatians sought to rid themselves of this overlordship. Pharnaces,
who appears as a cruel tyrant, set up garrisons in Galatia. He had also
overrun Paphlagonia and Cappadocia. The Galatians responded by an
alliance with their former enemy Eumenes II. Two Celtic chieftains,
Corsignatos and Gaizatorix, commanded Galatian troops in his army
and were still fighting with Eumenes in 179 BC. The alliance finally
drove Pharnaces out of Galatia.

In 167 BC, however we find the Galatians fighting for Prusias II
(180–149 BC) of Bithynia. Under their chieftain Advertas they invaded Pergamum and almost overthrew Eumenes. At this point, the
Roman Governor stepped in to mediate. Livy records that the Romans
allowed both the Galatians and Prusias of Bithynia the opportunity to
submit a list of grievances to them. After some negotiations, in 165 BC,
Eumenes, with Roman support, managed to expel the Galatians from
Pergamum but, by treaty, he was forced to recognize that Pergamum
had no control over Galatia.

From 164 to 160 BC there followed a series of border disputes
between Galatia and neighbouring Cappadocia. The Trocmi, with the
approval of the Romans, tried to seize a stretch of Cappodocian land.
Ariarathes V (162–131 BC), the Cappadocian King, eventually bribed
the Romans in order to be allowed to retain this territory. But the
Galatians continued their southward expansion until 123 BC, adding
parts of Lycaonia to their control.

The fluctuations between the power of Pergamum and that of Pontus ensured, for a time, the relative independence of Galatia. However, Manlius Aquillius, the Roman Consul in Asia Minor, declared that Mithridates IV (160–120 BC) of Pontus had a legal claim to control Phrygia, or the Galatian territory. In 126 BC the senate declared Manlius Aquillius' decision null and void. However, Mithridates IV continued to claim control. In 120 BC he was assassinated.

Mithridates V, called 'the Great', succeeded him and set about making the kingdom of Pontus into a small empire. He was a minor when he became King and for eight years devoted himself to the study of languages (he is reported to have mastered twenty-five) and to the development of physical prowess. At the age of twenty he set out to create an empire, adding Armenia Minor, Colchis, the eastern coast of the Black Sea, the Crimea (Cheronesus Taurica) and the entire region to the River Dniester. With those he felt unable to conquer, he merely entered into alliances, giving his sister Laodice in marriage to Ariarathes, King of Cappadocia, and his daughter Cleopatra to Tigranes, King of Armenia Major. In 102 BC he made an alliance with Nicomedes II of Bithynia and was able to partition and add Paphlagonia to his territory. In spite of his sister's marriage to Ariarathes, he eventually felt strong enough to attack Cappadocia and place his nephew, as Ariarathes VII, on the throne. Perhaps his nephew showed too much independence, for not long afterwards he had him murdered and set up his own eight-year-old son as King. Cappadocia finally revolted in 93 BC and managed to reassert her independence.

It was inevitable that Mithridates would turn to the Celts of Galatia. He decided to neutralize the Galatian leadership by an act of treachery. In 88 BC he invited some sixty leading Celtic chieftains to his court, ostensibly to dine and discuss his intentions towards their country. Here Mithridates displayed a knowledge of Celtic social customs and it is highly likely that Celtic was one of the twenty-five languages which he had acquired in his youth. He knew that the rules of hospitality were sacred to the Celt and that no Celt went into his host's dining hall armed. Mithridates waited until the feast had started and then had his soldiers kill them.

One chieftain escaped from the mass murder – Deiotaros, son of Dumnorix of the Tolistoboii.

Three other Galatian chieftains had either refused or not been able to attend Mithridates' feast, but the King of Pontus sent assassins to their fortress to seek hospitality, pretending to be travellers, with orders to slay the chieftains when the moment arose. They succeeded in killing one of these chieftains, so that, out of all the Galatian tribes and septs, three chieftains only survived. It was not the first time, nor would it be the last, that the Celtic attitude to the sacred laws of hospitality was cynically exploited by their enemies. Mithridates had obviously wanted to cut off the head and brains of Celtic government in Galatia so that he could move in, exploiting the ensuing power vacuum. Indeed, he had not omitted to kill supporters and friends of the Galatians within his own camp. However, while he had used his knowledge of Celtic custom to good effect, he does not appear to have considered the inherent democracy of the Celtic system, which allowed for the immediate election of new chieftains by the tribal assemblies.

Deiotaros, whose name means divine bull, soon emerged as the leader unifying the Galatian tribes and septs. He now managed to do what Ortagion had unsuccessfully tried to do one hundred years before – unite the Celts of Galatia. The war between the Celts and Pontus was long for it was not until 74 BC that Deiotaros finally drove out Zeumachus, whom Mithridates had sent as Governor of Galatia, and the troops of Pontus. Deiotaros had achieved this by political alliances as well as force. The mistake Mithridates had made was entering into a war with Rome.

Mithridates' war against Rome took three stages. The first was from 88 to 84 BC, the second from 83 to 82 BC and the third from 74 to 65 BC. Mithridates had attempted to invade Europe and was promptly defeated there by Lucius Cornelius Sulla, who had been made Consul in 88 BC and sent by the senate to throw back Mithridates' troops, who were in Greece. By 86 BC he had driven Mithridates out of Greece, and he crossed into Asia Minor and came to terms with him in 84 BC. Mithridates used the treaty as a breathing space to consolidate fresh troops, inviting punitive attacks from the Proconsul Lucius Murena. Another peace was made.

The war was eventually renewed in 74 BC when Mithridates attacked Bithynia, which had been bequeathed to Rome in 75 BC by Nicomedes II. Deiotaros and the Galatians made alliances with Rome and soon Mithridates was retreating. The Consul Lucius Licinius Lucullus invaded Pontus and Mithridates fled to the Crimea. Faced with surrender to Rome, in 63 BC Mithridates attempted to take his own life. The poison he used was ineffectual. There was a poetic justice in the fact that a Celtic warrior delivered the death blow with his sword.

Deiotaros moved the Galatians into the Roman orbit. It would appear that the Romans were doing their best to woo the Celts, finding the Celtic culture of Galatia potentially advantageous to them in a sea of Hellenistic states. With an independent Galatia, there would be a check to the rise of a major Hellenistic power in the area, such as Pergamum or Pontus, which might topple Roman influence.

In 66 BC Gnaeus Magnus Pompeius (Pompey the Great) was sent as Consul to take command of the area. He formed an alliance with Galatia, becoming a friend of Deiotaros, and, under Roman suzerainty, allowed them to retain their native organization of independent tribal cantons under the rulership of native chieftains. He recognized a triumvirate of three chieftains as ruling Galatia – Deiotaros of the Tolistoboii, Brogitarios of the Trocmi and an unnamed chieftain of the Tectosages. The Galatian chieftains were even granted, as compensation for Mithridates' ravages, concessions of lands in Pontus and Armenia Minor. Deiotaros was given Gazelonitis. Having secured Galatia as an ally, Pompey embarked on a campaign of conquest against the surrounding states which was then unprecedented in the annals of the Roman republic. By 63 BC Asia Minor and its kingdoms were firmly under Roman rule.

Deiotaros once again emerges as an astute and able politician. During the wars against Mithridates he had been the single unifying leader of the Galatians. Pompey, not wishing to give him too much power, had reinstituted the triune leadership. Deiotaros therefore married one of his daughters to Brogitarios of the Trocmi and another to Castor, son of the chieftain of the Tectosages. Soon he appears as undisputed ruler of the Galatians. He introduced the Roman methods of military training, organization and tactics into his army. He also became interested in the Roman art of estate management. He was respected by the Romans for his political ability and formed successful relationships with such powerful Romans of differing temperaments as Lucius Cornelius Sulla, Marcus Calpurnius Bibulus, Gaius Julius Caesar and Marcus Tullius Cicero. But it was recorded that Deiotaros never undertook an important decision without consulting the auguries, in traditional Celtic fashion.

His one major error of strategy was to give his support to the Roman senate and the old republican party during the Roman civil war from 49 to 45 BC. Deiotaros took the side of Pompey against Julius Caesar. The civil war was, of course, a Roman quarrel but Deiotaros was obviously attempting to make use of it to further the interests of Galatian independence. From his viewpoint, Pompey was a more sympathetic friend than Julius Caesar. And it is hardly likely that Deiotaros, the Celtic king of a Celtic people, was unaware of Caesar's recent campaign of conquests against the Celts of Gaul during 58–51 BC. By the time the civil war erupted Deiotaros was already an elderly man and it was reported that he was so feeble that he could not mount a horse without assistance. Yet he fought at Pompey's side at Pharsalus.

With Julius Caesar's victory, Deiotaros found new enemies. His own grandson Castor and his wife – sometimes confused with his son-in-law Castor and his daughter – accused him of plotting against the life of Caesar. In 47 BC Deiotaros was tried before a Roman court. He was able to call upon the skill of his friend Marcus Tullius Cicero, who had been Governor of Cilicia, south of Galatia, from 51 to 50 BC and had become a friend of the Galatian King during this period. Cicero himself had taken Pompey's side against Caesar but had been reconciled with Caesar just before the trial. Cicero was successful in his defence of the old Celtic ruler. However, Deiotaros, on his release, decided to ensure no further betrayal by his grandson and his wife by having them executed.

Deiotaros is said to have died at an advanced age and was succeeded by his surviving son, also named Deiotaros. Deiotaros II also managed to commit himself to the wrong side during the next phase of Rome's civil war – the struggle between Marcus Antonius (Mark Antony) and Octavian, eventually to become the first emperor, Augustus. Marcus Antonius gave Deiotaros II lands in Armenia for his help against Octavian. When Octavian emerged victorious, which seems to have coincided with Deiotaros II's death – whether from natural causes, battle or execution we do not know – a chieftain named Amyntas opportunistically made himself King of Galatia.

In 25 BC Galatia became a Roman province ruled by a propraetor appointed directly from Rome. Coincidentally, in AD 14, a monument was set up at a temple raised to Augustus and Rome in Ancyra which records the names of two British Celtic kings who came to him as suppliants in Rome. They are Tincommios and Dumnovelaunos. Little is subsequently recorded of Galatia until Paul of Tarsus, which city is in neighbouring Cilicia, visited the country on a Christian mission some time between AD 40 and 50. He was suffering a sickness at the time and stayed in Pessinus, the chief city of the Tolistoboii. He was apparently surprised by the warmhearted Celtic hospitality which he received. He also succeeded in converting many of the Galatians to his new faith – Christianity.

The Galatians have received a permanent place in Christian history through the famous letter which Paul wrote to them from Rome some time between AD 50 and 55. Paul was angry with them. 'You stupid Galatians! You must have been bewitched!' Apparently, not long after Paul had made his converts among the Galatians, other Christians arrived belonging to another 'school' of Christianity and drew the Galatians into their philosophy. This was the movement led by the original disciples of Jesus who still saw themselves as part of the Judaic faith, believing in Jesus as the last of the Jewish messiahs. Paul, who had not known Jesus while he was alive, had abrogated Judaic law, introduced the 'salvation doctrine' and gnosticism. The bulk of his followers came from a pagan Hellenistic background, which enabled them to respond to the gnostic aspects of his teachings.

This had brought him into bitter conflict with the original Christian, or Nazarene, leaders such as Jacob (James), John and Simon Bar-Jonah, nicknamed 'The Rock' – Kephas in Greek and Petra in Latin, and it is by the Latin, Peter, that he is known to Christendom. Paul freely admits his quarrel with them and speaks of a face-to-face confrontation with Peter. To compilers of the New Testament it seemed unseemly that Paul could quarrel with the man designated by Jesus himself to lead the movement. To get round this, they left the Greek Kephas in the contentious passages while translating the name to the Latin Peter in others. Thus, in places, Kephas and Peter appear as two different people instead of the same man – Simon Bar-Jonah.

Paul himself, claiming authority for his 'breakaway' Christian sect, wrote to the Galatians that Jacob, John and Peter had given him approval. They:

> acknowledged that I had been entrusted with the Gospel for the Gentiles as surely as Peter had been entrusted with the Gospel for the Jews. For God whose action made Peter an apostle to the Jews, also made me an apostle to the Gentiles.

Recognizing, then, the favour bestowed on me, those reputed pillars of our society, James [Jacob], Peter and John, accepted Barnabus and myself as partners and shook hands upon it, agreeing that we should go to the Gentiles while they went to the Jews.

But, from the evidence of the later conflict between Paul and the original disciples of Jesus, it was obvious that they were appalled that Paul was surrendering their teaching to pagan idolatry, as they saw it. In this conflict the Nazarenes, as they were known, sent out missions in an attempt to counteract Paul's teachings. The Celtic Galatians, therefore, were among the first of Paul's converts to take notice of the Nazarenes and brought forth Paul's angry letter to them.

I am astonished to find you turning so quickly away from him who called you by grace, and following a different Gospel. Not that it is in fact another Gospel, only there are persons who unsettle your minds by trying to distort the Gospel of Christ.

The Nazarene movement continued to exist as late as the fifth century AD, following the teachings of Jesus' original disciples. But Paul's 'breakaway' movement, the 'Gentile Christians', eventually constituted the bulk of the Christian movement and took the opportunity to declare the Nazarene sect 'heretical'. The Nazarenes' Gospels were suppressed, although fragments have been found. To the end they taught that Jesus was the last Jewish Messiah but not a divinity and that Paul was the heretic who had perverted the real teachings of Christ and merged them with pagan Hellenistic philosophy.

Whether Paul's somewhat abusive letter to the Galatians succeeded in reconverting them back to his form of Christianity is not known.

In AD 74 the Romans decided to unite Galatia with Cappadocia as a single province. In AD 106 the Emperor Trajan separated them again as two distinct administrative units. As we have already seen St Jerome (Eusebius Hieronymous), visiting Galatia and staying in Ancyra, reported that the Galatians still spoke their Celtic language and likened it to the Celtic spoken by the Treveri in northern Gaul, which he had also visited. Nothing more is known of the Galatians until a passing reference which indicated that Galatia existed as a separate unit as late as the eighth century AD. When the Celtic language of Galatia, the culture, customs and historical traditions, ceased to exist is difficult to estimate. Perhaps the language was dead by the eighth century, the century when the earliest records of the precursor of modern Turkish are to be found; this language is now the official language of Turkey, which covers the former Celtic territory of Galatia.

[7]

The Celts in North Africa

D IONYSIOS I (405–367 BC), ruler of Syracuse, was the first recorded Mediterranean monarch to employ Celtic warriors as mercenaries. Syracuse had been founded as a colony by Corinth on the south coast of Sicily in the late eighth century BC. When Dionysios came to the throne of Syracuse he began to pursue an expansionist policy and made himself master of half of Sicily and over many of the Greek city states on the Italian mainland. He encountered roving bands of Celtic warriors about 379 BC while he was besieging Croton, a Greek colony on the Gulf of Tarentum (Taranto). These Celts were fairly well south and must have wandered there after their successes against Rome. Dionysios sent 2,000 of them to Sparta to help her in her war against Thebes. But others he recruited into his own army.

Celts were serving in the army of Syracuse several generations later when Agathocles made himself ruler, in 317 BC. Agathocles was a demagogue who continued Dionysios' policy of expansion and his attacks on the western Sicilian cities. These cities called in the assistance of Carthage. The Carthaginians landed an army in Sicily and, in 311 BC, laid siege to Syracuse. Agathocles, a daring military commander, decided to relieve the pressure on his city by shipping part of his army from the harbour of Syracuse across to the North African coast and attacking Carthage itself. In this audacious venture it is recorded that he transported the first body of Celtic warriors to North Africa in 307 BC. The attack worked, for in 306 BC Carthage agreed to Agathocles' peace terms.

The Carthaginians apparently learned something of the qualities of the Celtic warriors, because forty years later, in 263 BC, Polybius tells us Carthage recruited a force of 3,000 Celtic warriors. Apparently they were from Cisalpine Gaul. The force was recruited in the year before the First Punic War opened, when the rising power of Rome was checked by the Carthaginian empire. The Celtic force was shipped to Agrigentum (Acragas), the Carthaginian city on the south-west coast of Sicily. When the war started going badly for Carthage, the Celts decided to loot the city for themselves. However, the Romans took control, made the Celts take service in their army and sent them to Illyria.

Carthage had, however, recruited other bodies of Celtic warriors, who remained loyal to them throughout the war. At the conclusion of this first war between Carthage and Rome, the Celtic mercenaries, led by their chieftain Antaros, who spoke excellent Punic according to Polybius, mutinied over lack of payment. They appealed to Rome to help them and this gave Rome the pretext for renewing hostilities and annexing Corsica, Sardinia and the Sicilian possessions.

In spite of their experience with Celtic mercenary groups, Carthage continued to recruit the Celts from Iberia, Gaul and Cisalpine Gaul during the Second Punic War. Indeed, Hannibal's policies relied on alliances with Celtic tribes. Without the Celts, he could never have launched his famous invasion of the Italian peninsula.

Other Celtic bands were arriving in North Africa. Ptolemy I Lagi, one-time General of Alexander the Great, had established his rule in Egypt, becoming Pharaoh and founding a dynasty which was to last for nearly 300 years, ending with the death of Cleopatra (51–30 BC). He it was who began the collection of the great library at Alexandria and also established a museum there, making Alexandria a magnificent university, inviting men of learning from all parts of the world to come to live there. His son Ptolemy II Philadelphios (b. 308 BC) ruled Egypt as Pharaoh from 283 to 246 BC. Through Antigonus Gonatas, King of Macedonia, Ptolemy recruited a large body of Celtic warriors from Greece to serve in his army.

Ptolemy had a brother called Magas, who rebelled against his rule, seeking the throne of the pharaohs for himself. This may well have been the reason why Ptolemy sought a corps of Celtic mercenaries to serve him, not being able to trust his own troops for fear of desertion to his brother. Pausanius records a corps of 4,000 Celtic warriors arriving in Egypt to serve Ptolemy II. Using the Celts, Ptolemy defeated his brother but was unable to follow up this victory and consolidate his position because the Celts mutinied. This was about 259 BC and it gave

Magas sufficient breathing-space to secure his rule over Cyrenaica, a Greek colony in what is now Libya, a few miles inland. It was a prosperous trading colony founded about 630 BC. Cyrenaica became a Roman province in 74 BC.

What was the cause of the Celtic mutiny? According to Pausanius, the Celts conspired to overthrow Ptolemy II and rule the Egyptian kingdom for themselves. If this was so, it was an ambitious and daring plan and one doomed to failure. Some 4,000 Celtic warriors against the might of Egypt seems improbable odds. The real motive probably lies with the reason put forward by Callimachos, the Greek scholar (c.310/305–c.240 BC), who was from Cyrene. He lived through the event and was actually at Alexandria at the time, having been commissioned by Ptolemy II to catalogue all the books in the famous library. During this time he produced several scholarly works including *Hymn to Delos*, in which he celebrates the defeat of the Celts. Callimachos speaks of a Celtic conspiracy to steal the treasures of Ptolemy while he was distracted by the affair of his brother Magas.

The Celtic mutiny was put down with severity by Ptolemy II, who had the prisoners taken to an island in the Sebennytic arm of the Nile and left there to languish. The Celts perished on the island, either by starvation or by ritual suicide. The suppression of the Celtic mutiny was considered of sufficient importance to be commemorated. Ptolemy had a coin struck which depicted a Celtic shield. A monument was raised of which only fragments now survive: a piece depicting the head of a Celt with an intense expression of pain is now in the Cairo Museum. There is also a younger Celtic head showing anguish and a headless body of a fallen warrior. The pieces are said to have come from one whole monument which represented the scene of mass suicide and, in its original form, must have been a magnificent illustration of the epic of these Celtic warriors. Other smaller monuments showing the Celtic defeat have also been discovered.

Ptolemy II did not harbour grudges against peoples for we are told that he recruited more Celtic warriors into the Egyptian army when he was developing commerce between the Nile and the Red Sea, reopening a canal originally excavated by Rameses II and building a road from Coptos, near Thebes, to northern Berenice and establishing commerce with Arabia, Ethiopia and India.

Ptolemy III Euergetes ascended the throne of Egypt in 247 BC and continued to recruit Celtic warriors to serve in the armies of the

Pharaoh. He took them with him on his invasion of Syria in 245 BC when he defeated Seleucos Callincos, captured Antioch and overran Mesopotamia, Babylon, Media and much of Persia.

When Ptolemy IV Philopator (222–205 BC) ruled Egypt, the Celtic presence in the Egyptian army was still strong. Bands of Celts, with their women and children, had settled in Egypt. Perhaps there was a degree of intermarriage, for Polybius speaks of them as the Katoikoi and their descendants as Epigovoi. Some of their graves, with painted tombstones, have been found in the cemetery of Hadra, south-east of Alexandria. It is recorded that 4,000 of these Egyptian–Celts fought at the battle of Raphia in 217 BC when Antiochus II marched against the Egyptian empire of Ptolemy IV.

Antiochus of Syria had an army of 20,000 men, including many Celtic mercenaries. They met up with the army of Ptolemy at Raphia (Rafa) on the Palestine–Egyptian border. Ptolemy's army numbered 25,000. As well as the 4,000 Egyptian–Celts, there were 10,000 Celts recruited from Thrace. The overwhelming composition of the Egyptian army was, therefore, Celtic. As Ptolemy's men attacked, the Syrian phalanxes became disorganized. Another charge and the Syrians were completely routed. Antiochus' Syrian army lost 14,000 men killed and some 4,000 captured.

At this time it was a common saying that no prince of the eastern world could do without his corps of Celtic warriors. In a curious repetition of those days, it was said in Europe of the eighteenth century that no European monarch could do without his Irish brigade – for Irish brigades saw lengthy and distinguished service in the armies of France, Spain and Austria. The Scottish regiment with the oldest history still remains the Gardes Ecossaises, the Scots Guards of the French army formed in AD 1420 and disbanded in the 1830s.

The last record of Celts serving in the Egyptian army was during 186/185 BC when Ptolemy V Epiphanes was Pharaoh. Ptolemy V had been only five years old when his father died and during his minority the affairs of Egypt were badly managed by his guardians Agathocles and Tlepolemus. Philip of Macedonia and Antiochus of Syria were able to combine together to strip Egypt of her European and Asiatic dominions. Antiochus had his daughter Cleopatra marry the boy king of Egypt. Even after Ptolemy V attained adulthood there was considerable unrest. A revolt in Upper Egypt was the reason why Ptolemy V sent an army of Celtic mercenaries up the Nile Valley in 186/185 BC.

From this campaign survives one of the most intriguing monuments from the ancient Celtic world. In the small chapel of Horus, in the temple of Seti I at the Great Temple of Karnak, a pharaoh who had reigned some time prior to 1400 BC, four Celtic warriors inscribed a piece of graffiti. 'Of the Galatians,' they wrote in Greek, 'we, Thoas, Callistratos, Acannon and Apollonios, came, and a fox we caught here.' It is a fascinating inscription. Four Celtic warriors, serving in the army of Ptolemy V, had taken time off from putting down the revolt in Upper Egypt to wander into the tomb in idle curiosity, caught a jackal, which they mistook for a European fox, and recorded what they had done and their names. Once again, it is interesting, and underlines the cultural point, that they did not think of writing in Celtic. They wrote in straightforward Greek, so correct that Henri Hubert demonstrates that it was an acquired language and not a mother-tongue, and also gave Greek forms of their names.

And with this intriguing piece of Celtic graffiti in the tomb of an ancient pharaoh, the Celtic mercenaries of the Egyptian army disappear from historical record.

Just before this time, further west along the coast of North Africa, the Celts were serving in the Carthaginian army. The battle of Ilipia in 206 BC had resulted in a Carthaginian withdrawal from the Iberian peninsula. When the Carthaginians withdrew to North Africa, many Celtiberians and Celts followed them. In spite of Scipio Africanus' conquest of the Iberian peninsula, the Roman senate was reluctant to let him take the advantage and pursue the Carthaginians to their home territory. It was not until 204 BC that they finally gave him permission and in the midsummer of that year he, with a large Roman army, landed at Utica, some twenty miles from Carthage. Almost immediately he found himself hemmed in near the coast by Hasdrubal, son of Gisco, with a body of Carthaginians and their allies commanded by Syphax of Numidia, a North African kingdom neighbouring Carthage. Syphax was elderly but had been won to the Carthaginian cause by Hasdrubal giving his young daughter Sophonisba in marriage to him.

Scipio and his Romans erected strong defensive positions around the city of Utica and made an alliance with another Numidian chieftain named Masinissa, who was envious of Syphax's marriage to the beautiful Sophonisba. In the spring of 203 BC Scipio launched an offensive against the Carthaginian army from his beachhead. The

Carthaginians and Numidians fell back inland towards an area known as the Great Plain.

In fact, they were in full flight approaching the town of Abba when they met a contingent of 4,000 Celtic warriors. The sight of these warriors, observes Polybius, raised the spirits of Hasdrubal's army and persuaded them to halt their retreat. 'The arrival of the Celts put fresh heart into the Carthaginians. Their numbers were reported in the capital [Carthage] as 10,000 instead of 4,000 and it was said that their courage and the excellence of their weapons made them irresistible in the field.'

The arrival of the Celts saved the city of Carthage from falling into Roman hands.

However, Scipio was an aggressive enemy and he took 16,000 men on a five-day forced march into the interior and fell on the new Carthaginian encampment. Hasdrubal had prior warning of the attack and had drawn up his men in readiness. The Celts he placed in the centre of his army, opposite the tough Roman legions, with Numidian cavalry to his left and Carthaginians to his right. While the Numidians were immediately driven back in the opening Roman assault, the Carthaginians wavered for a while until they also fell back. Polybius says: 'The Celts, on the other hand, fought splendidly and held their ground against the Roman centre.'

Scipio, realizing that the power of the Carthaginian army lay in the Celtic contingents, threw all his forces against them, slowly encircling them. When the Celts saw that they were on their own, Carthaginians and Numidians having fled from the battlefield, they surrendered. Scipio refused to accept their surrender and massacred them all. 'Thus perished the Celts, but they nevertheless rendered the greatest service to the Carthaginians not only during the fighting, but also in the rout, for if the Romans had not encountered their resistance, but had immediately pursued the fugitives, very few of the enemy would have got away.'

Hasdrubal was able to reach the walls of Carthage with the remnants of his army. Syphax was captured. He was eventually taken to Rome to be paraded in a triumph before ceremonial execution. The treacherous Numidian, Masinissa, took Syphax's wife, Sophonisba, who had been waiting at the Numidian capital of Cirta. Scipio disapproved and was going to despatch her in chains to Rome so Masinissa sent her poison to save her from the disgrace.

Scipio now turned on Carthage, seizing a portion of the Bay of Tunis, and establishing his army in siege positions. He offered terms to the city for its surrender: all prisoners and deserters were to be restored to Rome; the Carthaginian forces in Italy were to be withdrawn; the Carthaginian forces from Cisalpine Gaul were to be withdrawn; and Carthage was to give up her possessions in the Mediterranean islands as well as to reduce her naval fleet to only twenty ships. The Carthaginian parliament decided to accept in principle and started negotiations; at the same time, they sent to Hannibal, still in Italy, to return immediately with his army to save Carthage.

In June 203 BC, Hannibal slipped out of the port of Croton, in the Gulf of Tarentum, with the bulk of his 12,000-man army, including his Celtic allies. He had crossed the Alps into Italy when he was twenty-nine years old. Now he was forty-five. Hearing word of his coming, Carthage broke off negotiations with the Romans and Hasdrubal was able to seize 200 Roman transport ships. Hannibal landed on the east coast of what is now Tunisia, about eighty miles from Carthage, in October 203 BC. He immediately threw himself into the task of forging a new army to face Scipio. Hannibal's brother Mago, who was in Cisalpine Gaul with a medium-sized army, mainly of Celts, also arrived and joined him.

Scipio marched up to the Bagradas (Merjerda) river, arriving at Hannibal's outposts in the spring of 202 BC. Near the village of Zama, Scipio and Hannibal met. Scipio had placed his Roman legions in the centre with Masinissa and 6,000 Numidian horse on his right flank and Laelius and a contingent of Latin horse to the left.

Hannibal placed his eighty elephants in the front line while giving pride of the centre ranks to the Celts, directly behind the elephants. Hanno was commanding Ligurian, African and Carthaginian troops placed behind the Celts. Numidian horse were on the left flank and Carthaginian horse on the right.

The first Roman assault scattered the elephants and it became a battle of the centre footsoldiers – Roman legionaries against Celtic warriors. These Celtic troops were mainly from Mago's army. After fierce hand-to-hand fighting, the Celts were slowly forced backwards and, on a prearranged signal, they retired to the flanks.

Scipio now ordered his centre to fall back to encourage Hannibal to think he was wavering. As Hannibal's troops pressed forward, Scipio unleashed his flanking cavalry. The battle became a massacre and by the end of the day 20,000 lay dead on the field while a further 20,000 were captured in the pursuit. It was the battle which caused the Roman senate to award Scipio with the title 'Africanus'. The battle of Zama brought to an end the Second Punic War, which had lasted for nearly seventeen years. It marked the defeat of Hannibal and the collapse of Carthaginian power.

The battle of Zama was also important for the Celtic world. Aside from the Celts who had fought in the Carthaginian armies, the Celts of Cisalpine Gaul had had strong political motives for supporting Carthage. With Carthage defeated, and Rome's power in the ascendant, there was nothing to stop Rome continuing her policy of conquering and Romanizing Cisalpine Gaul. As we have seen,* Rome turned on Cisalpine Gaul and succeeded in conquering it after a campaign of twenty years. Once Cisalpine Gaul was part of the Roman empire, it was a short march across the mountains to the rich lands of Transalpine Gaul.

* See Chapter 4.

[8]

The Province

AFTER the conquest of Cisalpine Gaul, Rome could look beyond the Alps. With her new acquisitions in Spain in almost constant rebellion, there was a need for a supply route along which men, equipment and provisions could be shipped. Hannibal had demonstrated that one possibility could be an overland route. Rome had now established friendly relations with Massilia (Marseilles), the Greek colony founded by Phocaea, east of the River Rhône, about 600 BC. Massilia had become an important trading port and the gateway for Celtic trade from the hinterlands of the Celtic world to the Mediterranean. Her sphere of influence along the coast as far as Genoa was recognized by Rome. Massilots had established settlements in Gaul as far inland as Arles and along the modern Riviera coast at Agathem (Agde), Antipolis (Antibes) and Nicae (Nice) to her eastern side, and westward to Pyrene (hence Pyrenees) and to the future Malaga. Massilia had become one of the great centres of the Greek commercial world.

In 154 BC the Salyes, a tribe differentiated by ancient writers from the rest of the Celtic world by being designated Celto-Ligurian, launched an attack on Massilia. Rome, as a gesture of friendship, sent troops to aid the Massilots, who drove the Salyes back. In 125 BC the Salyes attacked again. This time the Romans saw an opportunity to annex Massilia to their empire without coming into conflict with the Greek population of the Massilot settlements. Roman terms to aid Massilia against the Celto-Ligurians were the annexation of the coastal area from Cisalpine Gaul to Massilia. The Massilots, to whom security and trade meant everything, accepted the proposal. Rome sent M. Fulvius Flaccus, one of the consuls, with a military expedition. Flaccus drove the Salyes back.

Their chieftains took refuge with one of the powerful Celtic tribes to the north of Massilia, the Allobriges. The Allobriges were allied with another influential Celtic tribe, the Arverni. For giving the Salyes help, the Romans sent an army under their Consul Cn. Domitius Aheno-barbus up the Rhône to teach the Celtic tribes that Rome's emnity was something to be feared. This was in 122 BC. At Vindalum, a place near the confluence of the Sorgue, Ahenobarbus faced an army of 20,000 Celtic warriors commanded by Bituitis, son of Lovernios the Fox, chieftain of the Arverni. Ahenobarbus delayed the battle until he could be reinforced by a second army commanded by Q. Fabius Maximus. The battle proved another disaster for the Celts. Fabius Maximus then led a punitive expedition into the country of the Allobriges. Ahenobarbus began to conclude treaties with other Celtic tribes in the area as far apart as the Helvetii (of what is now Switzerland) and the Tectosages of Tolosa (Toulouse). A large area of southern Gaul had not accepted the 'friendship' of Rome.

Bituitis, who had escaped after his defeat at Vindalum, now con-tacted Rome and offered peace terms on behalf of the Arverni. His condition, however, was that he should deal with the senate of Rome in person. Rome was delighted to welcome the Celtic chieftain and had no intention of letting him go. Bituitis was, in fact, interned near Frascati on the northern slope of the Alban mountain, some thirteen miles south-east of Rome. Here, he was eventually joined by his son Congentiatos (sometimes referred to as Comm). Domitius Ahenobarbus set up a monument at Nîmes to celebrate his victory.

The Romans now stood master of the Celtic territory between the Alps and Massilia, stretching north near to Lake Geneva. They called the area simply 'the province', which name is retained in modern Provence. By 118 BC this territory was extended westward to the Pyrenees and Tolosa. A Roman colony was founded called Narbo (Narbonne) and the province's official name became Gallia Nar-bonensis. The great Via Domitia, or Domitius' road, was constructed from Genoa, running north of Massilia to Narbo and then onwards, skirting the eastern end of the Pyrenees down to Valencia and finally reaching New Carthage. The great land route had been officially opened up and Rome was master of this commercial and military highway.

The province had annexed much fertile and valuable land from the Celtic tribes and given Rome a strong foothold in the Celtic hinterland.

To safeguard their interests, the Romans made alliances with many tribes on the northern frontier of this province. One tribe especially, the Aedui – the name meaning the burners, found in the Old Irish *aed* (fire) – proved to be one of Rome's staunchest allies and were used as a cat's paw to protect her interests. But Rome was not satisfied with the territory she had gained. It would not be long before her imperial greed would push her further northward.

In 113 BC a people called the Cimbri, arriving from the north, came into conflict with the Boii, in Bohemia. They were considered by contemporary observers to be a Celtic people. Sextus Pompeius Festus, abridging a lexicon of Verrius Flaccus (d. AD 14), says the name derived from the Celtic word *cimber*, meaning brigand. Old Irish certainly has a word *cimb* for tribute and a word *combid* meaning prisoner. This supposes a formation of 'one who takes prisoners for tribute', which could easily be an act of brigandage. The recorded names of the leaders of the Cimbri, such as Claodicos, are Celtic.

In their later incursions the Cimbri were joined by another people called the Teutones. Today, of course, the word Teuton is synonymous with German. But at the time of their alliance with the Cimbri the Teutones were considered Celts as well. The name itself is simply the Latin form of the Celtic word meaning people, which emerges in the Gaulish deity Teutates and in the Irish *tuath*, a tribe. The Galatians had a sept called Teutobodiaci in the Tectosages. The leader of the Teutones was named Teutobodunos, a clearly Celtic name. Diodorus, Strabo and Pliny all refer to the fact that the Cimbri and the Teutones spoke a Celtic language, while Plutarch refers to the Ambrones as the 'crack corps' of the Teuton army, who are clearly identified by Sextus Pompeius Festus as a *gens Gallica* – a Celtic people.

In recent times, however, scholars have become uncertain whether to accept the contemporary evidence that the Cimbri and Teutones were Celts. They base their current scepticism on the belief that the ancient world had yet to distinguish between the Celts and Germans, as the Germans had only just made their first appearance into record. Henri Hubert, while admitting the evidence which showed that the Cimbri and Teutones were Celtic-speaking, came up with the remarkable theory that they could have been Germans who were Celticized by trade or policy during the third or second centuries BC. He argued that just as the Irish, Scots or Welsh have taken Anglo-Saxon names, or Anglicized their Celtic names, so the Cimbri and Teutones could have taken Celtic names, spoken Celtic but been German. The theory seems a little far-fetched. Quintus Sertorius, the General whom Gaius Marius appointed to discover what he could about them, learned Celtic and found that language sufficient in his dealings with them. But, in fairness to the 'German theory', Pytheas, in the fourth century BC, does record a people called Teutones in his day as living on the island of Abalum (Esel) off the Baltic coast and being engaged in the amber trade. That area is not generally considered one populated by the Celts. Additionally, in Augustus' time, a Roman expedition sent along the northern European coast found, in what is now Jutland, a remnant of the Cimbri. Strabo called Jutland the Cimbric Peninsula.

The contemporary evidence, however, seems clear enough. The Cimbri and the Teutones spoke Celtic, had Celtic names and used Celtic weapons. The very names of the two tribes were Celtic. They were, then, Celts. And, eventually, they formed alliances with other Celtic tribes, creating a large Celtic army which, once more, nearly brought about the downfall of Rome.

The Cimbri first appeared in 113 BC, when they spread into the land of the Boii in what is called Bohemia. They were said to have come from north-western Europe, so the discovery of remnants of the tribe in Jutland is not so amazing. Poseidonius connected them with the Cimmerians, who, according to Homer's *Odyssey*, were a people living on the edge of the world by the shore of Oceanus, a land shrouded by perpetual mist and darkness. Some nineteenth-century writers have tried to link the name with the Welsh Cymry. The Boii drove these Cimbri out of their lands. They next appeared in the lands of the Volcae Tectosages, who also drove them away. They then appeared in the lands of the Taurisci of Noricum, modern Austria. So the Romans began to concern themselves with the Cimbri, for anyone controlling this area could pass into the Po Valley and thence into Italy proper. The Consul for that year, Cn. Papirius Carbo, was hurriedly sent with an army to Illyria by sea and thence into Noricum, marching to the principal city of Noreia (Neumarkt).

The Cimbri did not want to fight the Romans and attempted to negotiate with them. Carbo dismissed their envoys and pressed on in battle formation. The Cimbri devastated his army and he was beaten back with considerable losses. The road to Italy lay open and un-defended. But the Cimbri moved away northwards and nothing more was heard of them for two years.

In 111 BC they appeared in the Rhône Valley and began recruiting local Celtic tribes into an alliance. They were moving southwards and it was clear that the Roman province of Gallia Narbonensis was under threat. However, in 109 BC envoys from the Cimbri arrived before the Roman Governor of the province, M. Junius Silanus, explaining that all they wanted was an area of fertile land in which to settle. Silanus passed on their request to the Roman senate. The senate instructed him to break off any discussions and attack them. Junius Silanus obeyed orders and was promptly cut to pieces, as Carbo had been. The armies of Rome had received their second major defeat at the hands of the Cimbri.

By 107 BC the Cimbri had been joined by the Teutones and many other Celtic tribes led by Boiorix, Lugios and Gaesorix. The Tectosages of Tolosa had now rebelled against Rome and had been joined by the Tigurini. They were besieging the Roman garrison at Tolosa. Rome had raised a fresh army commanded by one of the consuls for that year, L. Cassius Longinus. He was able to separate the Tigurini, commanded by a chieftain named Divico, and pressed forward on them. Divico withdrew down the Garonne Valley, finally making a stand near Agen, in the country of the Nitiobriges. Not only did Divico defeat the Roman army but the Consul Cassius Longinus was killed in the battle. Divico took the surrender of the remnants of the Roman soldiers. In fact, fifty years after this event, Divico was still alive and living in the land of the Helvetii and was known to Julius Caesar.

Another Roman army, commanded by Longinus' fellow Consul for 107 BC, Servilius Caepio, had followed him to Tolosa and managed to relieve the besieged Roman garrison there. He forced the Tectosages to surrender and took, as tribute, an estimated 200,000 pounds weight in gold from their holy temples. Other versions have it that the gold was discovered in a sacred lake and identified as the gold taken in the sack of Delphi. Caepio sent it under guard to Massilia, en route for Rome, but it never arrived. He was accused of complicity in the theft from the imperial coffers. However, it seems likely that a part of this treasure re-emerged in the find at Taillac-Libourne in 1893 when a horde of gold coins was discovered. The coins were mainly struck by the Celtic tribes of the Arverni, Bellovaci and Ambarri, while others are unidentifiable.

In spite of Caepio's success in rescuing the garrison at Tolosa, Rome was in turmoil. Three Roman armies had been defeated in as many major engagements by the Celts. In 105 BC Caepio, now the Governor of the province, was reinforced by a new Roman army commanded by Gaius Manlius. Manlius was a blunt, no-nonsense professional soldier who had risen through the ranks of the army. Caepio, on the other hand, was an aristocrat who had achieved his rank by virtue of his birth. Caepio clearly despised Manlius while Manlius regarded Caepio as a fool. The rift was to prove fatal. Manlius was all for launching an attack on the Cimbri and their allies, taking the offensive immediately. Soon after he had arrived at Massilia, on 6 October 105 BC, he had sent out an advance guard, commanded by his second-in-command, Scaurus, to scout the enemy positions. Caepio disapproved of Manlius' action and, while the two Roman generals were quarrelling, Scaurus and his command were wiped out. The Cimbri came bursting down on the main Roman army positions at Arausio (Orange) and they suffered a similar fate. A fourth Roman army had been destroyed and the road to Rome herself lay open and undefended. Panic reigned in the city, the Celtic sack of Rome in 390 BC was uppermost in the citizens' minds.

Inexplicably, the Cimbri and their allies, the Teutones, turned away, westward across the Pyrenees, while their other allies returned to their former agricultural pursuits. Rome was given a breathing-space while the Cimbri and Teutones raided into Iberia, perhaps still trying to find fertile land in which to settle; but after a couple of years they were driven out by the Celtiberians.

Rome, in the intervening period, was able to find a man equal to the task of defending it. The man was Gaius Marius (157–86 BC), who had fought the Celts before, serving as a young officer under Scipio Aemilianus during the siege of Numantia. He was married to Julia, who was to become aunt to Gaius Julius Caesar. Marius had just concluded a successful campaign against Jugurtha and the Numidians, who had been in rebellion against Rome, and was now called back from Africa to defend Rome against the Cimbri and their allies.

Marius, with the Cimbri in Spain, was given two years to reorganize the demoralized and defeated Roman forces. He was elected Consul and placed in sole charge of the operation. It is his methods of organization with which we associate the Roman army today: the legionary formations with their *aquila*, or eagle, as a means to raise regimental *esprit de corps*. The legion, regular pay, standard weapons and standard battle-tactics were all introduced by him. For the first time, the army became a career for aspiring young men, and for the first time Rome had a standing army, with terms of service and retirement pensions.

In 102 BC, with Marius being re-elected Consul for a fourth term, the news came that the Celts were on the move once again. The Cimbri were massing along the Brenner Pass and Quintus Lutatius Catulus, the second Consul for 102 BC, was sent with an army to prevent them emerging. The Cimbri were forced to fall back towards the River Athesis (Adige), from where they threatened to move through Gallia Narbonensis.

Meanwhile, the Teutones and the Ambrones had already moved through eastern Gallia Narbonensis and were now coming through the Alps towards the Po Valley. Marius marched his army to face them. Their initial encounter was a stalemate, but it gave the Romans a boost in morale for it was not a defeat for them. Encouraged, Marius went on the offensive, forcing the Teutones and Ambrones to fall back as far as Aquae Sextiae (Aix), where he effected a skilful encirclement. He attacked and gave his troops orders to spare no one. The attack became a massacre. Chronicles recorded that the butchery by the Romans was so tremendous that for many years the fields in the vicinity, saturated with so much blood, produced bumper corn crops. Only a small body of survivors escaped to the lands of another Celtic tribe, the Sequani, but the Sequani were forced to surrender them to the pursuing Romans, who promptly butchered them.

Marius returned to Rome to universal rejoicing by the citizens and was elected Consul for a fifth time. In the spring of 101 BC he marched north with fresh troops to reinforce the army of Catulus which had wintered in the Po Valley. The Cimbri were already moving across the Alps in large numbers, determined to have revenge on the Romans for the massacre of their compatriots at Aquae Sextiae. By August they had taken up positions near Vercellae, between Milan and Turin, on the Paudine Plain. It was reported that their battle line was enormous and stretched for three miles. The Celts opened the attack and, for a time, it seemed that the Roman line was going to break before their charge as it had done so often before. But Marius' newly reorganized army was better equipped and trained to meet the onslaught. In tight-knit formations, the Romans stood firm against the charges. The Cimbri wavered. Roman writers observed that it was an extremely hot day and that the heat sapped the northern vigour of the Celts. Their

lines broke. This was the moment Marius had waited for. His troops
now took the offensive. The Cimbri fell back and then the withdrawal
became a rout. Historians record that 120,000 were slaughtered. No
one escaped. Rome had been saved yet again and it was fully five
centuries before the Italian peninsula was to be invaded again.

Of the tribes that had caused such devastation to Rome, and
checked her imperial ambitions for a decade, little else is known. The
Teutones are heard of no more. The Ambrones also disappear,
although Latin grammarians of the late empire say the name survived
as a term of abuse, perhaps in much the same way the name of the
Vandals, the Germanic tribe who invaded Gaul and Spain in the fourth
and fifth centuries AD, has survived for someone ruthlessly destructive.
Only the Cimbri are heard of when the Roman expedition, during the
time of Augustus (63 BC – AD 14), discovered them in Jutland. The
Cimbri sent the Roman Emperor a gift – a cauldron. One cannot help
remarking that a cauldron, with its mystic significance, is a very Celtic
gift!

The tribes who had joined the Cimbri, Teutones and Ambrones –
the Arverni, Tectosages, Tigurini and others – settled once more to the
peaceful life of agriculture. For a couple of generations there was peace
on the northern frontiers of the Roman empire. But the marauding
expeditions had had a great effect on the Celtic world beyond Rome's
influence. During the decade social habits had changed. From 500 BC
the people of Gaul, from the country of the Belgae, Belgium in the
north, south to the newly created province of Gallia Narbonensis, had
enjoyed a settled and stable life as agricultural communities, living in
open villages and scattered farmsteads. The ancient hill-forts had
fallen into disuse. Trade was prosperous and many of the Celtic
tribes produced their own coinage. Highways crisscrossed the fertile
farmlands of the Celts.

At the start of the first century BC, at the time of Rome's defeat of the
Cimbri, the people of Gaul were back in the old hill-forts and were
rebuilding them, creating new ones and fortifying their townships.
Was it simply a response to the Cimbri expeditions through Gaul?

The answer was no. A new people were moving southwards in great
numbers at this period – the Germans, ancestors of the Germanic
peoples, including the English and the Franks. They had originated
from an undefined area, generally considered to be southern Scandin-
avia. Tacitus, in his work *Germania*, on the origins, geography and

institutions of the Germans, written about AD 98, says it was the Celts of Gaul who first encountered them and gave them the name Germani, which designated the entire group of tribes. We have seen that at Clastidium in 222 BC the Germans, making their first appearance in recorded history, were found fighting for the Celts against Rome.

By 120 BC the Germans were pushing into former Celtic territory and soon the eastern border of Gaul was the Rhine, the great Celtic river of Rhenos (meaning sea), whose valley was filled with Celtic place-names, indicative of the centuries of Celtic occupation. The Celts in what is now southern Germany, Austria and Czechoslovakia were isolated from the rest of the Celtic world and were eventually to disappear. Within a few years, the Germanic tribes were even attempting to cross the Rhine. As we have seen,* whereas once the Celts had achieved political predominance over some of the Germanic peoples, now it was the Germans' turn to assert their military superiority as they pressed south and west. And it was the movement of these peoples which was forcing the Celtic agricultural communities to fortify themselves against attack by retreating to a lifestyle which they had abandoned centuries before.

The Celtic world had started to diminish and its heartland, Gaul, was suddenly caught in a pincer movement – pressed by the Germanic tribes from the north-east and by the Romans from the south.

* See Chapter 2.

[9]

Caesar in Gaul

IN 71 BC the Sequani of Gaul, living on the western bank of the Rhine, were involved in a quarrel with the Aedui, who occupied central Gaul between the Upper Loire and Saône. The Aedui capital was the hill-fort of Bibracte, modern Autun. What the cause of this dispute was it is difficult to say. The dispute erupted into prolonged warfare. The Sequani looked for allies to help them and invited from the eastern bank a confederation of German tribes, known as the Seubi, under their chieftain Ariovistus. Taking advantage of this internal squabble, the Germans pressed across the Rhine and were soon seizing Celtic land and raiding deep into Celtic territory. Ariovistus defeated the Aedui in 61 BC and, by this time, many of the Celtic tribes of Gaul were forced to pay tribute to him.

In 60 BC the chieftain of the Aedui, Divitiacos, looked for a powerful ally to help him drive back the Germans. Instead of turning to the rest of the Celtic world, he turned his eyes south – to Rome. He made the journey there and was allowed to address the Roman senate with his proposal for an alliance. During his visit it appears that he was the guest of Quintus Tullius Cicero (102–43 BC), an able soldier and administrator and younger brother of Marcus Tullius Cicero (106–43 BC), the orator and statesman. Divitiacos met the elder Cicero, who mentions him in his letters. Interestingly, Cicero does not refer to the Aedui chieftain's political interests in Rome but he does mention that Divitiacos was not only a chieftain but a druid and that he was acquainted with natural philosophy and was able to predict the future. It is unclear whether Marcus Cicero, who had been Consul in 63–62 BC, supported Divitiacos when he spoke in the senate. It seems highly likely, for any alliance with the Aedui was opposed by Gaius Julius Caesar (100–44 BC), who had just returned from Spain, where he had been Governor. Caesar had achieved a reputation for his generalship in that country and was a rising power in Rome. Cicero, however, opposed what he saw as Caesar's 'unconstitutional attitudes'. Divitiacos must have received some vague promises from Rome for when he returned to Gaul he did all he could to promote an alliance of Rome with the Aedui.

The following year, in 59 BC, however, Caesar was appointed Consul of Rome with Marcus Calpurnius Bibulus. It was now that Caesar emerged as a man of determined ambition for he began to push through laws which his fellow Consul attempted to veto, as was his right. Bibulus, finding himself ineffectual against the determination of Caesar, was forced to shut himself in his house for the rest of the year of consulship and gave rise to the joke that it was the consulship not of Caesar and Bibulus but of Julius and Caesar. Caesar turned to Gaul and, having dismissed the idea of an alliance with the Celtic chieftain Divitiacos – perhaps on the ground that he had been promoted by Marcus Cicero, his enemy – asked the senate to recognize the German warlord Ariovistus as king and 'friend of the Roman people' (*rex atque amicus*). Finding his actions approved of by distant Rome, Ariovistus continued to carve a Germanic empire among the Celtic tribes of Gaul, overcoming all resistance.

Dumnorix, whose name means king of the world, the younger brother of Divitiacos, was opposed to his brother's pro-Roman attitude. He must have argued vehemently, especially when it became known that Rome was supporting the German Ariovistus. However, Divitiacos was not to be budged. Dumnorix was married to a daughter of Orgetorix, chieftain of the Helvetii. The Helvetii were a large and powerful Celtic tribe inhabiting the area of modern Switzerland (the name Helvetia is used as the name for Switzerland by the Swiss today). Dumnorix entered into a secret alliance with Orgetorix and also with Casticos, a son of the chieftain of the Sequani who had become disillusioned by his father's alliance with Ariovistus. The purpose behind this agreement was to attempt to unite the Celts of Gaul in an effort to drive the Germans back across the Rhine and to check the interference of Rome in the affairs of Gaul.

In 58 BC Caesar emerged as Proconsul but with Gnaeus Magnus Pompeius (Pompey) and Marcus Licinius Crassus as co-consuls, forming what became known as the First Triumvirate. Pompey had already been Consul with Crassus in 70 BC and had a reputation as being a more successful general than Caesar. He, too, was a man of great ambition. Crassus (115–53 BC) had achieved fame for suppressing the Spartacus uprising. These three powerful men, breaking with the senate, became virtual dictators of Rome. They divided up the spheres of influence they were to have and Caesar took for himself the governorship of Illyricum (Dalmatia), Cisalpine Gaul and Gallia Narbonensis. But he was an ambitious man and he wanted to achieve a military reputation as great, if not greater, than that of Pompey. In spite of his alliance with Pompey and Crassus, Caesar saw them as his rivals for power as well. Only new conquests could enhance his reputation in Rome, and he was clearly looking beyond Gallia Narbonensis towards the rest of Gaul, the mainly unchartered hinterland of the Celts.

Caesar had been assigned only four legions to keep his provinces under control. This did not meet with his ambitious plans and he set about raising two more as well as bodies of auxiliaries. The position of second-in-command was offered to Quintus Tullius Cicero to appease his political opponents. Cicero, however, declined the offer, though he was later to join Caesar as a legate, commanding a legion, taking part in the 54 BC invasion of Britain. The post of second-in-command went instead to Titus Atticus Labienus. Labienus came from Picenum, where his family had settled among the Cisalpine Celts as colonists. He had served as a tribune in 63 BC and achieved notoriety by prosecuting one Rabirius for a murder which had taken place in 100 BC; Cicero had acted as defence counsel. Cicero's *Pro Rabirio* (For Rabirius) is one of his more famous speeches. Labienus was to serve as Caesar's most trustworthy lieutenant through the Gallic wars but during the Roman civil war he sided with Pompey.

In the early months of 58 BC Caesar was offered the perfect excuse for intervention in Gaul. Orgetorix, the chieftain of the Helvetii, had died. The new leaders of the Helvetii, pressurized by the advancing Germans from the north and north-east and fully aware of the ambitions of Rome to the south, decided on a mass migration. The Boii had already moved themselves from what is now Bohemia, in Czechoslovakia, and settled for a short time in Noricum, or modern Austria, where they had joined the Taurisci. The advance of the Germanic tribes had forced both these peoples to move yet again to the country of the Helvetii. In fact, the Helvetii had, apparently, been preparing for their mass exodus for some time. Wagons with food and stores for the journey had been assembled and nearly 400,000 men, women and children, of whom 92,000 were fighting men, assembled. It was to be one of the last major Celtic migrations for five centuries, for not until the southern British Celts fled to Brittany and northern Spain in the fifth and sixth centuries AD was there to be a migration on such a scale. The aim of the Helvetii, with their Boii, Taurisci and Tigurini followers, seemed to be a search for 'living space' away from the Germanic tribes and Romans. They were to move westward. Dumnorix of the Aedui had persuaded Casticos of the Sequani to allow the Helvetii to pass through his tribal lands. They were to move westward, keeping to the south of the Jura Mountains and passing what is now Lake Geneva. On the appointed day the 400,000 Celts fired their villages, towns, farmsteads and fields, to prevent them falling into the hands of the incoming Germanic tribes, and began to move to the Pas de l'Ecluse.

Meanwhile Dumnorix's pro-Roman brother, Divitiacos, chieftain of the Aedui, had sent Caesar word of what was happening. Caesar was in Aquileia, in Cisalpine Gaul. He must have been delighted by an apparently heaven-sent opportunity to intervene. The movement of the Helvetii was seen as a threat to the 'peace' of the Roman province of Gallia Narbonensis and also to the lands to its north. The Romans could explain that their intervention had been requested by a friendly monarch – Divitiacos of the Aedui. Caesar immediately set off with the six legions to confront the Helvetii.

By 1 April, 58 BC, Caesar and his legions had reached the southern end of Lake Geneva while the Helvetian Celts were assembling to pass through the Pas de l'Ecluse. Caesar blocked them from turning south, where they would have crossed part of Gallia Narbonensis to swing round into Sequani territory. To avoid the Romans they turned north-west into the territory of the Aedui. It was all the same to Caesar. Whichever way the Helvetii moved, it was an invitation for the Romans to attack. Divitiacos had invited the Romans to 'protect' Aedui territory against the Helvetii. Caesar began to march after the Celts.

The Aedui, finding the Romans entering their territory, were now split between their chieftain's pro-Roman policy and the pro-Celtic policy of Dumnorix. Although Dumnorix was not the chieftain of the Aedui, he, like his brother, also appears to have been a druid, and possessed as much influence as his brother Divitiacos. Caesar, entering

Aedui territory, found many of them giving support to the Helvetii. Indeed, the Aedui kept the Helvetii informed of Caesar's movements and also prevented supplies of corn and other provisions from falling into Roman hands. Roman cavalry, sent by Caesar to cut off the advance of the Helvetii, were misdirected by the Aedui.

Caesar demanded a conference with the Aedui leadership and Divitiacos sent a chieftain named Liscos to meet the Roman General. Undoubtedly Caesar wanted Dumnorix caught and eliminated. However, as Caesar recounts, Divitiacos stood up for his brother, pointing out that the punishment of Dumnorix would alienate Divitiacos from the good opinion of his people and, interestingly enough, not only from the Aedui but from the people of all Gaul. Caesar had a meeting with Divitiacos and records that the interview took place through an interpreter.

It was inevitable that the Romans would eventually encounter the Helvetii. After all, the movement of 400,000 people, men, women and children, and the elderly, with their wagons and goods, was a slow process. Caesar, hearing that they were crossing the River Saône, crossed the river of Lugdunum, the fortress of Lugh, the Celtic god (Lyons) and moved rapidly along the western bank to intercept them. By the time he reached the spot he could see only the Tigurini still crossing. This was the tribe which, in earlier years, had decimated the army of Longinus. Caesar and his troops, catching them by surprise, cut them to pieces.

It became clear that, in trying to avoid the Romans, the Helvetii would pass Bibracte, the Aedui capital of Autun. Caesar, taking advantage of his greater mobility, marched his six legions towards Bibracte and positioned his men in readiness. The Helvetii marched slowly into the trap. The battle at Bibracte lasted from noon until nightfall. The Helvetii fought desperately against Caesar's ruthless legions. Finally, using the wagons to form defensive positions they made it as hard as possible for Caesar to overcome them. Some 6,000 were massacred during the first day's fighting. The next day found the Helvetii making a stand at nearby Langres. Caesar surrounded them and moved in. Of the nearly 400,000 who had started the exodus, only 100,000 survived.

While the remnants of the Boii were allowed to settle in the country of the Aedui, the Helvetii were forcibly returned to their former homeland, Helvetia, and made to rebuild their burned and devastated homes. Here they were eventually subjugated by the incoming Germanic tribes and through conquest and intermarriage they have vanished as a distinct Celtic people, leaving only the name Helvetia as a name for modern Switzerland to mark their passing.

The ruthlessness and efficiency demonstrated by the Romans clearly impressed the Celtic chieftains of Gaul. Many of them began arriving at the capital of the Aedui to make friends with Caesar and to see whether he would help them against Ariovistus and his Germans, who were still encroaching on their eastern borders. Their thinking was shortsighted: the enemy of your enemy is your friend. Using Divitiacos as their spokesman, the chieftains of the Celtic tribes of Gaul asked Caesar to aid them. It was precisely what Caesar wanted them to ask. He could claim that he was champion and protector of Gaul.

Caesar asked Ariovistus to meet him for a conference. Notwithstanding the fact that the German King had been proclaimed a 'friend of Rome', and at Caesar's instigation, it was clear that Rome, in the person of Caesar, set little store by treaties. Ariovistus declined to meet, suavely replying that if Caesar needed anything, he had only to ask. The German King added that, after all, he was 'a friend of Rome'. The gloves came off. Caesar demanded that the German King should return east of the Rhine, release all his Gaulish prisoners and cease any military excursions into Celtic territory. He added that the Celtic tribes of Gaul were now under Roman protection. Ariovistus answered that he had not interfered with the Romans or Roman possessions and therefore the Romans had no right to interfere with him. If Caesar wanted to press the matter, he, Ariovistus, would fight.

A large body of Germans started to cross the Rhine to swell Ariovistus' forces. Caesar at once moved his army to meet this challenge. The Germans were gathering in the country of the Sequani, formerly enemies of the Aedui and now enemies of Rome. Many of the Sequani Celts decided to join forces with Ariovistus. Caesar marched to their capital, Vesonito (Besançon), a hundred miles north-east of Bibracte.

After an initial skirmish, the Germans pressed on to Caesar's outposts. Caesar responded with an immediate attack and the Germans were put to flight. Publius Crassus, the son of Marcus Licinius Crassus, one of the triumvirate, pursued them with cavalry and pushed them back over the Rhine. Men, women and children were cut down and Ariovistus' defeat was total. The German threat to Gaul had been broken for the time being – but the Roman threat was now immediate. As Dumnorix had foreseen, the Romans were going to seize the whole of Gaul. While Labienus and the Roman army went into winter quarters in the land of the Sequani, Ceasar went to Cisalpine Gaul to raise two more legions on his own responsibility, look after administrative problems and prepare his campaign for the forthcoming year.

To the north, in that area which is still named after them – Belgium – a confederation of the Belgae Celtic tribes had witnessed with dismay the political naivety of Divitiacos and his friends. They realized that the might of Rome would be turned against them during the following year. The Belgae confederation had come into being to fight the encroachments of the Germans and had been hardened by years of border conflict. Their territory was bounded in the south by the rivers Marne and Seine, in the west by the sea and in the east and north by the Rhine. They were not susceptible to Roman bribes and duplicity.

In 57 BC Caesar, back in Gaul, commanding eight legions and with a large contingent of Aedui cavalry now at his service, with Divitiacos in tow as adviser and chief negotiator, marched northward. In fact, he made a forced march so that he arrived in the territory of the Belgic Remi (Reims being their tribal capital) before they knew he was near. The Remi, whose name means the first, were the most southerly of the Belgae confederation and the most exposed to the Roman advance. They had no time to prepare and were forced to surrender. Caesar took hostages and passed swiftly on to the River Aisne, to the north. The Suessiones, Bellovaci and Ambiana were prepared but, after some tough fighting, Caesar secured their submission. Moving westward he reached the River Sambre (Somme) and set up camp near Samarobriva (Amiens). He discovered that the leading tribes of the Belgae confederation, the Nervii and the Aduatùci, were awaiting him on the far bank of the river. The Nervii had a tremendous fighting reputation and even Caesar eventually admits admiration for them. They were an austere tribe who forbade wine to be brought among them as being injurious to their health.

Caesar sent his cavalry across the river to feel out the enemy positions. The Nervii quickly routed the cavalry and carried the attack to the far bank, swimming across the river in the darkness and engaging the main Roman infantry in a fierce hand-to-hand struggle. On Caesar's right flank, the VII and XII Legions were actually in danger of annihilation. Caesar took personal command in the area, managed to rally his men and launched a counter-attack which broke the Celtic advance. Soon the Celts were in retreat and the retreat became a rout. Roman archers and slingers poured a withering fire on them as they tried to recross the Somme. Of the 50,000 Celts who were said to have launched the attack, only 500 survived, according to Roman estimations.

The Aduatuci were now moving westward to reinforce the Nervii and they posed a threat to Caesar's eastern flank. He turned his legions to meet them and encountered them at Namur, where they withdrew into the great hill-fort there. Caesar now surrounded them and besieged them. Word reached the Aduatuci that, with the defeat of the Nervii, the Belgae confederation had asked for terms of surrender. Caesar promised the Aduatuci leaders that if they surrendered he would spare their lives. The Aduatuci leaders put down their weapons and opened the gates of the hill-fort. Caesar claimed they had betrayed the terms of the agreement and immediately slaughtered 4,000 of them and then rounded up the others, some 53,000 members of the tribe, for sale into slavery.

The Belgae confederation had been crushed as completely as the Helvetii in the previous year. Yet for the next thirty years the Roman conquest of the Belgic tribes was to be a tenuous one and the peace uneasy. Nevertheless, in two brief campaigns, Caesar had been able to claim the major part of Gaul under Roman control. The only area which was an unknown territory was Armorica, the Breton peninsula. Caesar sent Publius Crassus with a unit of the VII Legion to make a survey of it and seek alliances among the tribes there while he left the major part of his army in winter quarters at Chartres, Orléans and Blois. Then he returned to Rome.

It was in the wake of the defeat of the Belgae that Divitiacos of the Aedui vanished from the historical scene. Until this point he had been Caesar's constant companion in Gaul, urging his fellow Celts to submit to Rome. As the Roman army became increasingly successful, more and more Gauls joined it as mercenary cavalry. Caesar concludes his account of events with what he claims to be a verbatim report of speeches made by the Celtic ruler, although they appear to be Caesar's own impressions of the function of Divitiacos in regard to furthering Rome's interests in Gaul rather than the actual words of Divitiacos. Cicero had said that Divitiacos was a druid and yet there seems little of the qualities commonly associated with a druid in his speeches. Certainly Caesar does not refer to him as a druid, but Cicero's testimony is unquestionable and was based on a personal knowledge of the man.

Divitiacos is the antithesis of his brother Dumnorix, who, after the defeat of the Helvetii, is not referred to by Caesar until the year 54 BC when he emerges as the new chieftain of the Aedui and still Caesar's most implacable enemy. The brothers are chalk and cheese. The one, manipulative, trying to make the best deal of selling Gaulish freedom to the Romans; the other, fiercely Gaulish, a man of inflexible patriotism and entirely devoted to his native land and people, who would die rather than betray their trust.

When Caesar returned to Gaul in the spring of 56 BC, Divitiacos had vanished. Did he simply die, or was he assassinated by a Gaulish patriot? Unfortunately, Caesar does not say. Nor does he say what Dumnorix was doing during 58–54 BC, although when he does re-emerge as chieftain of the Aedui, he is a hostage of the Romans.

Publius Crassus had arrived in Rome early in 56 BC with some disturbing news for Caesar. He had reconnoitred the Armorican peninsula, taking some of the VII Legion, and had received token submissions and assurances of friendship from half-a-dozen tribes, including an important sea-faring people called the Veneti, whose capital at Vannes still bears their name. But no sooner had he passed on, leaving some of the officers of the VII Legion with them to act as emissaries, than the Veneti had risen up in defiance of Rome and made those officers their prisoners. Caesar was having a rough ride in the Roman senate at that time and so he took the opportunity to cut short his stay in Rome and rejoin his legions in Gaul. In the meantime he had sent orders for a fleet of Roman galleys to be built in the mouth of the Loire, and rowers, seamen and pilots were transported there from Massilia.

However, when he arrived in Gaul in the early spring, he discovered that the Veneti were not the only tribe threatening the Roman conquest. The Belgae were causing disturbances and Caesar ordered Titurius Sabinus to take three of the legions to occupy their country. Then there were the Germanic tribes making further incursions across the Rhine. He despatched Labienus with another three legions to check them. So, with the remaining two legions, Caesar set off for the country of the Veneti to teach them obedience to Rome.

The Veneti were a maritime power whose strongholds stood on the headlands and islands in Quiberon Bay. They were almost un-approachable from the land. The Veneti had a powerful fleet of ships, some 220 vessels according to Roman sources, with which they traded not only along the coast of Gaul but with Britain and Ireland. Much of their wealth originated from trading tin from the mines of Cornwall. It appeared that their opposition to the Romans derived not only from a reaction to foreign domination but from a rumour that the Romans were going to invade Britain; this would destroy the Veneti trade with that country.

The Veneti waited with equanimity as Caesar and his legions marched into their country. They realized that the Romans would find it difficult to attack from the landward side. Indeed, when Caesar and his legions attempted to capture some of their island fortresses by constructing huge dykes or causeways, the Veneti simply evacuated their people by ship to another stronghold. Caesar saw that the only way to defeat the Veneti was to use a Roman naval force to attack them. Word came that his fleet of galleys was now ready in the mouth of the Loire. He gave command of them to Decimus Junius Brutus, then a young man, distantly related to Marcus Brutus who was destined to become one of Caesar's assassins. The fleet sailed up into the Gulf of Morbihan to encounter the Veneti fleet. It was to be the first major sea battle Rome had fought in the Atlantic. Curiously, in 138 BC, a Roman consul of the same name – Decimus Junius Brutus – built a fleet with which he attacked the Celtiberian strongholds on the Atlantic coast of Iberia. Was this mere coincidence? Or did some historian of the earlier event confuse the name with the exploit of the later Brutus?

According to Caesar, the Veneti ships were powerful vessels:

> They have flat bottoms which enable them to sail in shallow coastal water. Their high prows and sterns protect them from heavy seas and violent storms, as do their strong hulls made entirely from oak. The cross timbers – beams a foot wide – are secured with iron nails as thick as a man's thumb. Their anchors are secured with chains not ropes, while their sails are made of rawhide or thin leather, so as to stand up to the violent Atlantic winds.

As the two fleets closed with one another, Caesar and his legions watched from the headlands. The naval engagement lasted from 10 a.m. until sunset. Brutus had examined the Veneti ships well and had scythes fastened on long poles so that his sailors could cut the rigging of the Celtic ships. With their sails fluttering helplessly, the Celtic vessels apparently lost control and were an easy prey to Roman boarding parties. One by one the Veneti ships were overwhelmed. Some of them tried to withdraw but a drop in the wind prevented them and the majority of sailors were captured. Such an easy victory by the Romans over the tough sea-faring Veneti does seem a little hard to swallow. However, perhaps the answer lies in Tim Newark's *Celtic Warriors*, 1986, which suggests that not only were Caesar's ships built by Gallic mercenaries but they were also manned by Gauls used to sailing against the types of ships being used by the Veneti. The victory does appear more plausible in these circumstances.

The defeat of the Veneti was a significant step in Caesar's Gaulish campaign. Using the excuse that the Veneti had 'rebelled' against Rome in that they had first accepted Roman authority and then wrongly imprisoned Roman officers, Caesar treated the tribe and their allies without mercy. All the tribal chieftains and leaders were executed on the spot while the rest were sold into slavery.

While the war against the Veneti was taking place, Titurius Sabinus and his three legions had managed to put down the rumblings of insurrection among the Belgae. Some of the tribes had actually turned on their pro-Roman chieftains and overthrown them. Sabinus had marched across the Seine to the area around Calais, where he defeated two such tribes, the Morini and Menapii. Labienus had achieved a similar success in checking the incursions of the Germanic tribes across the Rhine. In the south-east of Gaul, Publius Crassus had been carrying out Caesar's instructions, with a mobile force, moving down the western coastline and taking submissions of septs and tribes as far as the Pyrenees, including the powerful Aquitani. Not many years before, the Aquitani had defeated two Roman armies. They had not given in without a struggle, even seeking aid from the Celtiberians. But Crassus, using what troops he had, had stormed their hill-fort. Caesar was delighted. It seemed that the subjugation of all the Celtic tribes of Gaul was complete.

During the winter of 56/55 BC, however, the Germanic tribes were pressing over the Rhine again. The Seubi, of whom Ariovistus had been King, were in the forefront of a new movement, pushing over above the junction of the Rhine and Meuse. During a council of pro-Roman Gaulish chieftains in the spring of 55 BC, Caesar learned that some anti-Roman Gaulish chieftains had been trying to form an alliance with the Germans against Rome.

Caesar sent word to two Germanic tribes, the Usipetes and Tencteri, telling them to withdraw across the Rhine. When they did not, he marched to engage them. In spite of attempts by Caesar to negotiate first, a large body of Germans attacked the Roman advance guard but were driven off. When the German chiefs came into the Roman camp the next morning to ask for a truce, Caesar had them arrested. Then he launched an attack on the German forces. With their chiefs held prisoner, the Germans were in a state of confusion. The Roman troops had been worked up to fever pitch by tales of German treachery and bloodthirst and began to slaughter them without discrimination. Thousands of men, women and children were drowned as they attempted to flee back across the Rhine. Caesar complac ɪtly remarks that, of the 430,000 men, women and children of these tribes, only a few survivors remained. This massacre, rather than battle, occurred near Coblenz.

Caesar followed up his success with a determined effort to break the German ambition to invade Gaul. Caesar had secured alliances with certain Gaulish chieftains, who accepted Roman overlordship and were content that Gaul had a role in the empire of Rome. If the Germans were allowed to establish a foothold in Gaul, they could use it as a base to weaken Roman rule and perhaps even invade the Italian peninsula. Then there was the existence of the Gaulish patriotic party, probably centred around Dumnorix, who were seeking alliances against Rome. If Caesar acted with swiftness and savagery, it would teach both the Gauls and the Germans a lesson which would force them to accept the *pax Romana*.

While the Germans were still reeling from their defeat at Coblenz, Caesar threw a bridge over the Rhine in ten days. He marched his legions across and spent the next eighteen days east of the Rhine burning villages, taking hostages, extracting submissions and forcing other tribes, such as the Suebi and Sigambri, to retreat before him. When Caesar and his legions returned in triumph to Gaul at about the beginning of August 55 BC, burning the bridge across the Rhine behind them, all Gaul was quiet. There were no reports of any Celtic tribe in arms against the Roman presence. Yet there were still two full months in which the army could campaign.

Caesar, ever the man of ambition, looked westward – westward across a narrow strip of sea towards the island of Britain.

[10]

Britain

THE country with which Caesar's ambition now lay, the island of Britain, had become known to the Mediterranean peoples at least by the fifth century BC through the merchants of the ancient world. Britain was one of the few sources of tin in Europe, tin being a necessary component of bronze. The Phoenicians and Greeks knew of the Tin Islands lying to the north-west of the known world. In the second half of the fourth century BC Pytheas, the Greek explorer from Massilia, made a voyage north along the western coast of Europe and crossed to the islands, actually circumnavigating Britain, noting its neighbour, Ireland, and the main features of the island group.

The Greeks had named them the Cassiterides – the Tin Islands. It has been suggested that the name was Celtic and that the word for tin, first recorded by Homer – *kassiteros* – was borrowed from Celtic, as tin was a 'Celtic' material. The stem *cassi*, in Celtic, means esteem or love and appears several times in British Celtic names – for example Cassivelaunos, the lover of Belinos. But the argument that the Greek word for tin was a Celtic loan-word is doubtful, for the Irish word is *stan* and the Welsh word is *ystaen*. It is not likely that a word describing an important product of the Celtic world would have disappeared from the Celtic vocabulary, especially if supported by Greek usage.

Polybius, Strabo, Avienus refer to the Tin Islands as the Pretanic Islands, the form implying that the inhabitants were Pretani. The name seems to have been used first by the Gauls and then picked up by the Romans. During the Roman period, the name Brittones, perhaps a corruption of Pretani, was used, and hence Britain. The older form continued in use in Welsh texts to describe the island of Britain as a whole – Prydain – and, significantly, Pretani is used to refer to the people the Romans called Picti or Picts.

When Caesar arrived in Britain, Celtic was the universal language. It is perhaps astonishing that even today in the territory now known as England Celtic place-names are fairly commonplace. In spite of the conquests and occupations by the Romans, Angles, Saxons, Jutes, Danes and finally Normans, and the driving off or extinction of the original Celtic population, many of the place-names are still recognizably Celtic. Most of the rivers and streams bear Celtic names, especially the major rivers such as the Aire, Avon, Axe, Dee, Derwent, Don, Esk, Exe, Ouse, Severn, Stour, Tees, Thames, Trent and Wye. Most of the prominent hills and ranges, the Pennines for example, and forests, Kinver, Penge and Savernake, bear Celtic names. Some of the major towns, such as London, retain their Celtic names while others, such as Manchester, retain them in compound form. Territorial names, such as Kent, Thanet, Wight and Leeds, linger on. However, most villages and hamlets bear the names of the cultures which replaced the Celtic and are mainly Anglo-Saxon. Several Celtic words of topographical meaning also survive such as *cumb*, *coombe* (valley), *tor* (hill), *bourne* (a brook), *carr* (rock) as in Carham, *luh* (lake) as in Lutton, Lincolnshire, and so forth.

If the Urnfield Culture established the first Celtic societies in Britain, we can accept that the Celts were living in Britain by 1200 or 1000 BC. And if the theory of Celtic scholars, among them Henri Hubert, that Goidelic was the earliest form of Celtic is correct, it is reasonable to assume that a form of Goidelic was once spoken throughout Britain but a language-shift took place with the development of the P-Celtic, now known as Brythonic, form.

It was with the Iron Age culture that Britain began to emerge clearly in history. Pytheas records that the Celts of Britain were agricultural and pastoral farmers like their cousins in mainland Europe. Their main crop was wheat. 'This wheat the natives thresh, not on open floors, but in barns because they have so little sunshine and so much rain.' Inland, Pytheas was impressed by the large herds of cattle and sheep. In the Cornish peninsula he found that the Celts worked iron, tin and bronze, made fine pottery and were spinners and weavers of wool and cloth. He found that at this stage of their development they preferred to barter goods. 'They refuse to accept coin and insist on barter, preferring to exchange necessities rather than fix prices.' Coinage did not develop among the British Celts until the second century BC. Diodorus Siculus (d. 21 BC), citing several older authorities, records:

The inhabitants of that part of Britain which is called Belerion [Land's End] are very fond of strangers and, from their intercourse with foreign merchants, are civilized in their manner of life. They prepare tin, working very carefully the earth in which it is produced. The ground is rocky, but it contains earthy veins, the produce of which is ground down, smelted and purified. They beat the metal into masses, like *astragali*, and carry it to a certain island off Britain called Ictis . . . here, then, the merchants buy the tin from the natives and carry it over to Gaul, and after travelling overland for about thirty days, they finally bring their load on horse to the mouth of the Rhône.

Diodorus accurately describes the method of 'tin-streaming'.

Archaeology has discovered in Cornwall a wide variety of artefacts supporting a popular trade with Britain long before the arrival of Caesar, ranging from Iberian brooches to Grecian mirrors. In fact, Publius Crassus, Roman Governor of Spain *c.*95 BC, was credited by the Romans with making the sea route between south-west Britain and the Roman colonies in Spain more generally known and developing trade between them.

When Caesar marched his legions through southern Britain he found that 'the population is numerous beyond all counting, and very numerous also the houses. These closely resemble the houses of Gaul.' He identified timber as a main building material and noted half-timbered constructions, some three storeys high. However, we can still see the remains of stone structures, dating from the fourth to second centuries BC. In the north, brochs made of drystone walling still survive, rising to heights of forty feet with lintelled entrances, inward-tapering walls, sometimes fifteen feet thick, with chambers, galleries and stairs. An archaeological reconstruction of Clickhimin, a building dating back to the fourth century BC, has been called a 'revelation' by archaeologist Dr Patrick Crampton: 'The evidence of Clickhimin is so revolutionary that it will take years before its full implications can be realized.' Dr Crampton was comparing the evidence of the Clickhimin site with the traditional misconception of ancient Britons clad in skins, painting themselves and living in mud huts, which a too literal and selective reading of Caesar has bequeathed. References to such structures in early Irish and Welsh manuscripts, thought to be due to the imagination of the scribes, are now seen as accurate.

Northern Britain, which did not emerge into recorded history until Gnaeus Julius Agricola attempted to conquer it during AD 80–4, was also pictured as wild and barbaric. The only ground for this belief was that the Caledonians, as the Romans called the people living north of the Firth of Forth, would not meekly submit to the *pax Romana*. However, the archaeological evidence shows that the Celtic tribes of Caledonia were every bit as advanced as their Celtic cousins elsewhere.

A people emerging later in this area have been thought to be a pre-Celtic people. They bear the popular name Picts, from the Latin Picti, Painted People. Bede (AD *c.*673–735) certainly treated their language as different from Celtic. However, Professor Kenneth Jackson regards them, in the main, as an offshoot from the continental Celts, but 'whether these are a simple extension of the British occupiers of Britain up to the Forth and Clyde . . . or whether a rather more separate Celtic nation is uncertain, but perhaps the second.' Professor Jackson says of the linguistic evidence that it is not clear whether linguistic differences were merely a matter of dialect. They called themselves Priteni, which in the Goidelic form of Celtic became Cruthin, if one remembers the famous substitute of Q/C for the P sound. According to Professor Jackson:

There are no texts in their language extant, because when they learned to write, from the Church, they wrote in Latin, and we have only some scanty personal names and place-names to guide us. Most are unquestionably Celtic, and moreover what is called P-Celtic, that is sprung from the continental Celtic milieu from which the Britons also came, and not from the Q-Celtic which was the source of Irish and Scottish Gaelic. A remarkable piece of evidence for this is the place-names numerous all through Pictland, beginning with the Pictish *pett*, meaning something like a farming unit or a man-orial unit. This gives Pit – in hundreds of names like Pitlochry; it is related to the Gaulish source of French *pièce* (cf. parcel of land) and is clearly P-Celtic, i.e. not Gaelic. For personal names, Calgacos 'The Swordsman', a war-leader, and Argentocoxos 'Silver-Leg', a chief, are examples of undoubted Celtic names during the Roman period; and a post-Roman instance is the eighth-century King Unuist son of Wurguist, 'One Choice son of Super-Choice' (Oengus son of Forcus in early Gaelic).

While Pictish king-lists give a preponderance of rulers in the Brythonic form of Celtic, nevertheless as far back as scholastic research can penetrate Gaelic was the common language of the Picts. So the change from one branch of Celtic to another must have taken place about the start of the Christian era or soon afterwards. This would also account for the rapid integration of the Pictish kingdoms with that of the Gaelic Dál Riada to form the united kingdom of Alba (modern Scotland). Picts are recorded as dwelling in mid and northern Ireland for many centuries, the last reference occurring in the *Annals of Ulster* in AD 809.

It has been hypothesized that towards 1200–1000 BC the climate in Scotland began to worsen, becoming colder and more damp and so encouraging the growth of peat and causing less arable land to be available. The result of this was a pressure on the communities to protect their crops and livestock from less fortunate tribes, who resorted to raiding. Archaeological evidence does show an increase of weapons from this period and defensive building. By the seventh century BC the construction of great hill-forts was under way and even farmsteads appeared to be enclosed by stout timber stockades, although it must be added that many unenclosed settlements have also been excavated.

Timber-laced forts occur from the seventh century BC, dated by radiocarbon, but it is difficult to date drystone fortifications accurately. The Celts of Britain, both north and south, used the drystone method with great ability. Many of their magnificent constructions survive, such as the village of Chysauster, near Madron, Cornwall, which is one of the best examples of stone-built Celtic houses. There are over fifty surviving brochs in Scotland, round towers and fortifications, the two tallest being Mousa (still standing forty-three feet high) and Dun Troddan (standing twenty-five feet high). But one of the best known is Clickhimin, which developed from a fortified farmstead built around the seventh century BC.

As well as these examples of the ability of the Celts to build lasting stone constructions, there survive numerous examples of their complex and sophisticated hill-forts. One of the best known in the south of Britain is Maiden Castle, near Dorchester, which was reduced by the II Augusta Legion commanded by the future Emperor Titus Vespasian (AD 9–79). Maiden Castle, the name apparently deriving from Mai's fortress – Mai-dun – was erected about the first century BC, with massive triple ramparts and intricate defences guarding its two entrances. It enclosed an area two-thirds of a mile in length and one-third of a mile in breadth, with ramparts rising as high as a hundred feet. This appeared to be the tribal capital of the Durotriges.

In the north, however, there is also no lack of hill-forts and these are similar, and certainly equal, to those in the south. For example, the Caterthuns in Angus, known as the White Caterthun and the Brown Caterthun, stand almost two miles apart. The White Caterthun retains a stone-built rampart – the inner wall alone measuring forty feet thick and ten feet high. The outer wall is some twenty feet thick. The area enclosed measures 150 yards by 60, while outside the fortress further defensive lines are seen. The Brown Caterthun encloses a large area, some 100 yards by 60, but does not have the same impressive fortification survivals as the White Caterthun.

At the time when Caesar turned his mind to conquest, Britain was a prosperous country with flourishing agricultural communities, advanced in art, woollen and linen production, wheeled pottery and the production of jewellery. Its woollen goods were even exported to Rome where the possession of a British woollen cloak, a *sagum*, placed one in the height of fashion. It was a civilization advanced in metalworking, the production of iron, tin and copper, and even gold from Wales. Bronze-smelting was an advanced art. It was a civilization which had a widespread trade with Gaul and the Mediterranean world.

Why, then, did Caesar, in his justification for invading Britain, paint such an inaccurate picture of the country, and one which is popularly accepted today even though Caesar is entirely at odds with older and contemporary Greek and Roman writers on Britain? Caesar writes:

> Of all the Britons those that inhabit the lands of the Cantii [Kent] are the most civilized and it is a wholly maritime region. These Cantii differ but little from the Gauls in habits of life. But many of the inland Britons do not grow corn. They live on milk and flesh and are clothed in skins. All Britons stain their persons with a dye that produces a blue colour. This gives them a more terrible aspect in battle. They wear their hair long, shaving all the body except the head and upper lip.

It is especially surprising that Caesar seems ignorant of the fact that the woollen cloaks (*sagi*) from Britain were highly prized in the Rome of his day and were therefore indicative of a widespread knowledge of the high standard of the British woollen industry. Caesar's contemporary, Strabo, the Greek geographer, certainly mentions this thriving export in woollen garments to Rome as well as the export of linen and leatherwork. And at this time British artwork had reached a new height of development. Whereas art among the continental Celts was then in decline, the Celtic artists in Britain, around 100 BC to AD 43, were producing magnificent decorated bronze mirrors and other objects, especially enamelwork, showing some of the finest and most intricate examples of the precision of their craftsmanship. Like the Celtic illuminated manuscripts of a later period, it is almost impossible to compare this artform with any other. One such mirror, found at Birdlip, Gloucester, has highly sophisticated workings of enamel inlays on the handle, while the Mayer Mirror, recovered from the Thames, is simply breathtaking.

In the north of Britain, too, there was a flourishing school of Celtic art, centred in Dumfries, Scotland, which reached its highest development in the years immediately after the birth of Christ. Some of the finest examples of British Celtic artistry can be found on bronze sword scabbards of this period, such as the one found in Bugthorpe, Yorkshire.

Was Caesar's ignorance of the conditions in Britain feigned or genuine?

Caesar's plan to invade Britain had been formed as early as 57 BC when he was fighting the Belgae confederation. He had discovered that many of the Belgae, perhaps several entire septs, had fled to Britain rather than submit to the Romans. These Belgae claimed kinship with certain tribes in southern Britain who had settled there in the second century BC and maintained contact with the Belgae on the European mainland. Some chieftains actually claimed to rule tribes with septs on both sides of the Channel. Thus he found a Belgae chieftain named Commios of the Atrebates claiming suzerainty over a tribe of Atrebates in southern Britain. Caesar immediately set out to learn what he could about Britain. Did his informants provide him with a highly inaccurate and bleak picture of Britain in an attempt to dissuade him from his invasion? Did Caesar distort the picture for reasons of his own? Or was it merely a matter of an insensitive soldier not being the right sort of person to record such details accurately?

Before coming to Caesar, it can be asked: what of Britain's history?

It was not until the Christian era that the British Celts, like the Celts of Ireland, began to record their traditions in their own language. Like Celts elsewhere, the druids and bards were the repositories of learning – the law, history, philosophy and poetry. Apart from the traditions, therefore, recorded in Welsh, there is little surviving tradition of the history prior to the coming of the Romans – unless we are prepared to believe Geoffrey of Monmouth.

In AD 1137 Geoffrey, a scholar of Breton Celtic origin born and living in Wales, wrote a prose chronicle in twelve books which purported to be the history of Britain from earliest times – *Historia regnum Britanniae*, the history of the kings of Britain. For many centuries no one questioned its authenticity as an historical document. It was the source work for Raphael Holinshed (d. AD *c*.1580), whose *Chronicles* in turn provided a source for the plots of many Shakespearean plays. And the Arthurian legends have their major source in Geoffrey's work. Geoffrey never claimed to be anything more than a simple translator. He introduced his work with the explanation:

> Walter, Archdeacon of Oxford, a man skilled in the art of public-speaking and well informed about the history of foreign countries, presented me with a certain very ancient book written in the British language. The book, attractively composed to form a consecutive and orderly narrative, set out all the deeds of these men, from Brutus, the first king of the Britons, down to Cadwallader, the son of Cadwallo. At Walter's request I have taken the trouble to translate the book into Latin . . .

During the last hundred years Celtic scholars have dismissed Geoffrey's translation as a fake, maintaining that there is no Welsh composition which exists which could reasonably be looked upon as the original or groundwork of the book. They presume that such a work in Welsh would have survived. However, what is more intriguing is the fact that there does exist a copy of a twelfth-century poem by John of Cornwall in Latin hexameters called 'The Prophecy of Merlin'. John of Cornwall claims that it is simply a translation of an early Cornish manuscript and, in support, he gives notations in the original Cornish, which words belong to the Old Cornish period, some centuries before John's Latin version. The only known copy of this work is one dated 8 October AD 1474 surviving in the Vatican. There is some similarity between John's 'The Prophecy of Merlin' and

Geoffrey's chapter 'The Prophecies of Merlin'. So did the book in the British language exist as Geoffrey claimed? And does *Historia regnum Britanniae* have its provenance in the Cornish dialect of British rather than Welsh?

If this is so, does Geoffrey's work provide us with a genuine British Celtic tradition of history prior to the arrival of the Romans in Britain in the same way as the *Leabhar Gabhálá* provides us with the historical traditions of early Ireland?

Geoffrey's statement is clear. The Archdeacon of Oxford, Walter Mapes, 'a man learned in foreign histories', had discovered the ancient book, written in Brythonic Celtic, and had given it to Geoffrey, who understood the language, to translate. Geoffrey dedicated the work to Henry II's son, the Earl of Gloucester. What would be the reason for such a deception, the forgery of the work – as claimed by modern scholars – involving the venerable and highly respected Archdeacon of Oxford and himself? Surely other contemporary scholars would have demanded sight of the original work and we would have had some comment about its veracity long ago? No such comment was forthcoming and for centuries it remained a source work.

This is not to say, accepting that it is a genuine British Celtic tradition, that we can also accept that it is a reliable history, any more than we can accept the *Leabhar Gabhálá* as a reliable acount of the early history of Ireland. It is interesting that *Historia regnum Britanniae* has similarities to the Irish tradition in that both claim an ancestry of kings going back to the Trojans. While Parthalon is the Trojan who arrives in Ireland to found a dynasty after the fall of Troy, Brutus is said to be the Trojan who founds a similar dynasty in Britain. This probably indicates the Greek scholarship of the later Christian scribes in both countries.

There is another similarity in the emergence in the British tradition of Dunwallo Molmutius, son of Cloten, King of Cornwall, as a man who exerted his rule over the whole of Britain and established a law system, subsequently known as the Molmutine Laws. One can compare this to the claim that Ollamh Fodhla became High King of Ireland *c.*714 BC and codified the Brehon Law system.

No less intriguing is that Molmutius, who is said to have ruled for forty years, has two sons, Belinos and Brennos. They are said to have quarrelled and Brennos goes into exile in Gaul, among the Allobriges, and marries the daughter of Seginos, their chieftain. He returns to

Britain, tries to overthrow his brother, but their mother, Conwenna, manages to reconcile them.

The account then has it that Belinos and Brennos lead an army to Rome and sack it before returning to Britain. So Brennos, famous as the conqueror of Rome in 390–387 BC, returns to be buried in his native capital, the city of the Trinovantes – identified as London. The account goes on to record some forty-four kings until Cassivelaunos, who is said to have been one of three brothers – Lud, Cassivelaunos and Nennius. Lud is described as rebuilding the city of the Trinovantes and renaming it as his fortress – Lud's dun. When he died he was buried by one of the gates, henceforth called Ludgate. And so Britain then passed to the kingship of Cassivelaunos, who was to be Caesar's greatest opponent.

This, of course, is if we accept Geoffrey's work as an accurate rendering of British Celtic tradition and if we attach some validity to that tradition.

Caesar chose the VII and X Legions, a total force of 10,000 men, to attempt a reconnaissance in force in August 55 BC. For a usually careful general, Caesar's decision to make the journey on his return from his punitive expedition against the German tribes is a surprising one. He was, in fact, proposing an ill-prepared military expedition to a fairly unknown island late in the campaigning season. He left his main army in the hands of Sabinus and Cotta, which would imply that he took his second-in-command Titus Labienus with him to Britain. Some eighty transports were assembled at Portus Itius (Wissant), while eighteen more transports were gathered at Ambleteuse for cavalry.

Caesar sent two advance guards. An officer named Caius Volusenus was despatched across to the British coast in a fast war-galley to reconnoitre for a safe landing-place. Volusenus was to rendezvous with Caesar's fleet off the coast within five days. The second person he despatched was Commios, the Celtic chieftain of the Atrebates who was told to go to the British Atrebates and suggest they submit to Caesar. If they did so, Caesar promised he would recognize Commios as their chieftain as well as chieftain of the Gaulish Atrebates.

On the evening of 24 August 55 BC, the Roman invasion fleet set sail for the British coast. By 9 a.m. on the following morning they were clustered at anchor under the shadow of the great white cliffs of South Foreland. Along the cliff tops, as far as the eye could see, were massed thousands of British warriors, called together by the alarm of their coastal sentinels when the ships had first appeared in the early dawn light. Volusenus' war-galley made its rendezvous on time and the officer reported that there was an easier landing place further along the coast. This was the open beach between Walmer and Deal. Caesar summoned a meeting of staff officers on his flagship and discussed how best to secure the beachhead against the opposition which was gathering. He then waited until 3.30 p.m. for the cavalry to catch up, but the small fleet of ships transporting the cavalry did not appear.

On the open beaches at Walmer the Roman fleet swung inshore. This was the land of the Cantii, still remembered in the county name of Kent. They were a large tribe split into four septs under their chieftains Cingetorix, Carnilios, Taximagulos and Segonax. They had followed the movement of the Roman fleet along the coastline with their army, which contained massive war-chariots and cavalry. Through ignorance of the waters, Caesar chose to start his landing at low tide when his transports were unable to get close to the shore. His soldiers were faced with having to wade over 200 yards to dry land in the face of a withering fire from the British bowmen and slingshots.

Caesar records:

The soldiers, oppressed with the great weight of their arms, ignorant of the ground, and with their hands encumbered, were obliged to jump from their ships and to engage the enemy standing close in the waves, while they on the other hand, either from dry land or having advanced a very little into the water, with all their limbs perfectly free, were boldly hurling javelins from places with which they were all acquainted, and urging on horses inured to the service. Finding my men dismayed, and disorganized by this unaccustomed manner of fighting, I ordered my long boats or galleys to be rowed a little distance from our transports, so as to attack the open flank of the enemy, and to dislodge them from their positions by slings and arrows and other missiles. This manoeuvre was of great service, for the British, confused by my artillery, stopped and drew back, though but for a little space.

The soldiers still hesitated to leave their transports and the advantage Caesar had gained might have been thrown away but for the unnamed standard-bearer of the X Legion who called upon the gods for the success of his venture and cried: 'Leap forth, soldiers, unless you wish to betray your standard to the enemy! I, at any rate, shall have performed my duty to my country and my general!' The standard-bearer then jumped from his transport and began wading ashore towards the Celtic defenders. Fearing the disgrace of the loss of a Roman eagle, the soldiers began to follow.

One of the British weapons which unnerved the Romans was the heavy war-chariot. Chariots as a weapon of war had fallen into disuse among the Gaulish Celts. While Roman historians had referred to the Celtic war-chariots in early clashes, Caesar's soldiers had no experience of them. The Romans were faced with two-wheeled and even four-wheeled chariots. They were light wickerwork vehicles adorned with decorated metalwork. Scythes were fitted on the hubs of the wheels which were able to mow down the enemy. The war-chariots were to feature in insular Celtic literature when the historical traditions of these days came to be written. They were handled expertly, with the warriors driving into the shallows to engage in hand-to-hand combat with the invaders. Caesar observes: 'On seeing this, I ordered the boats belonging to the galleys and the supply boats to be filled with soldiers and sent to help those I saw in trouble. By thus bringing into action all my reserve troops, I, at length, revived the drooping courage of the legions.' It was not until 7 p.m. that a beachhead had been secured and the Celts had been pushed back.

The chieftains of the Cantii reviewed their strategy. Commios of the Atrebates had doubtless warned them of the skill of the Roman soldiers. He had probably told them of how easily Gaul had fallen to Caesar. Commios later told Caesar that he had been imprisoned by the Cantii chieftains to prevent his warning the Romans of their determination to fight Caesar on the beaches. Commios could well have been lying. He may simply have waited to see if the British were more successful in handling the Roman soldiers than had been his fellow Gauls. The British chieftains certainly supported Commios in his claim and added that they had been forced to challenge Caesar by the common people. This comment is simply another affirmation of the democratic character of the system under which the clan assemblies elected the chieftain: he was hemmed in by office and dependent on the support of his tribe, so it was usually easier for him to promote their interests and follow their wishes than to become despotic.

The next morning the chieftains of the Cantii, accompanied by Commios and some other envoys, arrived at Caesar's camp and began

Staigue Fort (fifth-century BC), a superb, circular, dry-stone construction, stands at the head of a valley near Sneem in the Iveragh Peninsula.

There are numerous brochs on the islands and mainland of Scotland, built by the Celts around the fifth to the first centuries BC. Mousa is a particularly good example of Celtic building ability, and still survives at a height of forty-five feet.

Dún Aengus, Aran Isles, Ireland: this is one of the most famous of the ancient Celtic fortresses and is situated on Inis Mór, the largest of the Aran Islands.

Left: Chysauster, a Celtic village near Madron, Cornwall was built during the second century BC and occupied from then until the third century AD when it was abandoned. *Right*: Maiden Castle, Dorset: an aerial view from the west. Maidun, the fortress of Mai, was a major hillfort of the Durotriges.

A victim of the Roman attack: a Celtic defender of Maiden Castle with a Roman *ballista* arrow lodged in his vertebra.

This war-chariot burial was discovered at Garton Slack, East Yorkshire in the country of the Brigantes. The grave is dated to the second century BC.

The Uffington white horse is 365 feet from nose to tail and one of several Celtic hill figures to survive. It is dated between the first century BC and the first century AD and is thought to be a product of Belgae craftsmanship.

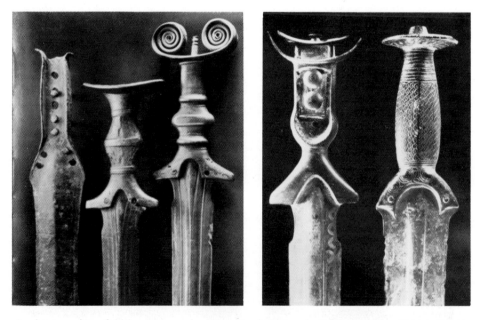

A selection of Urnfield bronze swords, now regarded as early Celtic or 'proto-Celtic'. Types of sword from left to right: Auvernier from Kirschgartenhausen; Riegsee from Egen; 'Griff-zungenschwert' from Hemigkofen; Morigen from Gailenkirchen; an 'antenna sword' from Schussenried. The swords date from the period 1200 to 700 BC.

An engraved iron and bronze scabbard, bearing remnants of coral studs, dated (400–350 BC). This is from the La Tène Celtic period although it was found at Hallstatt.

The Witham shield is made of intricately worked sheets of bronze originally mounted on a wooden frame. It is dated to the first century BC and was found in the River Witham, Lincolnshire.

A bronze-covered iron helmet, with gold-leaf and inlaid coral decorations (mid- to late fourth-century BC). A knob from the top has recently been discovered, and the cheek-piece (not visible in this picture) is decorated with coral inlay. The helmet was discovered in 1981 in a cave at Agris, Charente in France.

The Celts often placed wheeled objects in their graves. This warrior hunting
a wild boar, found in Merida, Spain, is from the second century BC.

'The Dying Gaul': a Roman marble copy of a bronze original. The original formed part of a
group raised by Attalos of Pergamum to commemorate his victory over the Galatian Celts in
241 BC.

Bronze helmet (first-century BC) found in the Thames by Waterloo Bridge, is one of the very few Celtic war helmets to have survived anywhere in Europe.

The Snettisham torc, found in a horde in Norfolk, England, during 1948–50 is dated to the mid-first century BC and is made of electrum.

The Desborough mirror dates to the late first century BC, and was found in 1908 near a hill-fort at Desborough, Northamptonshire.

A set of glass gaming pieces from a burial excavated at Welwyn Garden City, Hertfordshire (first-century BC). The pieces were found together with a much decayed gaming board.

to open negotiations. One of the envoys was a young man whom Caesar knew as Mandubratios. What the Romans did not know apparently was that the name was a derisory nickname. Mandubrad meant black traitor, the name still recognizable in a Welsh form, *du bradwr*. Accepting Geoffrey's British tradition, his real name was Avarwy. According to Caesar Mandubratios was the son of Imanuentios, chieftain of the Trinovantes, who had been slain by a chieftain called Cassivelaunos – meaning lover of Bel, but given in British tradition as Caswallon – of the Cassi. Mandubratios had come to ask Caesar if he would make him King of the Trinovantes.

The peace negotiations between Caesar and the Cantii chieftains went on for four days. Lacking cavalry, Caesar had made no attempt to explore the surrounding countryside. However, the cavalry finally arrived. But no sooner were their transports approaching the shore than a squall sprang up from the north-east. The transports were scattered before they could draw close to land. Most of them eventually made their way back to Gaul.

For Caesar this was a disaster. Not only had his cavalry reinforcement been lost but the infantry transport had been smashed in the same storm. The moon was full and the tide almost at the springs, with rollers racing each other up the sloping beaches and filling the hulls of the ships with water. The heavier transports were dragged at their anchors and many were simply smashed to pieces on the beach. Caesar reported:

> The result was that the warships, which had been beached, became waterlogged; as for the transports riding at anchor, they were dashed one against another, and it was impossible to manoeuvre them or do anything whatever to assist. Several ships broke up, and the remainder lost their cables, anchors and rigging.

The Celts were delighted. It must have seemed a good omen. The Cantii chieftains simply melted away from the negotiating table and went back to their arms.

Morale among the Romans was low. They were now cast away on a hostile shore, a small force of hungry men with no provisions, clothing or equipment for a protracted winter campaign. There were no facilities to repair or replace the transports and no reinforcements to rely upon.

Caesar ordered fatigue parties to venture out and reap neighbouring wheat crops, confiscating supplies and materials from the nearest settlements. The year had been fairly dry and good crops stood ready for harvesting. At the same time he ordered his engineers to demolish the worst of his damaged vessels and use them to repair the others. Twelve ships were totally beyond repair and were thus cannibalized to make good other ships.

The Celts were busy ambushing the foraging parties and isolated patrols and outposts. While members of the VII Legion were out foraging the sentries reported seeing an unusually large cloud of dust in the direction in which they had gone. A large force of British war-chariots had hidden in ambush in a wooded area between what is now Martin Hill and Ringwould and attacked the fatigue parties. Caesar issued immediate orders.

> The battalion on guard duty were detailed to go with me to the scene of the action, two others were ordered to relieve them and the rest to arm and follow on immediately. We had not been marching long before I noticed the VII Legion was in difficulties; they were only just managing to hold their own with their units closely packed under heavy fire.

Caesar now had a chance to see at first hand how expert the British were at using their war-chariots.

> Their manner of fighting from chariots is as follows: first of all they drive in all directions and hurl javelins, and so by the mere terror that the teams inspire and by the noise of the wheels they generally throw the ranks of soldiers into confusion. When they have worked their way in between the troops, they leap down from the chariots and fight on foot. Meanwhile their charioteers retire gradually from the battle, and place the chariots in such a fashion that, if the warriors are hard pressed by the enemy, they may have a ready means of retreat to their own side.
>   Thus they show in action the mobility of cavalry and the stability of infantry; and by daily use and practice they become so accomplished that they are ready to gallop their teams down the steepest slopes without loss of control, to check them and turn them in a moment, to run along the pole, stand on the yoke, and then, quick as lightning, to dart back into the chariot.

According to Geoffrey's British tradition, the leader of the attacking force was Nennius, the brother of Cassivelaunos. He is said personally to have attacked a detachment of the X Legion commanded by Caesar himself, which was hard pressed to save its standard from capture. The tradition has it that the sword of the Roman General buried itself in the shield of Nennius and, before Caesar could extricate it, the tide of battle had separated the combatants, leaving the weapon as a trophy for the British. True or not, Caesar succeeded in achieving no more than an orderly retreat back to his fortified encampment. The Romans were unable to prevent the Celts carrying off a large number of prisoners and weapons.

A period of extremely bad weather now set in. 'For many days in succession,' says Caesar, 'tempestuous weather prevented both armies from resuming hostilities.' Then came a period of fine, clear weather. The Celtic forces marched to the fortified Roman positions. Caesar and his men, backs to the sea, supported by their heavy artillery – *catapulta* and *ballistae*, taken from the dismantled ships – stood ready to receive the Celtic charge. It swept up to the Roman lines and, as so often in the past, broke. Caesar gave the word for his disciplined ranks to move forward. The Celts were routed. Caesar reports dryly:

> Envoys came to sue for peace. They were met with a demand for twice as many hostages as before and were ordered to bring them over to the continent, because the equinox was close at hand and the ill condition of our ships made it inadvisable to postpone the voyage until winter. Taking advantage of the fair weather, we set sail a little after midnight, and the whole fleet reached the mainland in safety.

From the Roman military viewpoint, the expedition was disappointing. More than once does an apologetic note creep into Caesar's narrative. In his defence he maintains that he had embarked on what had been merely a military reconnaissance by which he meant to learn something about the country in preparation for a full-scale invasion. Already, as his war galleys and transports pulled away from the British coastline, the Roman General was planning that invasion with at least three times as many troops and more extensive equipment – a sufficient force to conquer the entire island.

[11]

Caesar's Invasion of Britain

DURING the winter of 55/54 BC Caesar quartered his troops in the country of the Belgae while he was called to deal with disturbances which had broken out in Illyria. In March 54 BC Caesar was due to give up his governorship of Gaul, but he persuaded the senate to vote him a further five years. He wanted to carry on with the unfinished business of launching an invasion of Britain and had already left orders with his second-in-command, Labienus, to build the necessary transports and prepare the troops and equipment for an invasion force using three times the men taken in his first expedition. Caesar returned to Gaul in April and found 600 transports and 28 war-galleys ready for him.

However, there was unrest in the country of the Belgae. This time it was among the Treveri, a powerful tribe which had not submitted to Rome. Their tribal lands stood on the Moselle, with their chief town at modern-day Trier. Caesar took four legions and 800 cavalry and marched into their territory. The trouble was that two chieftains of the Treveri were contending for the overall leadership of the tribe – Indutiomaros and Cingetorix. Caesar discovered which of them was pro-Roman – in this case it was Cingetorix – and promptly provided him with military aid to overcome Indutiomaros, who, with his followers, was driven off. Cingetorix, whose name means the king who marched against the foe, thereafter proved supportive to Caesar.

Caesar was under no illusion that Gaul was entirely pacified. At any time it could erupt into insurrection against Rome and especially during his absence in Britain a signal might well be given for a general uprising. He decided to pre-empt such plans by rounding up Gaulish hostages from the anti-Roman factions. Among them was the chieftain of the Aedui, Dumnorix. Dumnorix was still preaching the co-operation of all the Celtic tribes of Gaul in the attempt to throw out the Romans and the Germans. He was appalled at his fellow Celts fighting each other while the Romans reaped the benefit of their petty squabbles and divisions. He appeared to have great popularity among the Gauls and had forged diplomatic connections with all the anti-Roman elements among the Gaulish leaders. If a general uprising were to take place, it was obvious that Dumnorix would be its leader.

Under military escort, and accompanied by a small Aedui retinue, Dumnorix was brought to Portus Itius, where he was joined by other Gaulish chieftains whose loyalties were similarly suspect. When they were told they were being taken as hostages with the Roman forces to Britain, Dumnorix became the spokesman for all of them. He told them that Caesar 'wanted to take them to Britain and murder them all' because he dared not put them to death in front of their people in case it caused an uprising. Indeed, this may well have been Caesar's plan. It was certainly a convenient way for the Romans to dispose of the subversive element among the Gaulish leaders. Dumnorix and his fellow hostages refused to embark.

On the day before the invasion fleet was due to sail, the sixth day of the month of Quintilis, soon to be renamed in Caesar's honour as the month of Julius, Dumnorix and some of his followers managed to evade the Roman guards, seize some horses and ride off. Caesar immediately halted the embarkation process and despatched cavalry after the Celts with orders to bring Dumnorix back – dead or alive. The Roman cavalry caught up with the Celts, managed to head them off and called on them to surrender. The Celts would do no such thing and drew their longswords. The Romans closed in and soon Dumnorix was overpowered and slain, crying out to the last that he was a free man of a free nation.

Even in the hostile eyes of Rome, Dumnorix was an extraordinary personality. An able Celtic leader, he was inflexible in his patriotism and an implacable foe to Rome's imperial expansion in his country. His death was to serve as a rallying point for the Gaulish people who, within a few months, rose up in a war of liberation which was to last for four years. By this token it can be argued that, in precipitating the Gaulish insurrection, the death of Dumnorix also cut short Caesar's plans for a full-scale conquest of Britain.

For his second attempt to conquer Britain, Caesar gathered a total of

30,000 men, consisting of five legions and 2,000 cavalry, packing them into 540 transports and 200 vessels confiscated from the Gauls. Unfortunately, we do not know which legions he took. Caesar mentions only the VII Legion but it would be unusual for him not to have taken his favourite X Legion, which had already seen service in Britain. We also know that Cicero's brother, Quintus Tullius Cicero, had been given command of the XIV Legon and that Cicero went to Britain. We can confidently presume that his legion went also. However, we do not know what other legions went except that one was commanded by an officer named Caius Trebonius. Titus Atticus Labienus was left in command of Gaul with three legions and 2,000 cavalry, with the specific duty of protecting the harbours to ensure Caesar's safe return.

The invasion fleet sailed on the ebb tide with a gentle south-westerly wind shortly before sunset, at 8 p.m., on the sixth day of the month of Quintilis (July). With Caesar went Mandubratios, who had arrived in the Roman General's camp in Britain the previous year. Caesar had promised to make him ruler of the British Trinovantes, and Mandubratios in return acted as Caesar's interpreter and chief negotiator with the British Celts.

At first light on 7 July, around 4 a.m., the Romans noticed that the tide was carrying them further northwards than they had intended. The order was issued to get out the oars and, after some tiring rowing, the tide turned and to Caesar's relief the fleet was carried towards the British coastline. Once more Caesar found himself off the great white cliffs of South Foreland. He recorded: 'The soldiers worked splendidly and by continuous rowing they enabled the heavily laden transports to keep up with the warships. The whole fleet reached Britain about noon . . .'

The landings were unopposed and took place in the vicinity of Walmer, the name given in later Saxon times, meaning mere of the Welsh, 'Welsh' being the Saxon word for foreigners, and given to the British Celts. 'The enemy was nowhere to be seen. We therefore disembarked and chose a site for the camp.' Traces of such a camp have been found near the old church in Walmer. Caesar's scouts managed to bring in some prisoners and they told him that initially a large army had gathered on the shore to meet the Romans on the beaches. Observing the size of the Roman fleet, they had retired inland.

By the evening of 7 July, Caesar and his 30,000 troops had

established their beachhead. The base camp was placed under the command of Quintus Atrius with ten cohorts (5,000 men) drawn from all the legions. Some 300 cavalry were also placed under his command. Caesar then ordered a night march to seek out the enemy forces. He records: 'After a night march of about twelve miles I came in sight of the forces of the enemy.'

The Celtic commanders had established a position by the Great Stour river, near Thanington. The Stour, cognate with Stura in Cisalpine Gaul, meaning strong and powerful river, was fordable but the Celts had retired to the opposite bank and were prepared to defend the crossing. Caesar writes: 'They came down with cavalry and war-chariots and, by attacking from higher ground, tried to bar our passage of the river. Repulsed by our cavalry, they retired to the woods where they had a strongly fortified position of great natural strength.' Caesar was fighting the Cantii, the Celtic tribe of the area. The Romans had caused many of them to retire into a nearby hill-fort, since identified with the remains at Bigbury Wood. The Celts had apparently prepared for a siege and most of the approaches to the hill-fort had been obstructed by the felling of trees. With their main body inside the hill-fort, the Cantii chieftains sent out small groups to harry the invaders.

Caesar inspected the fortifications. The ramparts and palisades rose some twenty feet above a defensive ditch surrounding the earthen banks on which the walls were built. He detached the VII Legion and gave them orders to storm it. Bowmen and slingmen started a fusillade to keep the heads of the Celts down while a *testudo* (tortoise) was formed by legionaries with their shields. They marched to the walls with a pioneer corps company who began to pile earth against the walls so that the legionaries could scramble upwards. Soon cohort after cohort was pouring into the fortress. It was taken with only small losses to the Romans. Celtic hill-forts never appeared to present a problem to the Romans in Britain.

However, in the confusion, the Cantii chieftains and their main forces managed to escape, but Caesar forbade any attempt at pursuit. His troops had already gone two nights without rest and he realized that if the Celts gathered to attack en masse his troops would be in no shape to repulse them. Additionally, he was unsure of the situation in the surrounding countryside.

On the next day, however, the Romans sent out cavalry

detachments which actually made contact with the rearguard of the retiring Celtic army. Then a messenger came from Atrius at the base camp. On the night of 8/9 July an easterly gale had whipped up from the sea and nearly all the vessels had been dragged. The coastline was littered with transports which had been driven ashore. 'The anchors and cables had parted, seamen and pilots had been helpless and heavy damage had been suffered as a result of collision.'

The very thing that had robbed Caesar of victory during the preceding summer had occurred again. He withdrew his army back to the base camp. An inspection showed that forty transports were beyond repair. The others were pulled ashore within a line of fortifications to prevent any attack on them by the Celts. The ships were to be repaired as well as possible. At the same time a war-galley was despatched to Portus Itius with orders for Labienus to build replacement transports.

It must have been a gloomy birthday for the forty-eight-year-old Caesar, celebrating it on the shore of the territory of the Cantii on 12 July. It became even gloomier when the war-galley returned from Labienus with news from Rome that Caesar's twenty-seven-year-old daughter Julia had died. Julia was Caesar's only child and was married to his rival Pompey. Her child, Caesar's grandson, had also died. The joint heir of Caesar and Pompey might well have prevented the coming civil war between them as each strove to make himself dictator of the Roman empire. It was another personal loss for Caesar for that year his mother, Aurelia, who had played such a dominant role in his life, had also died.

It was not until 19 July that Caesar was able to march his troops into the interior of Britain.

Caesar's landing and the capture of Bigbury, the most important fortress in the country of the Cantii – according to archaeological evidence – had been a severe blow to the Celts of Britain. The chieftains of the Cantii had been in contact with Cassivelaunos of the Cassivelauni, both names signifying lover of Belinos, singular and plural. Caesar tells us that Cassivelaunos had his tribal territory some seventy-five miles from the sea, north of a river called the Tamesis (Thames). The Celtic tribes of southern Britain 'had unanimously agreed to confer upon him the supreme command', says Caesar. We can presume, with a fair degree of certainty, that the bestowing of supreme command on Cassivelaunos was due to the fact that he was already overall King, the High King, at least of southern Britain at this time.

Unfortunately, little is known about Cassivelaunos except that in him the Romans found a very astute military commander. His territory appears to have stretched through Middlesex, Hertfordshire and Oxfordshire. His capital was a hill-fort which can still be traced at Wheathampstead, a little to the north of St Albans.

Caesar's first march inland had met with no resistance until he reached the Great Stour. Now, on 19 July, his second march into the British interior was not so peaceful. He immediately felt the different personality of the new Celtic commander. He had marched only a few miles inland when he found his troops engaged in running battles with British cavalry and war-chariots. It was soon obvious that Cassivelaunos' tactics were to harry and slow the Roman march as much as possible without engaging in an all-out battle. Time and again, his war-chariots and cavalry would swoop down, attacking vanguard or rearguard, scouting parties, foraging parties or flanking detachments. Time and again, the Romans would halt to meet the offensive only to find the Celts had vanished as quickly as they had come. Sometimes, junior officers were carried away by their enthusiasm and let their men chase the Celts into the forests. Each time this happened it spelt disaster for the Romans, for they found their units cut off by hidden British marksmen and inevitably they suffered heavy losses.

At the end of the first day's march, the Romans stopped to build a night camp. Cassivelaunos would not let them rest so easily. His troops burst out of the surrounding woods and attacked the fatigue parties and outposts. Caesar recalled that heavy fighting ensued and he had to order the first cohorts (the crack troops) of two legions to attempt to rescue the outposts under threat. The first cohorts contained veterans and were at double strength, so, in all, they totalled 2,000 men. The rescue was nearly a disaster for even these crack troops became cut off and involved in fierce fighting. Caesar begrudgingly praised the Celtic tactics and bravery. He tried to encircle them but the Celts withdrew. During this skirmish Caesar lost one of his senior commanders, Quintus Laberius Durus. British tradition, recorded centuries later, says it was the brother of Cassivelaunos, Nennius, leader of the attack on the VII Legion during the previous year, who commanded this particular attack. But 'the success of the day was dearly purchased by the death of Nennius, who fell in the last onset of the enemy.'

Caesar records:

In the whole of this kind of battle, since it was fought under the eyes of all and before the camp, it was perceived that our men, on account of the weight of their arms (inasmuch as they could neither follow those who were giving war, nor dared to depart from their standards) were little suited for an enemy of this kind; that the cavalry manoeuvre fought with great danger, because they [the enemy] would oft-times retreat even designedly, and, when they had drawn off our horse a little way from the legions, would leap down from their chariots and fight on foot in unequal combat. But this system of cavalry engagement is wont to bring equal disaster, and of the same kind to both those retreating and those pursuing.

He adds: 'The enemy never fought in close order, but in small parties and at considerable distances, and had detachments placed about, and some, in turn, took the place of others, and the vigorous and fresh troops succeeded those who were weary.' The brilliant hit-and-run guerilla tactics of the Celts certainly took their toll of Roman lives. Cassivelaunos now sent out small detachments of warriors who 'took up their position at a distance from the camp, on the hills, and began to show themselves in small parties, and with less spirit than on the day before, to provoke our horsemen to combat,' says Caesar. He forbade his troops to make any foolhardy answer to this provocation.

The Romans now found themselves running out of supplies because their foraging parties had been unable to move far afield and the native population had removed themselves and their livestock out of the route of the Roman march. Caesar ordered Caius Trebonius, an officer who was destined to be one of his assassins, to take command of the foraging parties and scour the countryside as far as possible. It was just such a move that Cassivelaunos had been waiting for. His warriors fell on Trebonius' men as they searched for provisions. Trebonius managed to withdraw his men back to the protection of the main encampment with a considerable loss of life.

Caesar, warned of the retreat of his foraging parties, decided to launch an attack on the pursuing Celtic warriors with three entire legions 'nor did they cease from pursuing them [the Celts] until the horse, confident of support since they saw the legions behind them, drove the enemy headlong and, slaying a great number of them, gave them no opportunity of rallying or halting or of leaping down from their chariots'. Caesar was able to report with satisfaction: 'Immediately after this retreat, the British auxiliaries who had assembled from all sides, departed, nor after that time did the enemy engage us in great numbers . . .' Caesar, by use of the word 'auxiliaries', referred to the tribes who had come to the aid of the Cantii, such as the Atrebates, Cassivelauni, Trinovantes and others.

Cassivelaunos resumed his devastating guerilla tactics, harrying and delaying the Roman advance. It seems that at no time in his campaign did Cassivelaunos use infantry against the Romans. His plan appears to have been simply to wear down the Roman troops, cutting them off from their base camp and supply lines. The legions none the less managed to forage and raid the numerous rich farming settlements along the line of their march, putting them to the torch. Cassivelaunos, observing that these farming settlements were Caesar's main source of supply, ordered a scorched-earth policy. Not only were the farmers to withdraw out of the way of the Roman army but they were to fire their own farmsteads and drive off their flocks and herds, destroying their grain stores and crops.

By now Caesar had learned the name of his formidable opponent and the location of his capital. Mandubratios had obviously identified him as the man who had driven his father, Imanuentios, from the kingship of the Trinovantes. The chieftains of the Cantii had now come to believe that they, and Cassivelaunos, were fighting a losing war against the Romans. Chieftains of five southern and eastern septs came into Caesar's camp to discuss terms. They wanted to end the conflict as quickly as possible to save their livestock and crops. It would seem that the scorched-earth policy of Cassivelaunos was not popular. Through the mediation of Mandubratios these chieftains gave Caesar much valuable military information. 'They told me we were not far away from Cassivelaunos' stronghold, which was strategically placed among woods and marshlands, and that large numbers of men and cattle were gathered there.'

Caesar and his legions crossed the Medway – a compound river-name still retaining the original Celtic root *medu*, the mead-coloured river. They crossed the river at Rochester, whose name at that time was Durobrivae, deriving from the Celtic for bridge of the stronghold.

Caesar reports that he eventually arrived at the River Tamesis, whose name could mean either the dark river or the sluggish river – the stem is still found in the Irish *támáilte*. Cassivelaunos was already waiting on the northern bank of the Tamesis with a force of 4,000 war-chariots, ready to dispute the Roman crossing. We can only surmise that his chariots had crossed by a bridge at this point, for Caesar must have been in the area of a trading settlement of the Trinovantes: London, which seems to have been called the wild place from the Celtic *londo*, found in the Old Irish word *lond*, wild. There is, of course, the argument that the name derived from the fortress (*dun*) of Lugh, as in Lugdunum (Lyons) in Gaul. If Cassivelaunos had crossed with his chariots, he must have destroyed the bridge behind him.

Caesar remarks: 'The river can be forded only at one point and even there the crossing was difficult.' Two possible fords have been suggested as the place where Caesar decided to cross. One was by Westminster, the other by Brentford. Archaeological evidence favours Brentford, which still retains, in part, its Celtic name, cognate with Brigantia, meaning the high, or holy, river, which is where the River Brent flows into the Thames.

Caesar says: 'Large native forces appeared in battle order on the far bank, which was also defended by a line of pointed stakes; and some deserters in our custody revealed that more of these obstacles were placed underneath the river bed.'

The Roman cavalry moved over first and secured the far bank and then the legionaries suddenly began moving across. It was a deep crossing and at times only the heads of the footsoldiers were above the water. The Celts seemed unnerved and were easily pushed back from their defensive positions.

Crossing the Thames had placed Caesar in the land of the Cassivelauni and the guerilla warfare intensified as the Romans pushed onwards, moving along the Colne Valley, whose name meant roaring river. Taking this route they would have marched past Denham, Rickmansworth and Watford before reaching Wheathampstead. By this time Caesar admits that Cassivelaunos' guerillas were so successful that his cavalry could no longer venture out of touch with the main body of his troops and foraging parties could no longer be sent out. On all sides the forests were infested by watchful defenders awaiting their chance.

By the beginning of August the Roman army had cut their way

through the forest and marshland and gazed upon the ramparts of the hill-fort which was the capital of the Cassivelauni, the most powerful tribe in southern Britain. Caesar was proud of his troops. 'They did nothing unworthy of them,' he reported.

The hill-fort of the Cassivelauni, at Wheathampstead, enclosed one hundred acres with ramparts rising to thirty feet in height, being one hundred feet in width. Its remains are still traceable today. Cassivelaunos stood ready to face a Roman siege but, as at the Cantii hill-fort at Bigbury, the Romans stormed the ramparts on two sides with comparative ease. In the confusion, Cassivelaunos and some of his retinue escaped. Caesar was left the victor with livestock and provisions captured in the fortress.

The Trinovantes, whose tribal area bordered on that of the Cassivelauni to the east, had decided to make terms with Caesar and accepted Mandubratios as their chieftain. But Caesar knew that as long as Cassivelaunos refused to submit the war was not over. There were a dozen hill-forts in the vicinity and Caesar was faced with having to reduce them one by one. Moreover, Cassivelaunos was not simply 'on the run'. He was not yet defeated and still exerted considerable authority. It is a testimony to his unquestioned authority, and a reinforcement of the presumption that Cassivelaunos was High King, that he was able to send a messenger to the chieftains of the four Cantii septs – Cingetorix, Carnilius, Taximagulus and Segonax – telling them to gather their warriors and make an attack on Caesar's base camp. Cassivelaunos probably reasoned that an attack on his base would force Caesar and his troops back to the coast, relieve pressure on Cassivelaunos himself and allow him time to reorganize his army.

The chieftains of the Cantii obeyed his instructions and gathered an army which launched an attack on the base camp at Walmer. Quintus Atrius made a resolute defence. British tradition has it that Cingetorix was captured, yet Caesar mentions only the capture of a chieftain named Lugotorix. It is Quintus Tullius Cicero who gives us the vital information that this attack did, indeed, send Caesar hastening back to the base camp but leaving his main force, commanded by Trebonius, encamped around the Cassivelauni capital at Wheathampstead. Cicero mentions this in a letter to his brother Marcus. So Cassivelaunos' ruse was unsuccessful. Caesar was at Walmer for only a few days, ensuring that Atrius had things under control, before returning to Wheathampstead.

This must have been a blow for Cassivelaunos, who was now faced with the Romans raiding his farming settlements and townships. Caesar reports with some satisfaction: 'So many losses having been received, his territories devastated, and being distressed most of all by the defections of the tribes, he sent ambassadors to me to treat through Commios, the Atrebatian, concerning surrender.'

So once again the intriguing figure of Commios, the ruler of the Gaulish Atrebates, whom Caesar had taken to Britain to make ruler of the British Atrebates, emerges at Caesar's camp. Where had he been during Caesar's second landing in Britain? Certainly he was not in Caesar's camp. The fact that Caesar says Cassivelaunos used Commios as an ambassador suggests that he was with the Cassivelauni and that his British Atrebates might have been part of Cassivelaunos' army. Commios appears as no unpopular pro-Roman ruler imposed by the Romans. He had ruled the British Atrebates for a year and they seemed happy with his rule.

Caesar's demands were brief. 'I demanded hostages, I fixed annual tribute payable by Britain into the Roman treasury, and I strictly forbade Cassivelaunos to interfere with Mandubratios and the Trinovantes. After receiving these hostages, we returned to the coast.'

The actual negotiations appear to have taken some time for Caesar and his legions did not return to their base camp at Walmer until the end of August. With them they took the remainder of the cattle herds of the Cassivelauni and large numbers of hostages – the first of countless British Celts who, over the next four centuries, were to be sold into slavery by Rome, never to see their native land again.

Labienus, in Gaul, had despatched sixty newly built transports to replace those destroyed, but because of the bad weather only a small number of these managed to reach Britain. For some time, until mid-September, Caesar waited anxiously for the arrival of the rest of the transports. The equinox was now approaching and he decided to split his army, sending half of them to Gaul in the available transports with orders for those transports to return for the second half. The reason for this was not only that the Romans had fewer ships but that they had more people, the hostages, to transport to Rome. It was from the sale of these hostages that Caesar would finance his expedition.

On 26 September 54 BC, Caesar records: 'We weighed anchor at 9 p.m. and the whole fleet reached land safely at dawn.'

It was fairly obvious that Caesar's ambitions for a military conquest and annexation of Britain did not end there. His mind was probably full of ideas for a further campaign during the next year and the establishment of a permanent garrison in Britain. But the situation in Gaul was to drive all such thoughts from his mind. The subsequent uprising against Rome cancelled any plans he might have had and Britain was to retain her independence for a further century. Cassivelaunos returned to his position of pre-eminence among the British chieftains and was able to take advantage of the situation in Gaul to ignore the provisions of the treaty with Caesar. No annual tribute was paid to Rome and no further hostages were sent. Britain returned to being one of the most prosperous of the surviving independent Celtic countries.

[12]

Insurrection in Gaul

A RRIVING back in Gaul at the end of September, Caesar went to Samarobriva (Amiens) to attend a council of pro-Roman Gaulish chieftains. The harvest in Gaul during that summer of 54 BC had been a bad one, adding fuel to the discontent felt in the country. Caesar told the chieftains that he was dispersing his troops over a wide area for winter quarters in order not to put too great a strain on any particular tribe. There were eight legions and several unattached cohorts consisting of nearly 80,000 men. He stationed them within a circle of 200-mile diameter, with Bavay as its centre. Lucius Roscius was given a command at Séex in Normandy; Quintus Tullius Cicero was placed at Charleroy; Titus Labienus was at Lavacherie on the Curthe; Sabinus and Cotta were at Tongres; Caius Fabius was at St Pol, between Calais and Arras; Trebonius was at Amiens, which was Caesar's general headquarters; Marcus Crassus was at Montididier and Munatius Plancus was on the Oise near Compiègne. Caesar, who usually went to Italy for the winter, remained at Amiens. It would seem obvious that he had been warned of the seething discontent in Gaul.

Indutiomaros of the Treveri, whom Caesar had chased out by helping his pro-Roman brother Cingetorix gain the chieftainship of the tribe, was behind the immediate unrest. The tribes were ready to rise against Rome, stung into action by the death of Dumnorix of the Aedui. Indutiomaros, however, knew that he must break the belief that the Roman legions were invincible. He entered into an alliance with Ambiorix and Catavolos, chieftains of the Eburones, a tribe whose country lay between Liège and Cologne. They took their name from *eburos*, the yew, which was one of the most sacred Celtic trees.

He convinced them that if one Roman legion was destroyed then all Gaul would rise up.

Ambiorix took command and decided to launch an attack on Tongres, where Sabinus and Cotta were quartered. Caesar, from his biased viewpoint, says the attack was carried out by treachery. Ambiorix appeared before the Roman encampment with an over-whelming force of Gauls. Caesar maintains that Ambiorix gave the Roman commanders a guarantee of safe passage to the nearest Roman fortress at Namur, some fifty miles away. When Sabinus and Cotta, with their 9,000 troops, were moving towards it in marching order, Ambiorix is said to have ambushed them. The entire legion, including Sabinus and Cotta, were wiped out.

Ambiorix's success produced the effect which Indutiomaros had calculated. As soon as the news of the annihilation of the legion spread, the country began to revolt. The Nervii and several smaller tribes along the Meuse and Somme rose up. Quintus Cicero, com-manding the XIV Legion at the fortress of Namur (Charleroy), was surrounded by some 60,000 Gauls. He sent a messenger to Caesar, 120 miles away, who issued orders to Marcus Crassus at Montididier, Caius Fabius at St Pol and Titus Labienus at Lavacherie to relieve Namur.

Meanwhile, Indutiomaros, having overthrown his pro-Roman brother Cingetorix, was now at the head of the Treveri and he marched them against Titus Labienus, preventing him from reaching Namur.

The country was aflame. For the first time since Caesar had used the Helvetii as an excuse to intervene in the affairs of Gaul, the tribes appeared united against Rome. Finally, Caesar himself marched from Amiens to relieve Cicero's fortress. He was able to break the siege but, of Cicero's garrison, two men out of every three had been wounded.

As the winter of 54/53 BC progressed, Indutiomaros was busy trying to build up a united Gaulish army. His hill-fort in the land of the Treveri at Trier became the centre for Gaulish resistance to Rome. A council was held to which the chieftains of all the tribes of Gaul were invited to send representatives.

The Romans, having identified Indutiomaros as a leader of the insurrection, offered a reward for him – dead or alive. Soon after-wards, Indutiomaros, besieging Titus Labienus at Lavacherie, was ambushed while crossing a ford on the Curthe; a Gaulish traitor killed him and claimed the reward from the Romans. This was a blow to the

Gaulish resistance movement. However, Ambiorix continued to inflict punishment on the legions.

Caesar, realizing how strong resistance now was, sent to the south to raise two fresh legions and asked Pompey if he could borrow a third legion from his command in Spain. During the summer of 53 BC he marched with four legions into the country of the Nervii and conducted a ruthless campaign, burning farmsteads and villages, seizing livestock, destroying crops, slaughtering men, women and children and carrying off survivors to be sold into slavery. Soon the countryside was depopulated, and only burnt ruins marked the passage of the Roman army.

During that summer Caesar called a council of the Gaulish chieftains at Amiens. Only a few pro-Roman chieftains attended and most of their tribes had already rejected their leadership and were in arms against Rome. Caesar, determined to crush resistance, set off in the direction of the area of modern Paris – named after the Celtic tribe, the Parisii. After a lightning campaign, he forced the Senones and Carnutes to sue for peace.

Then he turned towards the country of the Treveri, where Ambiorix appears to have established his headquarters. Caesar had taken Ambiorix's destruction of Sabinus and Cotta and their legion very much to heart. They had been among his favourite commanders. While Ambiorix lived, it was a personal affront. It seems that Ambiorix had persuaded some of the Germanic tribes along the Rhine to join the Celts in making war on Rome, probably having little need to remind them of how Caesar had devastated their country in previous years.

Caesar, however, turned on the Germans, once more throwing a bridge over the Rhine and taking his men to wreak havoc in their territory. But his main concern was to catch up with Ambiorix. He had ordered Cicero and the XIV Legion to occupy the defensive positions at Tongres, the same positions which Sabinus and Cotta had held, while he marched the rest of his troops north to seek out Ambiorix. Cicero thought he could relax. However, his encampment came under a surprise attack from 2,000 Germans seeking revenge on Rome. The camp was nearly overrun, and by the time the Romans had repelled the attack their casualties were very high.

Caesar must have been infuriated. He returned from his punitive expedition without encountering Ambiorix, who was never to be captured by Rome. But Caesar had his revenge in the massacre of many of Ambiorix's Eburones as well as the Carnutes and Senones. Acco, the chieftain of the Carnutes, was put to death as a warning to other chieftains who preached rebellion against Rome.

After such a devastating campaign, Gaul settled to an uneasy quiet during the autumn of 53 BC. Caesar seemed satisfied that the military threat to Roman rule was now over. He returned to Italy for the winter and set about discussing the political organization of the new province of the empire.

But the Celts were learning fast about co-operation against a common enemy. All the chieftains of the major tribes of Gaul were in contact with each other. They had been deeply affected by Caesar's execution of Acco. While nothing is known about this chieftain, he must have had some reputation which caused Caesar to use his execution as a warning to the rest of the Gaulish chiefs and for them to have responded with such outrage. Even the Aedui, which had once had a strong pro-Roman faction and had been the weak link which had allowed Rome to intervene in Gaul, were solidly anti-Roman now. While Caesar rested in Italy, the Gaulish chieftains were planning a universal uprising. A system of signals had been arranged and the spark was to be the uprising of the Carnutes. An armed band of Carnutes slaughtered a party of Roman officials at Gien, above Orléans, on the Loire. It was, they said, in revenge for the execution of their chieftain Acco. Within a few hours the spirit of revolt had spread across the country.

There now emerged the most formidable Celtic leader to take on the might of Rome. Vercingetorix, whose name means the high king who marched against the foe, was chieftain of the Arverni. Their principal town was at Gergovia, four miles from Clermont on the Allier in the Puy-de-Dôme. Vercingetorix, who had been accepted as the head of a national confederation of the tribes of Gaul, had been building up a Gaulish army during the autumn period, requesting each tribe to supply arms and bodies of men. He also devised a general plan of campaign. He wanted to prevent Caesar from returning to Gaul and thereby cut him off from his legions, which had been put into winter quarters in the country of the Belgae in the north. Obviously Vercingetorix recognized Caesar as a formidable military strategist. Therefore he wanted to prevent him from exercising control.

It had been the height of winter, with snow still on the ground, when the Carnutes had given the signal for the general uprising. Caesar immediately returned across the Alps and came marching swiftly up the valleys of the Rhône and Saône into the country of the Aedui, marching day and night. Vercingetorix's Celtic army were unable to make contact with him before he reached Cenabum (Orléans) and crossed the Loire to the south to surround Avaricum (Bourges), which was the principal town of the Bituriges, which tribal name means kings of the world.

Vercingetorix had ordered that a scorched-earth policy should be maintained against the Romans and that they should be prevented from gaining any supplies and provisions. All tribes were to fall back before Caesar, not only to wear him out but so that no contact with the legions in battle formation should occur before Vercingetorix was ready. However, the Bituriges had refused to evacuate their township and they now shut themselves in. Caesar laid siege to Avaricum. Attacks by Vercingetorix to relieve the town proved futile. The Romans eventually stormed it, slaughtering all but 800 of the 4,000 inhabitants. The survivors were taken to be sold as slaves.

The massacre of Avaricum underscored Vercingetorix's orders about a scorched-earth policy. Caesar's slaughter convinced the Celts to consent to a universal sacrifice and they began to burn their farmsteads, villages and townships before the Roman advance. It is reported that the Bituriges burned twenty of their towns in a single day. Adjoining tribes copied their example. The horizon at night was a ring of blazing fires as the Gauls sought to deprive the Romans of supplies and booty. Vercingetorix now had thousands of patriotic young Gauls, on their light war-horses, harrying the Romans' supply lines and communications.

Caesar, in his determination to crush the insurrection, decided to strike at the heartland of his enemy. He had learned that Gergovia was the chief town of the Arverni. He wanted to smash it and, at the same time, the new military leader who had emerged among the Gauls.

Gergovia stood on a high plateau where the rivers rise which run into the Loire on the one side and the Dordogne on the other. The sides of the hill were steep, and accessible in only a few places. Caesar, reinforced with six full-strength legions, decided to ascend from the right bank of the Allier.

The Celtic commander was fairly confident that his hill-fort was impregnable to attack. He had stationed his army outside Gergovia but in such a position that to attack it would put the enemy at a disadvantage. He was determined that Gergovia would not suffer a fate similar to that of Avaricum.

Caesar's assault troops managed to capture two heights outside the city but Vercingetorix made his counter-attack with such success that they were driven back. This brilliant Celtic strategist followed up the attack and soon Caesar's army was in flight from the field, with some 46 officers and 700 men dead. The Romans were routed. Only a fierce rearguard action by men of the X Legion prevented Caesar's army from complete annihilation. Caesar's own personal record of invincibility was smashed. For the first time, Rome's most formidable General had been beaten in battle by a Celt.

News of his defeat spread throughout Gaul. Even those tribes who had submitted to the Romans and promised them supplies turned and began destroying the provisions intended for Roman troops. Caesar's army was withdrawing northward now in an attempt to link up with Titus Labienus and his four legions which were in the Seine Valley.

Labienus had been having his own problems. He had, at the start of the uprising, moved his legions from his headquarters at Agendicum (Sens) to attack the Gaulish forces within the vicinity of Paris. Hearing the news from the south, however, Labienus decided to return to the safety of Agendicum. Camulogenos, the Gaulish leader in the area, made an attempt to cut off Labienus from his base by taking up a position just south of the Seine while ordering part of his army into a position to the north. Labienus, on the north bank, was caught between the two Celtic armies.

Labienus, however, was able to make a surprise move, crossing the Seine and attacking Camulogenos' positions. The Celtic leader had been informed that Labienus was trying to move north. The Roman attack, therefore, was a complete surprise and Labienus was able to cut his way through the Celts and reach Agendicum in safety. Camulogenos was killed in the attack. Labienus shut himself into his fortified position to await developments.

Caesar arrived with his legions not long afterwards and the two commands were united. Vercingetorix's main tactical error was allowing this unification, for Caesar was now confident enough to turn his force and moved south to seek out Vercingetorix's army. The Celtic commander was observing the march of the Roman army from positions ten miles away. There was no faulting the strategy of his decision to attack the Romans while they were on the march and strung out. He chose for the encounter the valley of Vingeanne, no more than a stream which descended into the Saône. As the Celtic cavalry attacked the marching legions, they responded swiftly by forming squares. After some brisk fighting the Celts were repelled and Caesar ordered his own cavalry to chase them before they had a chance to reform.

Vercingetorix withdrew towards Alesia, a fortress of the Mandubians, just north of Dijon, which is now called Alise Ste-Reine on the Côte d'Or. With Caesar close behind, Vercingetorix had little choice but to move into the fortified position and prepare for a siege. Like Gergovia, Alesia stood on a hill with precipitous slopes between two small rivers, the Ose and Oserain, which ran into the Brenne and thence into the Seine. Therefore, Alesia was actually a peninsula and well protected with a good water supply.

Vercingetorix was well aware of the Roman reputation for slaughtering non-combatants, women, children and the elderly, as they had done at Avaricum. He gathered all the women, children and old people, along with any Mandubii menfolk who chose not to fight with him, and allowed them to leave. Caesar, whose troops already surrounded the town, simply turned them round. No one would be allowed out of Alesia until Vercingetorix surrendered or until the Romans reduced it.

Only 50,000 Celtic warriors were in the town, facing well over twice that number of Roman soldiers and a considerable number of mercenaries, whom the Romans appear to have recruited from the Germanic tribes. Caesar was more cautious than he had been at Gergovia. He had obviously learned a lesson from that disaster. He began to build up siegeworks. Vercingetorix sent out daily and nightly raids to delay their construction while, at the same time, he issued a call for all the Gaulish tribes to gather and attack the Romans.

The call was answered. Some 100,000 footsoldiers and 8,000 cavalry began to converge on a point about a mile west of Caesar's army. Among those who commanded this great Celtic army were Vercingetorix's son-in-law Vercassivelaunos (his name meaning the great lover of Belinos) and Commios of the Atrebates, now showing clearly that he was no friend of Caesar.

Caesar quickly positioned his troops as the first attack swept upon them. The fighting lasted most of the day, with the legionaries keeping the Celts in check. That night members of the Celtic army scattered through the countryside in order to get materials to make ladders for an attack on Caesar's siegeworks. As the fight resumed the next day, led by Vercassivelaunos, Caesar ordered Mark Antony and Caius Trebonius to command cohorts which were to hold themselves ready to move from point to point, wherever Celtic pressures looked like breaking the Roman lines. Caesar was also using heavy artillery weapons such as the *catapulta* and *ballista* and the Celts fell in large numbers, unused to these sophisticated weapons.

On the third day the siege had not been raised and Vercingetorix and those in Alesia had been unable to break out. Now Vercassivelaunos launched an attack on the north side of the Roman siegeworks about midday, using some 60,000 warriors. The attack coincided with a determined thrust from Vercingetorix from Alesia. The idea was to catch the Romans between two fires. Caesar, however, saw the peril and sent Labienus with six cohorts to reinforce the two legions which held this northern line at Mont Rea.

The Celts struggled determinedly to break this line and Caesar had to send more reinforcements under Decimus Brutus and Caius Fabius. Even so, Caesar himself eventually had to take his remaining reserves to join the action. The Celtic attack wavered and finally broke. The German mercenaries were let loose, hewing down the Celts as they struggled to disengage. Caesar reports that seventy-four tribal standards were captured and brought to him and that his cavalry, chasing the Celts from the field, captured them in their thousands.

Vercingetorix had withdrawn back into Alesia. The relief army of Celts had been defeated and scattered. He now called a council of chieftains. He had gone to war to regain the liberty of his country, he told them. Now they were faced with the prospect of starvation. The Romans had them enclosed. He had attempted to get the non-combatants out of the fortress but the Romans had refused to let them pass. They all knew what would happen once the Romans broke in. It would not be simply the fighting men who would be killed but the elderly, the women and children. Maybe the bards could recite stories of what had happened a century before to the Celts besieged in the hill-fort of Numantia. Vercingetorix offered his followers a choice. They could kill him and send his head to the Roman commander by way of appeasement or they could send him to Caesar alive. The chieftains did neither but agreed to send ambassadors to Caesar asking for terms of surrender.

Caesar's demand was for unconditional surrender. The chieftains accepted. Caesar sat amid the devastation before the hill-fort as the chieftains were brought one by one before him and surrendered. Vercingetorix was to be taken in chains to Rome. He spent some years as a prisoner there in the dark underground cells of the Tullanium below the Capitol. There, during Caesar's official triumph of 46 BC, the last great continental Celtic ruler was beheaded. In 40 BC a silver *denarius* was struck in celebration by Rome showing the head of Vercingetorix.

During the winter of 52/51 BC Caesar decided to stamp the military lesson into the Gaulish psyche to ensure that Gaul would never rise again. He began his winter campaign in the land of the Carnutes, who had started the insurrection. Guturatos had replaced the executed Acco as chieftain. Caesar marched through their lands, burning, taking prisoners for selling into slavery, and destroying farmsteads and villages wholesale. Guturatos joined the Bituriges and the Bellovaci in a combined army whose leader was none other than Commios the Atrebate. Throughout the winter Commios fought Caesar with considerable skill. Finally, unable to fight any more, he fled across the Rhine while Guturatos was captured. Caesar had the Carnutes chieftain flogged into insensibility and then decapitated, his head being sent round Gaul as a warning of Roman vengeance.

By the spring of 51 BC Gaul was fairly submissive, its spirit nearly broken. Yet some of Vercingetorix's own tribe were still attempting to hold out. In the south-west of the Arverni territory in the Dordogne stood the hill-fort of Exellodunum. The name indicates its position on an inaccessible rock, for *uxellos* means high, cognate with the Irish form *uasal*. This, then, was the high fortress. It was well provisioned and watered. Here the spark of Gaulish resistance remained. The Romans took a long time to reduce the fortress, finally mining tunnels through the rock under its fortifications. Eventually, by finding a way to cut off its water supply, they forced the garrison to surrender.

Caesar now held a council of Gaulish chieftains and lectured them on the future of Gaul as a dutiful province of the Roman empire. He was to spend another year in Gaul as Governor and commander-in-chief, organizing the administration of the different districts and assigning troops and officers for the various military commands. Then he left Gaul, in which he had made his reputation, to meet his own destiny of violence and death. Having lived by the sword, he was to die by the assassin's dagger on 15 March 44 BC in the senate at Rome.

Gaul was never again to rise up as a united country against Rome. Small isolated revolts occurred, such as the rising of the Bellovaci in 46 BC, apparently in response to the news of Vercingetorix's execution in Rome. In 44 BC the Allobriges rose up and in 33 BC and 30 BC the Aquitani and Morini, while between 25 BC and 7 BC a series of campaigns had to be mounted to contain disturbances among the tribes of south-east Gaul.

Roman settlers soon began to pour into the country, but the popular notion that Gaul suddenly ceased to be Celtic and started speaking Latin in the years following the Roman conquest is entirely mistaken. As late as the fifth century AD, a Gaul could write that it was only in his day that the *leading families* of Gaul were trying to 'throw off the scurf of Celtic speech'. If the leading families were only then trying to rid themselves of the language one can assume that the vast majority of the people were still speaking Celtic.

At the time of the conquest, Gaul had been moving towards literacy in its own language in spite of the prohibitions of the druids. And it is from Gaul that one of the earliest extensive texts in a Celtic language survives – the Calendar of Coligny, which is now in the Palais des Arts in Lyons. As we have already mentioned, it consists of a huge bronze plate on which is engraved a calendar of sixty-two consecutive months. The lettering is Latin but the language is Gaulish. Place-names, personal names and inscriptions on the calendar testify to a literacy in this language. The calendar also confirms Caesar's observation that the Celts reckoned periods of time by nights. The Coligny Calendar is a masterpiece of calendrical computation, which also confirms many remarks made by Greek observers about the skill of the druids in astronomical observation.

New finds are continuing to advance our knowledge about Gaulish literacy. A new Gaulish inscription was found in 1983 in a Gaulish cemetery in L'Hospitalet du Larzac (Aveyron) in the neighbourhood of Millau. The inscription, written in Latin cursive on a lead tablet, gives us the longest-known Gaulish text to date.

By the fourth century AD the Gauls were using Latin to produce a literature of some distinction from the rest of the Latin world. Decimus Magnus Ausonius (AD c.310–393) became one of the literary giants of his day. Born in Burdigalia (Bordeaux), where he taught rhetoric, he was appointed tutor to the son of the Emperor Valentinian I. He rose to become Consul of the Gallic province. He wrote mainly in Latin but also in Greek. There were other writers such as (among many others) Sulpicius Severus of the Aquitani, author of a biography of Martin of Tours; Eutropius, the historian; Hilario, who wrote a history of the world; and Claudius Rutilius Namantianus.

It has been argued that, when Christianity took a strong hold on the Celts of Gaul in the fourth century AD, Latin, as the vehicle of the new religion, caused a rapid decline of the Celtic language of Gaul. But by the fourth century the Gaulish Church was well established as a powerful organization and the Celtic concept of Christianity, based on the distinctive Celtic philosophies, was already showing contentious differences from the philosophies preached at Rome. Pope Innocent I (AD 401–17) had to write to Victricius, Bishop of Rouen, forbidding the Gauls to write about their theological differences from other Christian provinces. Already the conflict between the Celtic Church and the Church of Rome was beginning. Yet some of the great early Christian philosophers emerged from Gaul, such as Hilary of Poitiers (AD 315–67), who wrote the theological discourse *De Trinitate*, expressing the concept of the Holy Trinity, which he derived from the Celtic triune god concept.

But at what stage did Gaul cease to be Celtic? We have seen that St Jerome, during the later fourth century, wrote of the Galatians as speaking the same dialect as that spoken by the Treveri – and St Jerome had stayed in both Galatia and the land of the Treveri. His comment is not mere hearsay but first-hand evidence. Celtic was then still spoken among the Treveri of Gaul in the late fourth century AD. Added to that we have the evidence of Gaius Sollius Apollinaris Sidonius (AD *c.*430 – *c.*480), who became Bishop of the Arverni, once ruled over by Vercingetorix. Sidonius' letters and poems are acclaimed for the light they shed on life and conditions in fifth-century AD Gaul. It is Sidonius who remarks that the leading families of Gaul were, in his day, still trying to throw off 'the scurf', as he calls it, of Celtic speech. Therefore Celtic must have been widespread among the ordinary people.

The Celtic language of Gaul has actually survived to a considerable extent in the vocabulary of modern French. While the Académie Française grudgingly admits to about 500 Celtic loan-words in French, there is a much larger Celtic vocabulary awaiting acknowledgement. The *Dictionnaire Général* (ed. Adolphe Hatzfeld and Arsène

Darmesteter, 1890–1900) provided a large number of Celtic etymologies but many Celtic scholars have argued that much more remains to be acknowledged and that through the vehicle of Low Latin Celtic words survived into the Romance languages. It becomes obvious that when the Germanic Franks finally conquered and settled Gaul, giving it its modern name, they intermarried with the Romano-Celtic population and assimilated some part of their language to form modern French.

Gaul proper, however, had become lost to the Celtic world. In the third century AD there arose a series of 'Gaulish emperors' during a schism in the Roman empire. Postumus, calling himself 'Restorer of the Gauls' on his coinage, set himself up as Emperor with his capital at the capital of the Treveri, at Augusta Trevisorum (Trier) on the Moselle in AD 259. Tectricus was the last Gaulish Emperor, who, in AD 274, submitted to Aurelian. But these 'emperors' did not seriously envisage an independent Celtic Gaul re-emerging to challenge Rome.

The Armorican peninsula (modern Brittany) has remained Celtic and was never submerged either by Rome or by the later settlements of Norsemen and Franks. It was in a state of insurrection against Rome at the start of the fifth century AD. Zosimus tells us that in AD 409, 'encouraged by the example of the insular Britons, they had thrown off the Roman yoke.' The anonymous *Gaulish Chronicle* refers to a chieftain called Tibatto (AD *c*.435) as leader of an independence movement in Armorica. In AD 437 Tibatto is reported to have been captured and slain.

The Celts of Armorica were reinforced soon afterwards by a new Celtic population arriving from Britain, having been forced to migrate in the face of the ruthless conquest of their homelands by the Anglo-Saxons. They settled initially on the coast and then in the interior in the west of the peninsula. At first the Gallo-Romano towns of Nantes, Vannes and Rennes adopted defensive measures against them, enclosing their towns in fortifications. But soon the peninsula began to change its character. The Gauls were reinforced by their British cousins and a new strong Celtic nation emerged. By the sixth century AD Armorica (the land by the sea) had become Brittany (Little Britain). Weroc'h II (AD 577–94) of Brittany managed to turn back the invasion of the Franks from the east. When Nominoe of Brittany defeated the armies of Charles the Bald of France at Ballon on 22 November 845, he secured complete Breton independence until the fifteenth century, giving Brittany time to develop into one of the modern Celtic nations.

[13]

Ireland

THE Celts of Ireland were not to suffer conquest by Rome. References to Ireland before the rise of native literacy with the Christian period are brief and inaccurate. The native literary traditions do not commence until the sixth century AD, apart from memorial and boundary stones found mainly in the south of the country and written in the Ogham alphabet.* As we have seen elsewhere in the Celtic world, the transmission of learning was conducted orally. Again, it has to be emphasized that this was not done through ignorance of the art of writing but because of the conservative rules of the society. If there was any earlier written tradition, indicated by references to libraries of Ogham cut on wands, or rods of yew or oak, nothing has survived. Only Ogham inscriptions on stone have survived. It has been conjected that the wands were bound in the form of a fan, held together by a pivot at one end, to be conveniently opened or closed. Such Ogham books were referred to as *tamlorga filidh* (staves of the poets) or *flesc filidh* (poet's rods). In the tale about two ill-fated lovers, Baile and Aillinn, it is related that when a yew and an appletree grew over the lovers' graves, they were cut down and made into wand-books on which the bards cut their sad history in Ogham. Certainly the rhythmical syllabic verse of the sixth-century Irish remains points clearly to a long literary tradition, although some have argued that this might represent the archaic form of oral transmission rather than a written tradition.

The history of Ireland until the early Christian period is therefore obscure. The first Irish historian we know of was Sinlán Moccu Min, an abbot of Bangor, in Ulster (d. AD 607). He was working on the

* See p. 216–217.

Chronicle of Eusebius, a work of universal history written by the Bishop of Caesarea in the fourth century AD. To this work Sinlán added a chronology of Irish historical events. The oldest-surviving native historical record, and the most reliable, is the *Annals of Tighernach*, composed in the late eleventh century AD at Clonmacnoise. Tighernach (AD *c.*1020–88) wrote the history of Ireland down to his own times, attempting to correlate it with major events in Europe. Among other early surviving historical works are the *Annals of Innisfallen*, compiled between the eleventh and fourteenth centuries AD by Maelsuthan Ua Cerbaill (d. 1010) – a tutor of Brían Boroimhe (Brían Boru, the High King) – and the *Annals of Ulster*, compiled in 1498 AD by Cathal Mac Magnus (or Magnusa Mheg Uidhir).

During the twelfth century AD a new book appeared in Ireland called *Leabhar Gabhálá* – The Book of Invasions (or takings). This work gathered into a single volume most of the traditions of the past, presumably both oral and written, on the ancient history of Ireland, giving an account of the origins of the Irish, the various invasions and the formation of an Irish monarchy. While it is classed as a work of mythology there is undoubtedly much in it that is historically true. There are dim echoes of the Bronze Age and of the Iron Age. What is described in places is the society which the Romans found in Gaul in the first century BC.

When the *Lebor Laighnech* (Book of Leinster) was compiled by Aed Mac Crimthainn and Fionn Mac Gorman in the late twelfth century, the *Leabhar Gabhálá* held undisputed authority as the history of early Ireland. In the seventeenth century it was re-edited by Michéal Ó Cléirigh and was also used by Seathrún Céitinn (AD *c.*1570–1647) as a basis for the early part of his history *Foras Feasa ar Éirinn*. Professor Eoin Mac Neill has described the *Leabhar Gabhálá* as 'a true national epic'. Unfortunately, we cannot regard it as reliable history.

We know that as early as 3000 BC there were farming communities in Ireland and some of the earliest megaliths were then under construction. The Bronze Age in Ireland, starting around 1500 BC, saw Irish metalwork being exported to the European mainland. It is in the Bronze Age period that scholars place the origins of Celtic society. Yet there are still some Irish scholars who place the arrival of the Celts in Ireland at a very late date. Dr David Greene accepted the dating of the arrival of the Celts to the third century BC. He wrote: 'Eoin Mac Neill found that the early Irish historians writing in the eighth century AD placed the coming of the Gaels to Ireland in the same period as that of the conquests of Alexander the Great at 331 BC.' Dr Greene, admitting that neither traditional nor archaeological evidence is worth much in dealing with identification of a people speaking a particular language, felt that 300 BC was a reasonable date and one not likely to be more than two centuries out.

Yet Professor Kenneth Jackson has argued, along with other eminent Celtic scholars: 'It is probable that Gaelic represents a rather early offshoot from this [Common Celtic], whereas the speech of those Celts who remained on the continent evolved with time into what we call Gaulish.' Now if Goidelic, or Gaelic-speaking, Celts arrived in Ireland from Europe only in the third century BC, it would mean that the evolution of Celtic on the continent from Goidelic to Brythonic would have commenced at that time. Yet from the linguistic evidence on the continent we have seen that the development to what is popularly called the Brythonic form of Celtic, or Gaulish, had already taken place by the third century. How could the descendants of the Celts of Galatia, arriving in Galatia in the third century, have spoken a similar Gaulish to the Celts of northern Gaul if the language had not already evolved?

The Goidelic or Gaelic-speaking Celts had already departed from Europe long before the third century BC. And Professor Mac Neill was not entirely correct about ancient writings for the ancient king-lists of Ireland go back centuries prior to the third century BC. Heremon, or Eremon, for example, is listed as the nineteenth King of Ireland, being the first of the Milesians or Gaels, around 1015 BC. If the old king-lists could be regarded as evidence, then the date is more in accordance with the accepted theory that the Celts originated in the Bronze Age. However, the surviving king-lists date from the Christian era with Mael Muru (AD 820–884/6) as the first-known writer to deal with Irish kings in any depth.

The existence of Ireland was known in ancient Greece, which used the name Hierne (Ierne), obviously derived from the native genitive form of Éire (Éireann and Éirinn). Eratosthenes of Cyrene (c.285/280–194 BC) was head of the great library at Alexandria. He correctly placed Ireland on the map contained in his three books of *Geographica*, the first complete descriptions of the inhabited ancient world which survive. Poseidonius (c.135–50 BC) of Apamea in Syria, historian, scientist and philosopher, who became head of the Stoic

School at Rhodes, also wrote about Ireland. Nothing remains of his works, however, but we are indebted to quotations from them by Strabo (64 BC–AD c.24), a Greek geographer from Amasia in Pontus. Strabo quotes Poseidonius in his seventeen books of *Geography*, compiled about 7 BC.

Poseidonius' information on Ireland is pretty vague and he does admit that his authorities are not exactly trustworthy. Whereas later Roman writers supposed that Ireland lay between Britain and Spain, Poseidonius places it more accurately to the west of Britain. According to him, the Irish were cannibals and fiercer than the inhabitants of Britain. He also claims that the Iberians and Scythians were cannibals (Scythia being the ancient region extending over eastern Europe and Russia). Strabo adds very little to Poseidonius except that Ireland, which he thought extended farther northward than Britain, would have a much colder climate.

Julius Caesar was also aware of the existence of Ireland, which he Latinizes from the Greek as Hibernia. He estimated that the island was half the size of Britain and as far distant from Britain as Britain was from Gaul.

Pomponius Mela of Tingentera (near Gibraltar), writing during the first century AD, was the author of the earliest-surviving work in Latin on geography. *De Chorographia*, sometimes called *De situ orbis*, On Places, was a work in three books. It is invaluable because, for example, he gives information on the druids which is not found in any other sources. Mela also dealt with Ireland. He was writing about AD 43, at the time of the Claudian invasion of Britain, and may have obtained his information from Britons trading with Ireland or Irish exiles in Britain. He calls the country Iuverna, a close approach to the British Celtic form, which would indicate that his sources were Britons. Mela talks about the relative size of the country, about the climatic conditions and, very accurately, about the abundance of excellent pasture for cattle. However, Mela adds: 'The inhabitants of Ireland are uncivilized and beyond other nations are ignorant of all the virtues and extremely devoid of natural affection.'

Needless to say, the Roman view of Ireland was just as inaccurate when it came to the structure of society and the law system as was Caesar's account of the British Celtic society. Roman knowledge of Ireland continued to be hazy. Pliny the Elder (Gaius Plinius Secondus, AD 23/24–79) mentions Ireland but his source, Marcus Vipsanius

Agrippa (64–12 BC), had estimated Ireland at four times the size it actually was.

While native historical records of traditions are not contemporary sources, I believe we can reasonably look at some of the main personalities which emerge in them. Although we cannot treat them as entirely accurate we must remind ourselves that they were the end result of countless generations of oral tradition, handed down in strict rote, word-perfectly, by a professional class of historians from remote times. Why then should we discount them as historical sources simply because they were not written down?

As an example of the truths that may be found in Irish mythology we may take the story of Étain Echraidhe, the beautiful daughter of Ailill of Echraidhe in Ulster, with whom the god Midir the Proud fell in love. Midir's jealous first wife, Fuamnach, changed her into a fly. Ultimately, in the time of Conchobhar Mac Nessa, the fly alighted on the roof of a house in Ulster and fell through it into the cup of the wife of a warrior named Etar. Etar's wife drank and became pregnant. The child was a beautiful girl whom they called Étain. In this reincarnation tale we find the High King of Ireland, Eochaidh Airemh (Eochaidh signifies horse and Airemh ploughman), who, according to the king-lists, ruled around the fourth or third centuries BC, falling in love with and marrying Étain. Now in this story we find a reference to Eochaidh imposing a task on the clans who dwelt in Tethba, an area which includes parts of Longford and Westmeath – the task of building a road and causeway across the bog of Lamrach. The story tells how the foundation of the road was laid with the trunks of trees.

In 1985, during operations in a Co. Longford bog by Bord na Mona, evidence of a roadway was found. The Department of Archaeology of University College, Dublin, took over the excavation and discovered 1,000 yards of road which had a foundation of oak beams placed side by side on thin rails of oak, ash and alder. Radiocarbon dating placed the date of the road from approximately 200 to 150 BC. In this discovery we have not only further evidence of the sophisticated road-building of the ancient Celts but proof of a reference in a mythological tale.

Perhaps the first King of interest is Tigernmas, son of Follach, who is recorded as the twenty-sixth ruler of Ireland, commencing his reign in 939 BC. It is recorded that during his reign the mining of gold and silver was introduced and that he also introduced the wearing of variegated colours in the clothing of his people – that is, the tartan. The number of colours varied and went up according to the rank of the wearer. His name signifies lord of death and it is said he forsook the peaceful ways of the druids and introduced the worship of an idol called Cromm Croich (or Cromm Cruach – Bloody Crescent), which involved human sacrifice. The idol was worshipped on Magh Slecht (Plain of Adoration) at the feast of Samhain (31 October/1 November). Tigernmas is said to have been slain during the frenzied worship of the idol and the people then returned to the ways of the druids.

In 714 BC it is recorded that Ollamh Fodhla became King of Ireland and founded rule by legislature, giving the country a codified system of law. The term *ollamh* denoted the highest grade of bard, top of the seven grades, and it took a candidate nine to twelve years to memorize the 250 prime stories and 100 secondary stories to become an *ollamh*. *Ollamh*, in fact, remains the modern Irish word for a professor. Whether or not Ollamh Fodhla was entirely mythical and whether or not he had anything to do with the foundation of the Brehon Law system, when the Irish legal system was first codified in the early Christian era it was clear that it had evolved from centuries of careful oral preservation.

The ancient laws of Ireland, named from *breitheamh* – a judge – are the oldest-surviving law system in Europe. The laws are very sophisticated and complex, the result of many centuries of practice. Their roots are in ancient Indo-European custom and not in Roman law, from which other European systems have derived. In parts of Ireland this law system survived until its final suppression by England in the seventeenth century AD.

Ollamh Fodhla is also claimed as the founder of the great festival, held every three years, at Teamhair (Tara), the site in Co. Meath generally regarded as the capital of ancient Ireland and main royal residence of the high kings. Tara was certainly in use in 2000 BC. It seems to have declined in importance shortly after AD 734 when the high kings of the period tended to take up residence where they pleased, usually within the safety of their native province.

Another outstanding name in the early king-list is that of the female ruler Macha Mong Ruadh, or Macha of the Red Tresses. She is said to have commenced her reign in 377 BC, being the daughter of Aedh Ruadh. It is claimed that she built Emain Macha (Navan Fort), which became the capital of the kings of Ulster, the place where Conchobar

Mac Nessa ruled during the heady days of the *Táin* saga when the great Ulster champion Cúchulain single-handedly protected the province. Macha is also said to have built Ard Macha (Macha's Height, Anglicized as Armagh) and to have established the first hospital in Ireland Bron Bherg, the House of Sorrow), which was in use until its destruction in AD 22.

The Brehon Law system has a highly intricate section of laws dealing with the practice of medicine and the running of hospitals. Although St Fabiola is generally accorded a place in European history as founding the first hospital in Rome in the fourth century AD, we can be sure, judging from the evidence, that hospitals existed in Ireland long before this time. Hospitals, according to the Brehon Laws, should be staffed by qualified personnel, should be free from debt, should have four doors and fresh water, and should be freely available to the sick, feeble, elderly and also orphans. Under the Brehon Laws no one in early Irish society needed to fear illness. Not only were they assured of treatment and hospitalization, but the society would not let them or their dependants lack food or means of livelihood.

During the Dark Ages this long tradition of the practice of Irish medicine was widely known in Europe. The skill of Irish physicians was proverbial and the Irish medical schools were famous. The premier medical school of Europe during the period was that founded in the fifth century AD at Tuaim Brecain (Tomregan, Co. Cavan), where the eminent physician Bracan Mac Findloga was chief professor. From the medieval Irish medical tracts we can see that the skills and knowledge of the Irish physicians were highly advanced. The oldest-surviving medical tract is dated AD 1352. Most of the works date from between the fourteenth and sixteenth centuries. Yet from the myths and sagas, and from archaeological evidence, we can state categorically that physicians in ancient Ireland were skilled not only with herbal remedies but in performing Caesarean operations, amputations and even brain-surgery.

The surviving medical literature written in Irish is regarded as the largest collection of medical literature before the nineteenth century existing in any one tongue.

Another ruler of interest is Labraid Loinseach, the Mariner Who Speaks, who became King in 268 BC. Although he is regarded as a mythological personality, there is a degree of reality and plausibility in his story. He was the son of Ailill Aine, a king of Leinster. Ailill was poisoned by his brother Cobhthach. Cobhthach then forced his nephew to eat his father's heart, after which the boy was struck dumb in shock and revulsion and was eventually called Móen, signifying dumb. He was taken out of Ireland to save him from a worse fate at the hands of his evil uncle and resided first in Britain and then in Gaul. He eventually recovered the power of speech.

In Gaul he came to the kingdom of the Fir Morc, ruled by Scoriath. Scoriath had a beautiful daughter named Moriath. They fell in love and married. Scoriath then gave Móen an army of Gauls to accompany him back to Ireland to overthrow the evil Cobhthach. Fearful of the return of Móen, Cobhthach had sent an envoy to ask if the leader of the Gaulish army had the power of speech. He was told that the leader was Labraid Loinseach, the Mariner Who Speaks. Móen and his Gauls stormed Dinn Righ, the fortress of the King. There are two versions of the conclusion of the story. One is that Cobhthach surrendered and Móen made peace but subsequently killed him after more treachery. The second version is that Cobhthach and thirty of his warriors were shut into a hall and burned to death.

Now the name of Leinster, the kingdom where these events happened, in Irish is Laighin, said to be taken from the word for spearmen, being named after the Gaulish warriors who accompanied Móen. The Gauls were said to have used a broad-pointed spear called *laighen* made of a blue–green iron. The province had previously been called Galian but after Móen became King it was named Laighin. The termination -ster was added at the time of Norse settlement from *stadr* – a place – hence Laighin-ster or Leinster.

Contemporary with Cunobelinos, ruling in Britain before the Roman invasion, was Conaire Mór, recorded as ruling from AD 1 to 65. He was therefore also a contemporary of Boudicca. In the annals his story is firmly interwoven in myth – as the son of Nemglan, a mysterious bird-god, and of Mess Buachalla. He was slain at the siege of Da Derga's hostel, one of the great tales of the mythological sagas. Conaire Mór's successor was Lugaid Riab nDerg, Lugaid of the Red Stripes, who also had a supernatural birth. He was said to be the son of Clothra, a daughter of an earlier high king, who was a rather vicious lady. She drowned her own sister Ethne when she was pregnant and had affairs with each of her three brothers, then bearing a son named Lugaid. He was called Riab nDerg because his body was divided into three by two red stripes which proclaimed him to be the son of all three brothers. When he grew to manhood, Lugaid is said to have begotten a son by his own mother.

Lugaid's son was called Crimthann Nía Náir, the modest warrior, who was King when Agricola turned his speculative eyes towards Ireland and contemplated an invasion. Crimthann had succeeded in overthrowing the High King Conchobar Abrat Ruadh, of the Red Brows, in AD 73. Conchobar had succeeded Lugaid but appears to have been something of a tyrant. Crimthann ruled until AD 90. He might well have emerged into Roman history as forcibly as Caratacos had the Roman General Agricola followed his plan to invade Ireland.

Agricola (AD 40–90) was from Fréjus (Forum Julii) in Gaul, the same town as the poet Gallus, but, unlike Gallus', Agricola's family were Roman colonists who had settled in the area soon after the conquest of the Celts there. As a young military tribune he had served with Suetonius Paulinus in Britain during the Boudiccan uprising. In AD 71–3 he was commander of the XX Legion in Britain and then went to Gaul as Governor of the Aquitani. In 77/8 he returned to Britain as Governor, where he immediately set out to pacify the rebellious tribes and extend the influence of Rome into the north of the island.

Agricola's career is well known through the pen of his son-in-law, Publius Cornelius Tacitus (AD 56/57–117). Tacitus was, like his father-in-law, born in a former Celtic territory in Narbonensis Gaul. He married Agricola's daughter in AD 77 and subsequently was able, at first hand, to learn of Agricola's campaigns against the Celts in Britain. His biography of Agricola was produced in AD 98.

From AD 80 Agricola, as Governor of Britain, consolidated the Roman advance northwards by building a series of fortifications on a line between the Forth and Clyde. It was during the summer of his fifth campaign, in AD 82, that Agricola, having moved the Roman army into what is now southern Scotland, had a visitor from Ireland. According to Tacitus it was 'one of their petty kings, who had been forced to fly from the fury of a domestic faction'. This unnamed king was 'received by the Roman General, and, under a show of friendship, detained to be of use on some future occasion'. Agricola managed to gather a lot of intelligence about Ireland, although he thought it lay between Britain and Spain. 'By means of merchants resorting thither for the sake of commerce, the harbours and approaches to the coast are well known,' observed Tacitus. Agricola concentrated his troops on the coast, presumably at the site of modern-day Stranraer, in preparation for the invasion. Tacitus recalls: 'I have often heard Agricola declare that a single legion, with a moderate band of auxiliaries, would be sufficient to complete the conquest of Ireland.' While one must accept Agricola's credibility as a seasoned campaigner, it does seem a very sanguine estimation in the light of what we know about subsequent attempts to conquer the country.

Agricola's justification for a conquest was that 'he saw that Ireland, lying between Britain and Spain, and at the same time convenient to the ports of Gaul, might prove a valuable acquisition, capable of giving an easy communication and, of course, strength and union to provinces disjoined by nature.' In addition to its strategic value, 'such an event would contribute greatly to bridle the stubborn spirit of the Britons, who, in that case, would see, with dismay, the Roman arms triumphant, and every spark of liberty extinguished round their coast.'

However, Agricola did not launch his projected invasion. The Celtic tribes of the north, the area called Caledonia by the Romans, had united under their leader Galcagos, whose name means the Swordsman, and began to worry the Romans by skilful guerilla warfare. In AD 84 Agricola's army met the Celts in a pitched battle at Mons Graupius, a much sought battlefield site. The discovery of a large Roman encampment near Inverurie, in Aberdeen, suggests that the site of Mons Graupius is the mountain now called Bennachie. The speech which Tacitus put into the mouth of Galcagos, the Celtic leader, before the battle contains several phrases which became famous, such as *omne ignotum pro magnifico est* – what men know nothing about, they see as wonderful – and *ubi solitudinem faciunt, pacem appellant* – when they create a desolation, they call it peace.

Agricola's victory over Galcagos at Mons Graupius secured a precarious Roman foothold in northern Britain. But in AD 85, before he could consolidate his victory, Agricola was recalled to Rome. He lived long enough to see Rome abandon its claims on northern Britain, withdrawing to fortifications on a line of the Forth and Clyde. Then a wall was built during Hadrian's time, being started about AD 122 and finished by 127. Hadrian's Wall marked the border with the north. However, in AD 140–42 Quintus Lollius Urbricus, then Governor of Britain, tried to reclaim the north, moving into the Forth–Clyde isthmus. Here he built a second barrier, using Hadrian's Wall as a model, a continuing rampart stretching from sea to sea which became known as the Antonine Wall. This wall proved powerless against the attacks of the northern Celtic tribes and it was eventually abandoned about AD 180–4, when it was destroyed. The Romans fell back to Hadrian's Wall and held it for at least another century as the most northerly frontier of the Roman empire.

The fierce resistance of the Celts of Caledonia had gained for Ireland safety from Roman invasion. But Ireland was not cut off from the Roman world. Trade continued. Claudius Ptolemaeus, known as Ptolemy (AD c.100–178), a Greek astronomer and geographer, born in Ptolemais Hermius in Upper Egypt, and a citizen of the great cultural centre of Alexandria, wrote about Ireland in his *Geography*, a work of seven books. Ptolemy gave the most detailed account of his time of Ireland and it has been suggested that he was using the works of other writers which have not survived. At least half the names he gives to peoples and settlements of Ireland are authentic, other names, significantly on the western and northern coasts of Ireland, are not recorded in other sources.

Ptolemy named several estuaries, which showed that his informants were sea-going traders, informed about safe havens in which their ships could find shelter. Several townships are also named, like Tara and Emania (Navan). Eblana is listed as a city name in the area of Dublin and some think it an ancient name for Dublin. But Dublin was not constructed until the Norse fortified the area in AD 841. Also Eblana, according to Ptolemy's map, is further north on the coast of Co. Louth.

Julius Solinus (writing AD c.200) made an intriguing reference to Ireland when he edited a version of Pomponius Mela's *Geography*. 'Hibernia is barbarous in the manner of living of its inhabitants, but is so rich in pasture that the cattle, if they be not kept now and then from grazing, are put in danger from over-eating. There are no snakes.' So two centuries before St Patrick, Solinus has robbed the patron saint of Ireland of one of his traditional glories, the banishment of snakes from Ireland.

By the middle of the third century AD the Irish were raiding and settling Britain, particularly along the western coast from Cornwall to Wales and Scotland. In the middle of the second century AD certain clans from the southern province of Munster had fled from a famine during the kingship of Conaire Riada. They settled for a while in Ulster. Then they, the Dál Riada, crossed into Argyll (Airer Ghàidheal

– the seaboard of the Gael) and formed another Dál Riada kingdom. The name given to the Irish raiders of this period was Scotti, a name which was eventually to be applied to the people of northern Britain – Scotland and the Scots. Yet until the twelfth to fourteenth centuries AD, a Scot was usually an Irishman.

The Celtic people of Ireland were to emerge as a strong and cultured nation. It was not until AD 795 that Ireland was to suffer the first serious invasions from the Vikings, who established small city kingdoms there. But in AD 1014, at the battle of Clontarf near Dublin, the High King Brían Boroimhe defeated the combined Norse armies and repulsed the Norse threat to Ireland once and for all. The Norse enclaves remained but accepted the power of the high kings and eventually merged into a unified Irish state which then met the first Anglo-Norman invasion in AD 1169.

During the so-called Dark Ages, the Celts of Ireland were experiencing an age of great enlightenment and cultural achievement. Christianity had become widespread in the country during the fifth century AD and, while the European centres of Christendom had been devastated by the barbarian hordes sweeping through Europe, Ireland became a centre of learning. Soon monks were leaving Ireland to rekindle the Christian faith in Europe, establishing monasteries and churches as far east as Kiev in the Ukraine, as far south as Taranto in Italy and north to the Faroes and Iceland. Perhaps ironically it was Ireland which kept alive the learning and literacy of Greece and Rome until the Renaissance.

Irish is now recognized as the third-oldest written language after Greek and Latin. The Irish scribes and scholars prided themselves on their proficiency not only in their native tongue but in Greek, Latin and Hebrew, seeking out manuscripts in those languages and copying them for future use. Large libraries of such manuscripts were accumulated in Ireland, copies were made and redistributed to Europe. Copying manuscripts was an important part of the monastic occupation. The Irish monks were the innovators of the 'pocket book': liturgical works and religious tracts which had to be made small enough to allow them to be carried in a purse or satchel, or *tiag liubhair*. The *Stowe Missal*, for example, is only five and a half inches by four.

It was the Irish who brought Christianity and literacy to the ancestors of the English. Many of the English kings, for a while thereafter, would send their children to the monastic schools in Ireland for their education. Aldfrith of Northumbria, for example, was educated at Bangor, Co. Down, and was a poet in Irish, some of his poems surviving today. He is also said to have been the 'begetter' of *Beowulf*, the earliest epic written in English (or indeed any Germanic language). Celtic experts, Professor C. W. von Sydow and Professor Gerald Murphy, have argued that there are many extremely close similarities between *Beowulf* and the older Irish saga, the *Táin Bó Fraich*, which might be because the Irish saga was the model for the English one. However, few English commentators would admit to such a possibility. Perhaps there is an irony in Ireland's role in bringing Christianity and learning to England during the Dark Ages and England's subsequent role in Ireland.

[14]

The Roman Conquest of Britain

THE war in Gaul had saved Britain from further invasion and attempted conquest by the Romans. However, within a few years of the departure of Caesar, there came a new wave of emigration from Gaul which, in fact, was to be the final Celtic migration from the continent to Britain. Commios of the Atrebates, chieftain of the Atrebates both of Gaul and of Britain, had taken part in Vercingetorix's war against the Romans and he was subsequently named as one of four Gaulish chieftains whom the Romans wanted executed for 'rebellion'. Commios was one of the last to hold out against Caesar's conquest and when his position became untenable in the lands of the Gaulish Atrebates, he and his followers withdrew into German territory, where he continued to conduct a series of guerilla raids against the Romans.

Aulus Hirtius, who had been one of Caesar's officers during the Gaulish campaign and who became Consul of Rome in 43 BC with Vibius Pansa, wrote a continuation of Caesar's account of the Gallic War, *Commentario de bello Gallico*. He relates that Caesar's second-in-command, Titus Labienus, decided that if Commios could not be captured by Rome, an agent should be sent to attempt to assassinate him. Obviously, Commios was considered a major threat to Roman control of Gaul. To this end Labienus sent an officer named Caius Volusenus, the same officer despatched by Caesar to reconnoitre the coast of Britain before the 55 BC landing. Volusenus must have spoken excellent Gaulish to have been chosen for both missions. Nevertheless, he failed in his later mission, although he did meet with Commios and apparently befriended him, for when Commios discovered Volusenus' intention he vowed never to speak to a Roman again. Subsequently, Commios met Volusenus in single combat and wounded him.

About 51/50 BC, realizing that Gaul now lay firmly under the Roman yoke, Commios decided to withdraw his Gaulish Atrebates to the lands of the British Atrebates in southern Britain. The migration is confirmed by archaeological evidence. The Atrebates consolidated their tribal lands in Hampshire and the Belgae kingdom grew strong. Their main city was recorded by Ptolemy as Kaleoua (related to the Welsh *ceilli*, a wood), which became Silchester. The tribal lands also spread into Sussex. About the time of this migration the old hill-fort of Trundle was abandoned and the prosperous Atrebates built another township which the Romans were to call Noviomagus, which is modern Chichester. The Atrebate kingdom spread as far east as the River Adur in Sussex, north to Swindon, along the crest of the Marlborough Downs from Ashdown to Devizes, and east to Bourne-mouth. Hill-forts during this period were abandoned in favour of townships and a highly prosperous agricultural community sprang up.

Commios struck his own coinage using Latin characters on them. His descendants, regarded as his sons, also struck their own coinage. They were Tincios or Tincommios, Eppillos and Verica, or Virica. These coins likewise made use of the Latin alphabet. Eppillos had also exchanged a Celtic name-ending for a Latin ending, Eppill*us*, and the letters R and F on the coins are obviously abbreviations for *Rex* and *Filius*.

From the coins being struck in Britain we have a glimpse of other rulers. Dumnovelaunos was a chieftan of the Trinovantes and is thought to have been a son of Mandubratios, who had been installed as chieftain by Caesar. Then we have Addedormaros (*c*.15–1 BC), who may have been ruler of the Iceni. Further west there are coins of Antedrigos, Buduoc, Catti, Comux, Eisu and Voconoad.

However, in spite of these chieftains and their coins, Cassivelaunos was still regarded as the High King, striking his own distinctive coinage. He was succeeded by Andoco, and Andoco was in turn succeeded by Tasciovanos. The coinage of these chieftains is wide-spread and numerous, indicating long and prosperous terms of office and positions of power exceeding other chieftains, thus underlining the high-kingship theory.

Tasciovanos was succeeded about AD 10 by one of the most famous Celtic kings in popular folk memory – Cunobelinos, whose name means hound of Belinos and thence emerges into English literature as Shakespeare's Cymbeline. The modern Welsh name Cynfelyn derives from it. He became the figure of numerous medieval tales before being given his final degree of immortality by Shakespeare via Holinshed. Cunobelinos was, without doubt, a high king, exercising authority over a confederation of many southern British tribes. He had moved his capital from the fortress of Cassivelaunos at Wheathampstead to a prosperous township further east named the fortress of the Celtic god Camulos – Camulodunum (Colchester). Its defensive works occupied an area of twelve square miles.

Cunobelinos' authority might well have spread further than is known. Certainly he exercised authority over at least five tribal kingdoms from the Wash, on the east coast, to the Devon borders in the west and all south-east Britain. South of the Thames, his brother Eppaticos exercised authority on his behalf as far as Salisbury Plain.

During this period Britain was continuing her valued trade with the Mediterranean world, particularly with the Roman empire. Scholars are inclined to believe that Britain did not have her own fleet of commercial vessels nor any warships, such as the Venetii of Gaul had possessed. The reason for this assumption is that no such ships were used by Britain in attempting to repel Caesar's invasions. It is assumed that Britain relied on the merchant fleets from Gaul. But it seems remarkable that all Britain's trade with Greece and Rome could have been done through foreign intermediaries. A few centuries later we hear of the shipbuilding skills of the Celts in northern Britain. And who provided the large fleets involved in the massive migrations of the Celts? I would venture an informed guess that the British kingdoms did have their own merchant ships, for Strabo enumerates the tremendous exports from Britain at this time – wheat, cattle, gold, silver, iron, leather goods, hide and hunting dogs. The Britons were in the market for amber, glassware, jewellery and wine. Indeed, the wine trade was considerable for *amphorae*, in which wine was imported from the continent, are found in large quantities.

Some scholars consider that it was during this period of vastly increased trade, under Cunobelinos, that London grew to prominence as a trading port. Britain had become a leading commercial centre outside the Roman empire. Strabo (64–24 BC) argued that trade with Britain produced more revenue for Rome than would accrue if the island were to become a Roman province and the Roman treasury had to pay for a standing army and civil service to run the country. But the rulers of Rome were apparently not swayed by this powerful economic argument.

Augustus, the first Roman Emperor (63 BC–AD 14), born Gaius Octavius and known as Octavian until 27 BC when he became known by his title, had been adopted by Julius Caesar. According to Cassius Dio (AD *c*.150–235), the Roman historian from Nicaea in Bithynia, he actually set out to invade Britain 'in order to outdo the feats of his adoptive father'. However, Augustus had to abandon his plans because of insurrection in Dalmatia in 34 BC. Cassius Dio says that in 27 BC he made another attempt to invade Britain but became tied up in Gaul due to the unsettled nature of the country. Augustus expected envoys from the rulers of Britain to cross to Gaul to make submissions to him and became angry when they did not appear. He embarked on a third plan for invasion in 26 BC but, once again, it had to be postponed, because of insurrection in Spain. This third invasion plan is confirmed by a reference in the work of Horace (Quintus Horatius Flaccus, 65–8 BC) and in the writing of Virgil (Publius Vergilius Maro, 70–19 BC).

It appears that after the abortive attempt of 26 BC any further plans for the conquest of Britain were abandoned. Augustus, in his *Rex Gestae*, recorded the names of the various countries outside the Roman empire whose rulers had sought his friendship. Britain is not mentioned. However, the names of two exiled chieftains from Britain who sought Augustus' help in replacing them on their thrones are recorded – their names are Dumnovelaunos and Tincommios, whose names appear on several surviving coins from southern Britain.

Cunobelinos never sought Roman friendship but he certainly did nothing to excite Roman enmity. There is no record of him aiding his fellow Celts in Gaul to rise against Rome. Indeed, we find one act of friendship with Rome recorded. In AD 9 Quintilius Varus, a Roman general, had been sent to quell the Germanic tribes across the Rhine. He was given command of three legions – the XVII, XVIII and XIX. The German chieftain Arminius (known in German folklore as Hermann) ambushed Varus and annihilated his three legions; Varus committed suicide. Roman expansion into northern Germany was checked. Some time afterwards Nero Claudius Germanicus (15 BC –AD 19), nephew of the Emperor Tiberius, waged a successful war of revenge on the Germanic tribes. During this warfare, AD 14–16, a number of Roman soldiers sailing north along the coast of the

European mainland were blown off course and shipwrecked on the shore of Britain. Cunobelinos had them treated with traditional Celtic hospitality and sent back to Gaul.

At about the end of the fourth decade AD, when Cunobelinos was growing elderly, a quarrel appears to have occurred at his court. Pro- and anti-Roman parties seem to have been established among his sons. How many sons Cunobelinos had we do not know, although he must have had at least five. The pro-Roman party was led by Adminios and the anti-Roman party by Caratacos and Togodumnos. Adminios appears to have been swayed by the wealth and power of the Roman empire and believed that Britain would be better off within it. About AD 39/40 Cunobelinos took the step of banishing Adminios from Britain. Adminios went straight to Gaul and contacted the Romans. The Emperor Gaius was then ruling Rome. He is better known by his nickname – Caligula, or 'little boots' (AD 12–41). Caligula suffered from some mental illness which was marked by an increasing despotism, wild extravagance, arbitrary executions and aspirations towards deification. He was finally murdered by his bodyguard. Emperor Gaius was campaigning against the Germans and was encamped at Mainz when Adminios was brought to him. He immediately broke off his German campaign and marched his legions to the Gaulish coast opposite Britain. It is said that he prepared for an invasion by ordering a lighthouse to be built at Boulogne. However, instead of ordering his legions to embark in the ships, he told them to march down to the seashore and cast their spears into the water, slashing at it with their swords. Then they were told to gather seashells in their helmets as spoils of the battle. Solemnly the mad Emperor told them that they had won a great victory over Neptune, the ocean god.

Adminios may well have had second thoughts about seeking an alliance with an empire which could be ruled by such a madman. However, he seems to have remained in exile. Cassius Dio mentions that he was joined by another British chieftain named Bericos, who might well have been the Verica of British coins. Bericos sought refuge with Claudius, who had become Emperor on the death of Gaius, and his arrival provided Rome with a diplomatic excuse for her invasion.

Some time between AD 40 and 43 Cunobelinos died. Perhaps it was the death of Cunobelinos which prompted Rome to seize her chance. Caratacos had succeeded his father, and some coins of his confirm his kingship. Britain was still a powerful kingdom. Just how powerful it was appears in an interesting glimpse given by Gaius Suetonius Tranquillus (b. AD c.70), one of our two main sources for the account of the Claudian invasion. As a reason for the invasion he says 'the Britons were now threatening vengeance because the [Roman] senate refused to extradite certain deserters who had landed in Gaul during Caligula's reign'. This can only be a reference to Adminios and Bericos. Is Suetonius using an excuse or did Britain really feel secure enough to make threats against the powerful empire of Rome?

Claudius (10 BC – AD 54) approved the invasion in AD 43. He appointed Aulus Plautius as commander of the expedition. According to Cassius Dio, Plautius was 'a senator of great renown'. Unfortunately, unlike Caesar's expeditions, for this invasion we have no first-hand account, and our sources are Suetonius, writing fifty years afterwards, and Cassius Dio, writing over one hundred years afterwards, although they are doubtless using contemporary sources which are now lost.

Aulus Plautius selected four legions: the II Augusta, the XIV Gemina, the XX Valeria and the IX Hispania. All the legions were tough frontier troops. The II Legion, for example, was serving at Argentorate (Strasbourg), the XIV Legion was at Mogontiacu, (Mainz) and the XX Legion was at Novaesium (Cologne), keeping the warlike Germanic tribes from flooding into Gaul. The IX Legion was in Pannonia. The total Roman legionary force numbered 25,000 men. In addition to these troops an auxiliary force was raised, mostly cavalry, which came from various parts of the empire. The total invasion force was somewhere in the region of 40,000 to 50,000 men. According to Suetonius, when Aulus Plautius was within sight of a major victory against the Britons, he, by prearrangement, was to halt and send for Claudius himself. The Emperor would arrive in Britain with his Praetorian Guard, the VIII Legion and a detachment of elephants. Thus Claudius would be accorded the victory. Suetonius comments: 'The senate had already voted him triumphal regalia but he thought it beneath his dignity to accept these, and decided that Britain was the country where a real triumph could be most readily earned.'

The troops were sent to their embarkation ports. But there was trouble. Britain lay on the borders of the known world and a rumour was spread, perhaps by British agents, that if one sailed too far one's ships would topple over into a bottomless abyss. Claudius sent to Gaul Narcissus (d. AD 54), a former Greek slave, but now a freedman and private secretary to the Emperor, who exercised great political influence. He was eventually forced to commit suicide upon the accession of Nero. Narcissus was told to reason with the troops. According to Cassius Dio:

> The soldiers were indignant at the thought of carrying on a campaign outside the limits of the known world, and would not yield obedience until Narcissus, who had been sent out by Claudius, mounted the tribunal of Plautius and attempted to address them. Then they became much angrier at this and would not allow Narcissus to say a word.

The tension was broken by some soldier with a sense of humour who cried out 'Io Saturnalia!' It was the greeting used on the feast of the Saturnalia (25 December) when slaves were allowed to dress in the robes of their masters and assume their functions. The tension broke and Narcissus managed to avert the mutiny.

Cassius Dio says that the invasion fleet sailed in three divisions so that they could outflank any attempt by the British to stop their landing on the beaches. The major landing was at a township called Routoupiaci by Ptolemy and Latinized as Rutupiae. The Celtic word-root seems to signify somewhere which is dug out. This is modern day Richborough, the 'burg' being added when the English arrived. The Romans eventually raised a marble monument here, the foundations of which still exist, to commemorate their landing. We are told that the landings were unopposed. It could not be that the British were caught unawares. There was enough intercourse with Gaul to know exactly from where and when the Roman fleet had sailed.

It became obvious immediately that the Romans were dealing with one military commander, Caratacos, and it seems that it was part of his policy, as it had been of his ancestor Cassivelaunos, not to come into open conflict with the Roman legions. Cassius Dio says that the Britons would not come close but withdrew into the forests 'hoping to wear out the invaders by fruitless effort, so that, just as in the days of Julius Caesar, they should sail back with nothing accomplished'.

After the initial beachhead had been secured, Plautius seemed to have established fortified ports at Rutupiae (Richborough), Dubris (Dover) and Lemanae (Lympne), obviously having taken to heart the lesson learned by Caesar when, on two occasions, his fleets were destroyed. Dubris was already in existence when the Romans came, for the name is Celtic, being Dobra, the plural of *dubro*, water (modern Welsh, Breton and Cornish forms are *dwfr*, *dovr* and *dour*). Streams met there and thus the meaning was the meeting of the waters. The name Lemanae (Lympne) was also given to the river there and meant the river by the elms.

With his base secured and supplies being landed, Plautius pushed his invasion force inland. As had Cassivelaunos before him, Caratacos and his brother Togodumnos began to harass the invaders. However, Aulus Plautius reached the Medway and here Caratacos decided to fight a major engagement. According to Cassius Dio:

> The Celts thought that the Romans would not be able to cross it without a bridge, and consequently bivouacked in rather careless fashion on the opposite bank; but he [Plautius] sent across a detachment of Batavi, who were accustomed to swim easily in full armour across the most turbulent streams. These fell unexpectedly on the enemy but instead of shooting at any of them they confined themselves to wounding the horses that drew their chariots; and in the confusion that followed not even the enemy's mounted warriors could save themselves.

The reference is of interest in that it also tells us that the Celts of Britain were still using war-chariots at this time.

Aulus Plautius now ordered Titus Flavius Sabinus Vespasianus (AD 9–79), commander of the II Augusta Legion, and the future Emperor of Rome, to cross the river further downstream and flank the Celts. According to Cassius Dio:

> So they too got across the river in some way and killed many of the foe, taking them by surprise. The survivors, however, did not take to flight, but on the next day joined issue with them again. The struggle was indecisive until Gnaeus Hosidius Geta, after narrowly missing being captured, finally managed to defeat the Celts so soundly that he received the *ornamenta triumphalia*.

After this defeat at the Medway, Caratacos and his army 'retired to the Tamesis, at a point where it empties into the ocean and at floodtide forms a lake'. This would appear to be a spot on the Thames Estuary.

But Cassius Dio's account is full of inconsistencies. For example, his account would have a tribe called the Bodunnu surrender to Aulus Plautius at the Medway. Is this simply a transposition for the well-known Dobunni, whose tribal area was in Gloucester? If so, why were they at the Medway? He also has the Romans crossing the Thames Estuary by a bridge! And he has Togodumnos being killed before the battle at the Medway. These inconsistencies seem to indicate that Cassius Dio was misinterpreting his original sources or, indeed, that those sources were also inaccurate.

Cassius Dio says that the Celts crossed the Thames easily enough 'because they knew where the firm ground and the easy passages were to be found; but the Romans, in attempting to follow them, were not so successful.' Once more he has the Batavi swim across and then others crossing by the bridge 'after which they assailed the Celts from several sides at once and cut down many of them'. He adds that the Romans got into difficulties when they pursued the Celts into swamps. This would indicate that the crossing was just west of Tilbury and that the swamps were probably Lea Marshes. It was during this conflict that Togodumnos, Caratacos' brother, was killed.

Caratacos withdrew to his fortified capital at Camulodunum. Aulus Plautius surrounded the township with its massive fortifications. Victory was in sight. This was the time to send for the Emperor, Claudius. The Emperor gathered his reinforcements and sailed from Ostia, the port of Rome, to Massilia, being nearly wrecked off the Ligurian coast, according to Suetonius. But he reached port safely. 'Thence,' says Cassius Dio, 'advancing partly by land and partly along the rivers, he came to the ocean and crossed over to Britain, where he joined the legions that were waiting for him near the Tamesis.'

With the Emperor in command, the Romans began their attack on Camulodunum. Although there is no full description of the taking of the city, it would appear that Caratacos had fought a battle outside the fortifications of the city and that Claudius' elephant detachment played a crucial role in turning the tide of the battle against the Celtic chieftain. Caratacos, his family, and many of his followers were able to escape to the west.

Claudius entered Camulodunum in triumph and spent a total of sixteen days in Britain taking the formal submission of several tribal chieftains. From the speech made by Caratacos nine years later, it would seem that Claudius offered a truce and was willing to make him a client king under Roman suzerainty. But Caratacos preferred to head westward to raise the tribes there against the invaders. Camulodunum was made the capital of the new Roman province and was garrisoned by troops of the XX Valeria Legion. Others troops of the same legion were despatched to Verulamium, near Wheathampstead, and a fortress was built there.

Adminios and Bericos appear to have been established by the Romans as client kings and we learn that Cogidumnos, an Atrebate chieftain whose capital was Noviomagus, was made 'rex et legatus Augusti', a rather unique title, and solemnly took a Romanized name, Tiberius Claudius Cogidumnus. His tribe was afterwards called the Regni. An inscribed stone, giving his title and name, was found in 1723 at Noviomagus, then Chichester, and is now part of the wall of Chichester town hall. Cogidumnus is said to have built the famous villa at Fishbourne. Among other submissions to Claudius was that of Prasutagos, King of a powerful tribe called the Iceni, whose lands were in East Anglia. His wife was Boudicca (Victory), who was eventually to fight the Romans with a savage fury nearly twenty years later.

When Claudius returned to Rome, Aulus Plautius set about securing the conquest. Titus Vespasianus (Vespasian) and his brother Sabinus, commanding the II Augusta Legion, were ordered to move south-west, moving through Sussex and Hampshire. It is recorded that the future Roman Emperor fought thirty battles and captured twenty fortresses during this campaign. He reduced Vectis (Isle of Wight), whose Celtic name means what rises above the sea (an island). He subsequently marched his legion westward to the River Frome (the Celtic name being cognate with the Welsh *ffraw* meaning fine, fair or brisk). Overlooking the Frome the Romans saw one of the strongest hill-forts in the country, *Mai-dun* (the fortress of Mai – Maiden Castle). This was one of the major hill-forts of the Durotriges with sevenfold ramparts rising one hundred feet in height enclosing an area two-thirds of a mile long by a third of a mile wide.

Having heard of the approach of the Romans, the Celtic chieftains had gathered their people into the enclosure and prepared to with-stand a siege. Now they watched as the Roman soldiers marched into position. Vespasian could see the complicated western gateway and realized that it would be a difficult obstacle to overcome. He marched his men to the eastern gateway and found it less strong. He set up his artillery – the *ballista*, which would machine-drive its arrows over longer ranges than the Celts were used to, and the *catapultae*, which could throw stones and boulders considerable distances. The chieftains of the Durotriges perhaps had no notion of the new weapons and their capability – perhaps they were mown down in the first barrage before they could reorganize their defences.

The hill-fort was also weakened by the fact that a cluster of dwellings of wood had been built up outside the east gate and these were soon set on fire by the Roman troops. Under cover of the smoke and barrage of machine arrows, the legionaries were able to rush each rampart, forcing their way over rather than entering through the gates. Once inside the great walls of Mai-dun, the soldiers seem to have lost their heads, for something caused them to start a massacre of the men, women and children. Archaeologists have discovered that people were killed with blows struck at their backs and that many bore signs of blows struck at them after they were dead.

By nightfall one of the strongest hill-forts in Britain had fallen to the Romans. The next day they marched on, leaving the few survivors to bury their dead in the ashes of the burnt buildings on the edge of the town. The hurry is proved by the shallowness of the graves and the way the corpses were tumbled in instead of being carefully placed according to custom. In this cemetery archaeologists found evidence of the use of the *ballistae*, with their heavy machine-driven arrows. In addition, some 20,000 pebble sling-shots were also found piled in one spot. Evidence also of the merciless killing is shown in the way one woman was buried, her arms pinioned behind her and her skull smashed in by three death-dealing blows. Many of the skulls were scarred with sword-cuts.

For a few years the survivors of Mai-dun eked out an existence in the ruins of the hill-fort but, finally, about AD 70, they left to live in the unfortified township of Dorcic (Dorchester), which name meant a bright or splendid place. To the Celtic name the Romans simply added their *ceastor*, signifying that it was a military station.

Unfortunately Tacitus' book, which covered this period and would have given a detailed account of the storming of Mai-dun, has been lost. So apart from the movement of Vespasian, we know little of the movements of the other legions. We know that the IX Hispania moved north and by about AD 47 had probably reached Lincoln, whose Celtic name Lindon meant a settlement by a lake. The XIV Gemina and units of the XX Valeria seem to have reached Deva (Chester), the settlement taking its name from the River Dee, on which it stood, its early Celtic form being Dubr-duiu, the holy river or the place of the river goddess. And Vespasian, in the south with his II Augusta, had reached Isca Silurum (Caerleon), a settlement of the Silures on the River Usk. Isca was the Latin pronunciation of the Usk, identical also with Axe, Esk, Isc, and meaning *easc* – water. The Romans later called the spot camp of the legion or Caerleon.

In the autumn of AD 47 a new governor arrived in Britain to continue the work of conquest. This was Publius Ostorius Scapula, a former consul. Caratacos was now in the mountains in the western peninsula across the River Severn (what is now Wales). Here he had the support of the Ordovices, Deceangli, Demetae, Cornovii and Silures. Among the place-names which this energetic Celtic leader left behind is Caradoc in Herefordshire, first recorded as Caer Caradoc, Caratacos' fortress. Tacitus says that Caratacos had established himself in a strong military and political position by the time Ostorius came to govern Britain and attempted to complete the work of conquest. Almost as soon as Ostorius arrived, Caratacos went on the offensive. In an aside, Tacitus tells us that the new Governor's son, Marcus Ostorius Scapula, who had come to serve as an officer under his father, won the Oak Leaf for saving a comrade's life in an encounter with the Celtic chieftain's forces. Marcus was later forced to commit suicide by the despotic Emperor Nero.

Ostorius countered Caratacos' offensive by making a punitive raid on the country of the Deceangli (modern Clwyd) because this was the area from where the Romans believed that Caratacos was conducting his campaign. A series of uprisings began from tribes across southern Britain, many of whom the Romans thought 'pacified'. Ostorius decided to disarm the Celtic tribes behind his 'front lines'. According to Tacitus, the Iceni were the first to rise up because of this policy. Their ruler, Prasutagos, was angered by this affront to his integrity, having sworn fidelity to Claudius.

The Dobunni of Gloucestershire began to harry the Romans, and the Silures joined them. Ostorius established a permanent garrison at Glevum – the bright or splendid place – modern Gloucester. The permanent garrison of the II Augusta was able to maintain control of the area. But the largest tribe in Britain, the Brigantes, in the north, had become active. Their tribal area reached from the Mersey and Humber as far north as the line of what was to become Hadrian's Wall. Roman troops had to move against them and finally a truce was made with their ruler, a chieftainess named Cartimandua, whose name means sleek pony.

About AD 50 the decisive battle of the initial Roman conquest took place. Caratacos had been an astute leader, realizing that a full-scale battle between the Roman legions and his united tribes was one to be avoided until he held the upper hand. His skill as a guerilla leader was unquestionable. Tacitus says: 'The natural ferocity of the inhabitants [the Celts] was intensified by their belief in the prowess of Caratacos, whose many undefeated battles, and even many victories, had made him pre-eminent among British chieftains.'

But now, with the Romans pressing closely into the western peninsula, Caratacos decided that an outright battle was inevitable. It had to be on ground of his own choosing. Scholars have attempted to identify the site of the battlefield from Tacitus' account but in the area described there are a number of hill-forts all of which fit his description equally well. One of the most likely spots is Criggion in Powys, although Tacitus seems to place it in the territory of the Ordovicians in Clwyd. Somewhere in those areas, perhaps on what is the modern Welsh–English border, Ostorius and Caratacos met in battle. Tacitus puts this speech into the mouth of the Celtic leader before the battle.

This day, my fellow warriors, this very day, decides the fate of Britain. The era of liberty, or eternal bondage, begins from this hour. Remember your brave and warlike ancestors, who met Julius Caesar in open combat, and chased him from the coast of Britain. They were the men who freed their country from a foreign yoke. Who delivered the land from taxations imposed at the will of a master; who banished from your sight the *fasces* and the Roman axes; and above all, who rescued your wives and daughters from violation.

Tacitus remarks that Ostorius was astonished at the spirit which animated the British army. Here was no easy victory, although the subsequent Roman account makes it seem like one. The battle cry of the Romans was 'all things give way to valour'. They marched forward and, we are told, the fighting was fierce. Eventually the Celts were pushed back. 'The Britons, having neither breastplates nor helmets, were not able to maintain the conflict,' says Tacitus. This seems a strange comment for we have evidence of the remarkable workmanship of Celtic helmets, shields and even horse armour at this period. However, the victory was decisive. Caratacos' brother, whose name we are not told, 'surrendered at discretion'. His wife and daughter were also taken captive.

Caratacos managed to escape and fled northwards, seeking refuge in the land of the Brigantes. Presumably he hoped to continue the struggle against Rome from there but the ruler of the Brigantes, Cartimandua, had done a deal with Rome. Betraying the sacred law of hospitality, she had Caratacos bound in chains and handed over to Ostorius.

Cartimandua, the sleek pony, was one of those powerful female Celtic rulers whose names have become almost legendary – Boudicca of the Iceni, Medb, the semi-mythical Queen of Connacht, Gráinne O Maillie, chieftainess of the tribes of West-Connacht, and many others. She remained loyal to Rome. Some years later in AD 68 she divorced her husband Venutios in favour of Vellocatos, his charioteer. Venutios put himself at the head of an anti-Roman faction and overthrew her. Aulus Didius Gallus, the new Governor, had to send legions north and succeeded in restoring her to her throne. Venutios managed to escape capture and some time later raised a new insurrection against Cartimandua. Yet again the Queen of the Brigantes appealed for Roman aid and this time Vettius Bolanus sent an army north. However, Venutios was so popular with the people of the Brigantes that all the Romans could do was rescue Cartimandua and leave the Brigantes in the hands of Venutios. It was not until AD 74 that Venutios and the Brigantes were finally subdued by Rome.

Thanks to Cartimandua's betrayal, Caratacos, his family and faithful retinue began their long journey to Rome in chains. Southern Britain was now firmly in Roman hands. It was the end of an epoch in Celtic history.

Epilogue

Celts, Etruscans and the New World

EW ancient civilizations have been so romantically portrayed as that of the Celts. From the nineteenth century there have been countless volumes which have merged fact and fiction, conjuring images of the Celts, on the one hand, as 'noble savages' – the American Indians of Europe – and, on the other, as all-wise, all-knowing ancient mystics who, in spite of their ancient wisdom, went under before the barbarity of the Roman Empire. There are, in fact, many similarities in the way the Celts have been treated by popular writers and the way the American Indian has been treated. The real history of the American Indian did not have an impact on popular consciousness until Dee Brown wrote *Bury My Heart at Wounded Knee: An Indian History of the American West* (1970). For the Celts, such an act of rehabilitation in history has yet to be made. The conqueror always writes the history books and for centuries the Celts have been almost edited out of their true place in the historical development of European civilization. Some recent popular works, such as *The Celts* by Frank Delaney (1986), have served merely to continue the confusion.

With the remnants of the ancient Celtic peoples giving way before the conquests of the English and French, much of their pre-Christian past was 'mislaid'. Rediscovery came accidentally during the European Renaissance when scholars began to examine the works of ancient Greek and Latin writers and found references to the Celts and their 'priesthood' – the druids. Soon a veritable 'druid industry' had mythologized them beyond recognition. The English and French began to seize hold of Celtic figures and weave them into their own national history-myth. Arthur, for example, was turned from a Celtic chieftain, fighting for the independence of his people against the invasion of the pagan Germanic ancestors of the English, into a suave medieval English king. Tristan and Iseult became part of French folklore. Boudicca (Boadicea) has even been referred to in an English history textbook for schools as 'Queen of the English'!

However, even the Celts themselves have contributed to some extent to this myth-making. A Welsh stonemason named Edward Williams, taking the name Iolo Morganwg, established a Gorsedd of Bards on 21 June 1792, maintaining that the Gorsedd was a traditional Celtic assembly, traceable into ancient times. In 1819 the Gorsedd became an integral part of the Eisteddfod, which in its modern form dates from 1789. Professor Gwyn Williams has said: 'The inventions of Iolo Morganwg in the eighteenth century . . . helped to throw a mist of unreliable antiquarianism about the subject which scholarship has not the means completely to dispel.' The Gorsedd is now an annual and almost integral part of the national life not only of Wales, but of Brittany, where a Gorsedd was formed in 1901, and in Cornwall, whose Gorsedd dates from 1928.

The 'Celtic Renaissance' of the nineteenth century in some ways did a disservice to ancient Celtic civilization for it saw the creation of a new era of myth-making as poets and novelists and musicians contributed to the production of a 'never-never world' of pre-Christian Celtic society. However, before concluding this history of the pre-Christian Celtic world, there are two pieces of historical myth-making which have been given serious consideration by scholars and which I feel need discussion. Both ideas seem to be gaining some credence in the mind of the general public. One idea is that the Etruscan civilization was, in fact, a Celtic one and that the so far undecipherable Etruscan written remains can be translated through the medium of a Celtic language. The second idea is that the Celts managed to navigate the Atlantic before the sixth century BC and established themselves on the North American continent. This second claim was the subject of a bestselling book by a Harvard professor in 1976.

Let us deal first with the Etruscan–Celtic theory.

The Etruscan civilization of northern Italy flourished in the period 700–400 BC and was engaged in a constant struggle with the Romans until the Etruscans were conquered and incorporated into the Roman state during the third century BC. Their language, which lasted a little longer, is represented in an alphabet of twenty-six characters whose history is unknown. In spite of over 10,000 surviving examples of Etruscan texts, mainly funerary inscriptions, linguistic identification and translation has not been successful. The Etruscan language remains one of the great mysteries of the ancient world.

In 1964 the Celtic polemicist and writer Domhnall Gruamach of Islay, Scotland, brought down the scorn and derision of the academic world when he suggested that Etruscan could be interpreted through the means of Celtic and, more particularly, through the Goidelic branch. In a contentious book, *The Foundations of Islay*, he used Scottish Gaelic word-roots to effect a translation of an Etruscan funerary inscription. Before publication of the book, the London *Times* noted the translation, and there followed a brief correspondence. The furore lasted a short while. Kenneth H. Jackson, Professor of Celtic Languages, Literature, History and Antiquities at the University of Edinburgh, dismissed Gruamach as 'a crank' and stated unequivocally that 'any Celtic origin for Etruscan is quite impossible.'

Gruamach and his supporters would deny the *impossibility* of the Etruscan–Celtic contention. The Celts were, of course, next-door neighbours of the Etruscans and the date of their move into northern Italy is still a matter of speculation, many scholars pushing it back to a period concurrent to the rise of the Etruscan civilization. Gruamach's argument is, why is it so *impossible* for the Etruscans to have been an earlier offshoot of Celtic migration?

Gruamach was not presenting an original thesis. The theory that the Etruscans were Celtic had been a popular one during the early nineteenth century. W. C. Taylor, of Trinity College, Dublin, in his introduction to Dr Goldsmith's popular *History of Rome* (thirteenth edition, 1834), stated: 'The Etruscans appear to have been Celts who descended from the Alps.' Some of the early Etruscan scholars, such as R. Lepsius and B. G. Neibhur, appear to have given their weight in support of this theory and another Etruscologist, Luigi Lanzi, mentions as early as 1806 (in his *Dei Vasi antichi dipinti volgamente chiamati etruschi*) that an attempt had been made to render Etruscan comprehensible through Celtic. It has proved impossible, to date, to trace this early attempt.

The thesis is supported by only one specific reference among 'classical' writers: Caius Sempronius Tuditanus, who distinguished himself as a young tribune in the Second Punic War, wrote: 'et Etruscos veteres Gallos conditos'. Yet even this reference is suspect. While the work of Sempronius is mentioned by Dionysius of Halicarnassus, it is generally regarded as lost. This reference occurs in a work published in Venice in 1498, the attribution of the text to Sempronius now being considered spurious. It is true, however, that some early writers were clearly confused about the relationship between the Etruscans and the Celts, a situation which caused that most trustworthy of historians of ancient Rome, the Greek Polybius (c.200–118 BC) to comment about 'the Celts, who *were much associated with the Etruscans because they were neighbours* . . .' (my italics). This, I believe, makes clear how confusion arose.

Apart from the unknown attempt at translation through Celtic referred to by Luigi Lanzi in 1806, the first attempt of which we have a record is a paper read to the Royal Irish Academy on 28 November 1836, which rendered some Etruscan place-names into English through the medium of Old Irish. This paper was read by Sir William Betham, who was vice-president of the Royal Dublin Society, fellow of the Antiquarian Society, member of the Royal Irish Academy, member of the Royal Academy of Sciences of Lisbon (Portugal) and recipient of several distinguished academic accolades. He was the author of such works as *Irish Antiquarian Studies*, *Gael and Cimbri* and *History of the Constitution of England and Ireland*. In short, Betham was no lightweight scholar. He is still remembered at the Public Record Office in Ireland for his diligent collections of Irish manuscripts.

Betham followed up his initial paper two years later with a more contentious one, this time clarifying his thesis that Etruscan could be translated through the medium of Old Irish. This time he translated the Eugubian Tables, a series of bronze tables found in La Scheggia, near Gubbio. Betham's paper was considered by the Academy's committee and rejected. According to the secretary of the day:

> With respect to the paper on the Eugubian Tables, the Committee are of the opinion that the alterations which you have made in the text of these tables (especially in the division of the words) are altogether arbitrary and unauthorized, and that the translation given (though composed of Irish roots) is not the Irish language either of the present day or any other period.

Indeed, when it is considered that the Irish Records are more than two thousand years more recent than the assumed date of these tables, and offer the greatest difficulties to the best Irish scholars, it is not to be supposed that the modern dialect of Irish could afford any clue to their interpretation even supposing them to be a language kindred to the Irish.

Betham, in annoyance, dismissed the committee of the Academy by saying that it did not, so far as he was aware, include 'any one who even pretended to be an Irish scholar, or at all to understand the language' and pressed on with his work. This resulted in a fascinating two-volume study published by Philip Dixon Hardy and Sons, Dublin, in 1842, entitled *Etruria–Celtica*. In the work, Betham transcribes not only the entire Eugubian Tables and the Perugian Inscription, but many smaller inscriptions. In view of the weight of Betham's scholastic reputation, his work was deserving of careful consideration and answer. However, it appeared to vanish without trace until Domhnall Gruamach reopened the controversy. Interestingly, when Gruamach made his contentions, he was totally unaware of Betham's work.

Let us take Gruamach's contentions, as the latest work in this field, first. He chose for his exercise an Etruscan tomb inscription from the Tomba degli Scudi at Tarquinia dated to the third or second century BC. In his study he does not give the original Etruscan lettering, but published his text in modern lettering. The original lettering can be found illustrated in *Corpus Inscriptionum Etruscarum*, II, 1.3 (1936), no. 5388.

ZILCI: VELUS: HUL
CNIESI: LARTH: VEL
CHAS: VELTHURS: APRTHNAL
C: CLAN: SACNISA: THU
IETH: SUTHITH: ACAZR

It is clear from the original inscription that the spacing between these groups of letters was intended and thus the letters comprise the actual Etruscan words. Gruamach decided to ignore this and make his own grouping of letters, reducing the inscription thus:

ZIL CIVEL U SHUL CNIES IL ARTH VEL
CHAS VEL THURSA PRTHN ALC CLAN
SACN IS A THUIETH SUTHITH A CAZR

Having completed this arbitrary exercise, he can then render the 'sounds' through Scottish Gaelic word-roots as follows:

ZIL(SIL) drop or shed	CIVEL(CIBHEAR) rain shower	U(UA) from	SHUL(SUIL) eye
CNIES(CNEIS) tender	IL(IL) in plenty	ARTH(ARTH) O god	VEL(BHEL) Bel
CHAS(CAS) pity	VEL(BHEL) O Bel	THURSA(TUIRSE) sorrow	
PRTH(PAIRTHEAN) of kindred	ALC(ALGA) noble		
CLAN(CLANN) tribe	SACN(SAGHAIN) Savin or Sabine	IS(IS) and	A(A) whom
THUIETH(TUAITH) northern	SUTHITH(SUID) warriors	A(A) to the	
CAZR(CASAIR) slaughter.			

Gruamach renders this as:

> Shed rain of tender tears in plenty O god Bel. Pity O Bel the sorrow of the noble kindred of the Sabine Tribe [and] whom Northern Warriors slaughtered.

Gruamach is so excited by his 'success' that he goes on to make several more contentious claims. For example, 'if the Tomba degli Scudi is an early name for this tomb, it is certainly a later rendering of the Gaelic Tuama de Sgudaigh, which means "Tomb of those cut off at one stroke".' Gruamach overlooks the fact that *tuama* (tomb) is a loan-word adopted into Irish from Latin in the Christian era, which, in its turn, was borrowed into Latin from the Greek τύμβος – *tymbos*.

The pitfalls into which Gruamach has blithely rushed will be obvious to philologists and, indeed, to any competent linguist. His methods are hopelessly unscientific. He has argued that this does not matter; only the results are important. However, Gruamach admitted that his only guide had been R. A. Armstrong's 1825 *Scottish–Gaelic Dictionary* and Edward Dwelly's *Scottish–Gaelic Dictionary* 1902–11. He has ignored the linguistic changes that have occurred in Scottish Gaelic since its divergence from Old Irish, which started about the tenth century AD. Not only this, Gruamach assumed that modern Scottish Gaelic resembled the language of the European Celts of the pre-Christian period. But both Goidelic and Brythonic branches of Celtic underwent cataclysmic changes in the centuries preceding their emergence into manuscript form *circa* the sixth century AD and, indeed, there is no simple way they can be compared with the older surviving fragments of continental Celtic, much less with any other language. One should compare Gruamach's attempts with the more painstaking analysis of continental Celtic inscriptions by, for example, Professor Karl Horst Schmidt in *Bulletin of the Board of Celtic Studies* (vols xxvi, xxviii and xxix). Looking at such work one gets an idea of how the Celtic language of pre-Christian times really looked. There is no word in them which could be equated with any modern Scottish Gaelic word without going through a process of linguistic analysis to account for the resemblances and differences between them.

Even on a simplistic level, the respacing of the letters by Gruamach into new groupings in order to arrive at ones which would fit his word-roots is quite arbitrary, and the exercise can be done to practically any language with similar results. I do not wish to imply that Gruamach was a charlatan, merely misguided. Having corresponded with him on the subject in the 1960s, I found that he sincerely believed in the accuracy of his method. But, in this matter, enthusiasm and lack of linguistic expertise overcame considered scholarship and his contentions cannot be taken seriously.

However, because Gruamach's contentions were backed by the more reputable scholarship of Sir William Betham, there are still many who take the thesis seriously. Did Betham, therefore, apply a more scientific basis to his work, or can it be similarly dimissed? The short answer is that Betham achieved his results by the same method as Gruamach. His comparison of Etruscan and Irish belongs to the pre-scientific period, and his knowledge of Irish is practically nil. Where Gruamach sought his word-roots in Armstrong's and Dwelly's dictionaries, Betham sought them in John O'Brien's and Edward O'Reilly's dictionaries. And it seems that it was O'Brien's dictionary which was Betham's main inspiration. Dr John O'Brien was Bishop of Cloyne, and published his dictionary primarily for the use of priests in Ireland. His *Focalóir Gaoidhlige-Sax Bhéarla* (An Irish–English Dictionary) was printed by Nicolas Francis Valleyre for the author in Paris in 1768. Betham may have had access to it through the second edition, revised and corrected by Robert Daly in Dublin in 1832. O'Reilly's *Irish–English Dictionary* was published in Dublin in 1817.

In reference to O'Brien's dictionary, Betham already demonstrates his inadequate knowledge of the Irish linguistic field when he calls O'Brien 'the compiler of the first published Irish Dictionary'. The first Irish dictionary had been published in 1643 in Louvain by the Franciscan Brother Micheál Ó Cleirigh and was entitled *Foclóir no Sanasán Nua*. Additionally, there was another English–Irish dictionary published in Paris thirty-six years before O'Brien, compiled by Father Conchobhar Ó Beaglaoich with the assistance of the poet Aodh Buidhe Mac Crutín (d. 1755), who was also the author of an *Irish Grammar*.

O'Brien, in his preface to his dictionary, makes the claim that the 'Umbrians, Sabines and others were certainly Celts'. Umbrians he equates with Etruscans. Betham, echoing this statement, adds: 'Dr O'Brien's acute notion that it [Etruscan] was a dialect of Celtic was never followed up with any farther [*sic*] investigation by himself, or as far as it is known by others.' This, then, was obviously the inspiration for Betham's claims in his work *Etruria–Celtica* (1842).

The major part of his first volume is devoted to an examination and translation of the Eugubian Tables. These tables were found in La Scheggia, near Gubbio, in 1444. It must have required tremendous effort in respacing letters until they fitted into a word pattern which resembled Irish and then in translating them from word-roots gleaned from his Irish dictionaries to make some sort of sense.

There is one immediate problem.

Though the first five tables are written in Etruscan lettering and the last two in Latin lettering of the third century BC, the Eugubian Tables are attested as Umbrian, which has been clearly identified now as an Italic language and a close relative of Latin, Faliscan and Oscan. It is not Etruscan. Admittedly the texts were known to be Umbrian in Betham's time, but Betham, along with Dr O'Brien, believed Umbrian was the same language as Etruscan. 'It is substantially the same as the Etruscan,' he claimed.

The fact that Betham could 'translate' an attested Italic language via Irish word roots by a regrouping of letters is enough to explain the philologists' criticism of his work. Perhaps one need not delve further, yet in fairness to Betham, we should at least consider his work on an attested Etruscan inscription.

As well as the Perugian Inscription and several minor ones, Betham devotes considerable space to an examination of the second-century BC tomb of the Volumnii family, which is the most outstanding tomb found in Perugia. Betham interprets the inscription on the door and on the six sarcophagi contained inside. To underline the spuriousness of Betham's translations, I chose at random one of these inscriptions for analysis and comment by Gearóid Mac Eoin, Professor of Old and Middle Irish and Celtic Philology at University College, Galway, Ireland, one of the most outstanding modern Celtic scholars. The result of this work was published in *The Incorporated Linguist* (Winter, 1984, vol. 23, no. 1). The inscription that I had chosen was from the fifth or principal sarcophagus which (remembering Etruscan reads right to left) was as follows:

ᛖᛃᚢᚱ : ᛗᚱᛁᛗᛁᛃᛰ : ᛟᛰᚼᚱ

Betham had respaced the letters to arrive at the Irish, reading left to right:

ᚪᚱ ᚪᛝ ᛏᛁ ᚠᛖᛚ ᛁ ᛗᚾᚪ ᛁᚱ ᚪ ᚢ ᛚᛠᚱ
Ar an ti fel i mná is a u leas

He translates this as: 'With the lamentations of women he was taken from the light.'

Taking the words of Betham's text one by one, Professor Mac Eoin translated and annotated them as if they were Irish, illustrating the wide divergence of both text and translation not only from Old Irish but from the more primitive form of the language which existed at the time the inscription on the Volumnii tomb was written in the second century BC:

ᚪᚱ *ar*: The Royal Irish Academy's *Dictionary of the Irish Language based mainly on the Old and Middle Irish materials* (1913–76) – henceforth *DIL* – lists about ten words spelt *ar/ár*, ranging in meaning from the prep. 'before', through the poss. pron. 1 plur., to nouns meaning 'ploughing' and 'slaughter'. Apart from the fact that none of them fits the context of Betham's translation, they have undergone major changes in form in the centuries between the 3rd and 6th AD, so that none of them would have appeared as *ar/ár* in the 2nd century BC.

⚛ɳ *an*: This might be said to resemble any of the nine words spelt *an/án* in *DIL*. The meanings range widely from the definite article to nouns meaning 'water' and 'drinking cup' and to adjectives meaning 'brilliant', 'swift' and 'true'. These words are of varying origin but they have all lost a second syllable during the period between the 3rd and 6th centuries AD. Authentic forms from the 2nd century BC would certainly show this syllable.

ᴄⳑ *ti*: *DIL* lists two nouns with this form: 1. 'cloak' and 2. 'line, circle'. These are regarded as one word by J. Vendryes, *Lexique étymologique de l'irlandais ancien*, T-56, and derived from earlier **tég-s* with the primary sense of 'covering'.

ⱡel *fel*: Apart from its occurrence as a rare variant spelling of *fil* 3 sg. rel. pres. ind. of the substantive verb, this has no existence in Irish as a real word. The medieval glossaries contain two words *fel* which were extracted by the glossarists from compounds of *fell* 'evil' or *fili* 'poet'. Neither of these had any place in the real language. Furthermore, the sound *f* did not exist in Irish before the 7th century AD.

ⳑ *i*: Superficially resembles the prep. *i n-* 'in' or the 3 sg. fem. personal pron. *í* or any one of several similar words listed in *DIL*. But these forms from the 8th century AD or later give no indication of the shape these words would have had in the 2nd century BC.

ⳍɳ⚛ *mna*: This is clearly one of the starting-points of Betham's translation. It resembles *mná* gen. sg. or nom. plur. of *ben* 'women'. But Betham's translation demands a gen. plur. which would be *ban* in the Irish of any period, up to and including most of the modern dialects. The form *mná* derives in the first instance from **bna*, more remotely from **gwnás*, and it is somewhere along this line of development that we would expect to find a form datable to the 2nd century BC, eight hundred years before the first attestation of *mná*.

ⳁⲧ *is*: Resembles the 3 sg. pres. ind. of the copula, *is*, in Irish. Apart from the fact that this derives from **esti* and one would have expected a more archaic form than *is* in the 2nd century BC, there is no place in Betham's translation for a copula form.

⚛ *a*: *DIL* lists 13 different words and particles with this form. They are all much reduced in form and none of them provides a meaning to suit Betham's translation.

u   *u*: No such word occurs in the Irish of any period, though the spelling *u* occurs infrequently as an irregular variant of *ua* 'grandson'.

leaꞇ   *leas*: This is the second of Betham's starting-points in his attempt at a translation. In form it resembles the Modern Irish spelling of the Old Irish *lés* 'light'. But this is considered by *DIL* to be a borrowing of Old Norse *ljós* 'light', which etymology is supported by early spellings of *leos*. If this is so, the word cannot have entered the Irish language until the 9th/10th century AD, excluding any connection of the Etruscan word with the Irish.

Therefore, only the words for 'women' and 'light' seem to correspond to Betham's rendering from Irish to English, and they are not valid in the given context. Given this examination of each word it is difficult to understand how Betham arrives at his translation in English. Professor Mac Eoin comments: 'In illustrating Betham's ignorance of Old Irish from the sentence you propose, I hardly know where to begin, because it contains so little that corresponds in any way to the translation he gives or indeed to any coherent sort of Irish.'

Professor Mac Eoin felt, as I do, that 'we cannot blame Betham for his methods. They were those of his time and comparative linguistics has come a long way since 1842.' It was only in 1853 that the publication of Johann Kasper Zeuss' volume *Grammatica Celtica* put the study of the Celtic languages on a sound scientific basis.

We can make one final comment on Betham's contention. He mentions that his study was inspired by discovering that the word for god in Etruscan was *aesar*.

> In reading in Suetonius, the Life of Augustus, I found that *Aesar*, in the Etruscan tongue, signified God. The import in Irish being the same, it struck me forcibly that this might not be accidental but that the Etruscan language might be essentially Celtic, and, therefore, capable of interpretation by Irish.

However, the *Royal Irish Academy's Dictionary of the Irish Language* lists no word found in Old or Middle Irish in any way similar to *aesar* for god. Betham might well have been confusing the word with *aesir*, plural of the Old Norse word *as*, a Norse god, inhabitant of Asgard, whose form is seen in survival in the proper names *Oswald* and *Osric*. If the word *aesar* had any currency in Irish, which seems unlikely, and Betham encountered it in some now forgotten manuscript gloss, its introduction could not have been made until the ninth or tenth century AD with the Norse settlements in Ireland – thus cancelling his contention.

Betham's work, more so than Gruamach's more recent study, remains fascinating and intriguing but totally misleading to unwary students and enthusiasts who have sometimes become so involved that they are enticed into this stagnant backwater when their time might be put to more fruitful pursuits. The Etruscan–Celtic theory has enjoyed a considerable following in the United States from where the second piece of historical myth-making has emanated.

In 1976 Professor Barry Fell of Harvard University caused a sensation with the publication of a book entitled *America BC: Ancient Settlers in the New World*. In this work, Professor Fell claimed: 'The evidence now in our hands furthermore shows that Celts in considerable numbers did settle here [America] particularly in New England.' The date of these Celtic settlements, according to Professor Fell, was about the eighth century BC and certainly no later than the sixth century BC. To sum up his argument, Professor Fell maintains that the Celtiberians, the Celts living in what is now Portugal and Spain, speaking a form of Goidelic Celtic, migrated to the New World.

Now the argument that the first Celtic settlers in the Iberian peninsula spoke a Goidelic form of Celtic is generally accepted among scholars who say that these first settlers were later absorbed when new waves of Gaulish-(Brythonic)-speaking Celts arrived at a later date. But Professor Fell says he has personally identified inscriptions dating from the eighth to sixth centuries BC in Spain and Portugal, especially in the Douro Valley, where the Duoro river flows from Spain, through Portugal and into the Atlantic at Porto. But what script did these Celts use, having regard to their custom not to commit their knowledge to writing? Professor Fell says the inscriptions are in Ogham.

Ogham (Ogam) is the earliest form of Irish writing in which alphabetical units are represented by varying numbers of strokes and notches marked on the edge of stone monuments; it may also have been used on lengths of wood or bone, although none has survived. It is a cipher based on the Latin alphabet and the bulk of survivals are dated around the fifth and sixth centuries AD. Ogham inscriptions do not date prior to the Christian period in Ireland. In fairness, the language of the inscriptions demonstrates an archaic form of Irish which caused Johann Kaspar Zeuss, the linguistic pioneer of Celtic studies, to believe that Ogham did exist before Christianity arrived in Ireland in the fifth century AD. There are 369 known Ogham inscriptions, the majority in Ireland, with the highest concentrations in the south-west. This has led Dr Máirtín Ó Murchú, former Professor of Irish at Trinity College, Dublin, to argue that Ogham actually originated in south-west Ireland.

But if Ogham originated in south-west Ireland during the early Christian era of the fifth century AD, how could Ogham be used on memorials in the Douro Valley in the Iberian peninsula in the eighth century BC?

First, let Professor Fell continue his thesis. Having ascertained that the 'Celtiberians' were writing Ogham, during the eighth century BC, which is surprisingly decipherable through modern Gaelic, Professor Fell transports them to the New World. He correctly points out that the Celts, at least in Caesar's time, had the nautical technology to sail the Atlantic. Therefore, it is easy to bring them across the Atlantic where, he maintains, they settled in concentrations in New England. We have, conjured before us, an amazing picture of druids in New England building monuments, standing stones and teaching Gaelic to the natives, such as the ancestors of the Algonquin Indians, so that pure Gaelic words are recognizable in Algonquin nearly three millennia later! Not only did the Celts leave tangible evidence in standing stones but they are also claimed to have carved inscriptions all over America, even in the West Indies, where at Barouaillie, St Vincent Island, Professor Fell identifies and translates the inscription as belonging to the eighth century BC. Many of the Algonquin place-names of New England are translated by Professor Fell using the medium of modern Scottish Gaelic.

Professor Fell's book proved a bestseller, perhaps naturally enough, as the Americans delightedly discovered that, thanks to the Professor, they now had an ancient European lineage. If his claims were true, then it was a truly epic and exciting story. However, the world of Celtic scholarship was not so credulous. Professor Mac Eoin summed up their view: 'The rock scratchings resemble Ogham script only insofar as they are lines on rocks . . . Dr Fell ignores completely the question of Celtic history.'

Indeed, the words which Professor Fell deciphered from his inscriptions bore even less resemblance to the early forms of Goidelic than

Betham's remarkable Etruscan translation. The alleged Celtic loan-words in Algonquin suffer from the same weakness as Betham's etymologies. Professor Fell had visualized the Celtic languages as somehow fixed in time, unalterable since their first historical appearance. All one needs to do is view the differing forms of Old, Middle and Modern Irish to see how a language is constantly evolving and changing. Yet the Goidelic Celtic spoken by Professor Fell's eighth-century BC intrepid Celtic navigators is still readily understandable to Scottish Gaelic speakers of today!

To illustrate the pitfalls, take the word *cuithe*, which Professor Fell claims was borrowed from the Celts into the Algonquin Indian language to survive today, its meaning being a gorge. He correctly points out that *cuithe* in modern Scottish Gaelic means a pit. But the word *cuithe* is in fact a loan-word from Latin into Old Irish, coming from the word *puteus*. This would put its appearance in Old Irish not much before the fifth or sixth centuries AD. How, then, could it have existed in the Celtic of Professor Fell's intrepid explorers of the eighth century BC? Once again we see a demonstration of the same linguistic inability which plagued the work of Betham and Gruamach. To make such contentious linguistic comparisons one would need to investigate the history of the words to be compared in both languages before declaring a relationship between them, much less a borrowing.

The lay readers who flocked to read Professor Fell's work were obviously impressed that it was a study by an eminent scholar – a Harvard professor. However, Barry Fell was a professor of zoology, not of Celtic studies nor even linguistics. Even so, one would have expected more detailed collation and evaluation, of the evidence, with advice from linguistic experts, before a scholar made such claims. Perhaps one should leave it to the Gaelic-speaking Celts to have a final word on Professor Fell's remarkable work. There is an old proverb in Irish – *oscar cách i gceird araili* – which means that everyone is agile at doing something but, uttered in sarcastic fashion, implies that every man is a beginner at another man's trade.

I have felt it necessary to make some comment upon these two popular myths about the pre-Christian Celts before drawing my history of the first millennium of Celtic civilization to a close.

In many ways, it is a sad history, especially in its later stages, with the Celts slowly being overtaken and absorbed by the ruthless efficiency of the Roman empire. History has a way of intruding on the present and the continued slow decline of the Celtic peoples, their languages, their cultures and their unique contribution to European civilization, has lasted until the present day.

The descendants of the ancient Celts, now confined in six small nationalities on the north-western seaboard of Europe, are reaching the ultimate crisis of their long march through history. Their languages and cultures, and even their histories, are all but lost. Of the sixteen millions who inhabit the Celtic area of Europe, scarcely two millions speak a Celtic language.

The Celts have been called the American Indians of Europe, and the comparison is valid for, over the centuries, they have been subjected to conquests and ruthless policies of genocide, such as Oliver Cromwell's 'solution' for Ireland and the notorious Highland Clearances in Scotland. Their languages have, over the years, been forbidden by law and, during the Victorian Age and afterwards, were literally beaten out of the children. Programmes of assimilation have sought to destroy their distinctive cultures. They, like the American Indians, have been subjected to greedy exploitation and violence which has all but destroyed their civilization – a civilization which has lasted 3,000 years. If it is now the sad fate of the Celts to plunge into the abyss of lost civilizations, for today they stand on the very edge of that bleak future, then it is my hope that this volume will, at least, have accorded them their proper place in the historical tapestry of ancient Europe.

Chronology

BC

c.1200–750	'Proto Celtic' (Urnfield) civilization of the Bronze Age.
c.750–500	Hallstatt (Iron Age) Celtic civilization.
c.500–100	La Tène (Iron Age) Celtic civilization.
c. sixth century	By this time settlements of Celts, migrating from the area of the headwaters of the Danube and Rhine, had been established through France and Spain, as far south as Cadiz, into the Po Valley of northern Italy and north-west to Belgium and the British Isles. It is generally accepted that Goidelic-speaking Celts, regarded as the more archaic form of Celtic, had settled in Spain, Ireland and Britain at least by the start of the first millennium BC. The ancestors of the Brythonic Group (including Gaulish) were part of a later expansion still continuing in the fourth century BC when Celts expanded eastwards along the Danube Valley.
c.474	Celts defeat Etruscans near the Ticino (north Italy).
396	Celts capture Melpum in Po Valley
c.390–387	Clusium, Etruscan city, besieged by Celtic army led by Brennos. Roman intervention. 18 July battle of Allia (twelve miles north of Rome). Celts defeat Roman army. Sack of Rome but Celts fail to capture Capitoline Hill. Rome pays ransom for Celtic withdrawal.
379	Dionysios I of Syracuse recruits Celtic mercenaries.
367	Celts besiege Rome for second time.
366	2,000 Celtic mercenaries serve Sparta in war against Thebes.
362	Battle of Maninea (Spartan–Theban War). Celtic cavalry play decisive role.
361–360	Celts in vicinity of Rome again. Roman army too weak to meet them in battle.

358	Celtic eastward movement reaches Carpathians.
c.350–300	Pytheas of Massilia, Greek explorer, surveys Britain.
349	Celtic raids as far south as Apulia in Italy but Roman army defeats them for the first time in battle.
340	Consul Titus Manlius Imperiosus Torquatus of Rome forbids Roman commanders to settle warfare by single-handed combat with Celtic chieftains (in Celtic tradition).
335–334	Alexander the Great meets Celtic chieftains on the Danube.
310	The Antariatae, largest of Illyrian (Bulgaria/Albania) nations, flee before the advance of the Celts led by Molistomos.
307	Celtic mercenaries serve Agathocles of Syracuse in war with Carthage.
c.300	Celts and Etruscans form alliance against Roman expansion. Celts in the east settle in Moravia region. Ireland correctly placed on map of world by Eratosthenes of Cyrene.
298	Celtic alliance with Samnites against Rome. Celtic–Samnite victory over Rome at Camerium, ninety miles north-east of Rome. Celts led by Cambaules conquer and settle Thrace. Thrace now a Celtic kingdom.
295	Roman victory over Celts and Samnites at Sentium.
284	Celts besiege Arettium. Defeat of Roman army of Caecilius, who is slain in battle. Celtic victory checked by new commander of Roman forces.
283	Defeat of Celts and Etruscans at Vadiomonian Lake, forty-five miles north of Rome.
280	Celtic alliance with Pyrrhus of Epirus against Rome during Pyrrhus' campaign to prevent Greek colonies of southern Italy falling under Roman domination. Roman defeat at battle of Heraclea in which Celts take part under Pyrrhus' command. Three Celtic armies of immense size gather on northern border of Macedonia.
279	Asculum. Romans defeated by Pyrrhus with strong Celtic element in his army. Celtic army of Bolgios defeats Macedonian army. Ptolemy Ceraunos, King of Macedonia, is slain in battle. Celtic army of Brennos and Acichorios enters Greece.

Battle of Thermopylae in which Brennos defeats a
combined Greek army, though predominantly Athenian,
commanded by Callippus, son of Moerocles.
Sanctuary of the oracle, the Pythia, priestess of Apollo at
Delphi, sacked by the Celts.
Celtic withdrawal – suicide of Brennos?
Greece devastated by Celtic victories. Panathenaea
(annual games) cancelled for 278 BC.

278 Celtic army of Cerethrios defeated by Antigonus
Gonatas, new King of Macedonia, near Gallipoli
peninsula.
Antigonus Gonatas recruits defeated Celts as mercenaries
for Macedonian army and also for the armies of
Nicomedes of Bithynia and Ptolemy of Egypt.
20,000 Celtic warriors and their families, the Tolistoboii,
Tectosages and Trocmi, led by Leonnorios and Lutarios,
cross into Asia Minor to serve Nicomedes of Bithynia
against Antiochus of Syria.

277/276 4,000 Celts arrive in Egypt to serve Ptolemy II.
275 Antiochus I of Syria defeats the Celts in Asia Minor and
they are settled in a central area to become known as
Galatia.
Roman victory over Pyrrhus at Beneventum, 130 miles
south-east of Rome, ending Pyrrhus' campaign. Pyrrhus
returns to Epirus.

265 Celts of Galatia defeat Antiochus I of Syria at Ephesus
and slay him in battle.

263 3,000 Celts serve in Carthaginian army during the First
Punic War between Carthage and Rome. They are
commanded by Antaros.

c.260 Timaeos first to use term 'Celtiberians' to describe Celts
living in Spain.

259 Celtic mercenaries in Egypt mutiny against Ptolemy II.
Imprisoned on island in Nile where they are starved to
death, some committing suicide.
Ptolemy strikes gold coin with Celtic motif.
Ptolemy recruits new Celtic mercenaries for his
army.

249 Antaros leads mutiny of Celtic mercenaries in
Carthaginian army at the end of the First Punic War,
causing Roman intervention and seizure of Carthaginian
territory.

245	Large recruitment of Celtic mercenaries by Egypt for war against Syria.
243	Celts of northern Italy seek Transalpine Celtic allies to protect them against Rome. Internal clashes in Cisalpine Gaul.
241	Attalos I of Pergamum throws off Galatian overlordship and defeats Celts of Galatia in battle near source of the Caioc.
237	Rome seizes territory of Senones Celts of Picenum for colonization.
	Carthage begins to build new empire in Spain, conquering Celtiberian territories.
232	Tolistoboii of Galatia are decisively defeated by Attalos I of Pergamum.
225	Celts of northern Italy seek new allies from Celts of Transalpine Gaul against Rome.
	Battle of Clusium, eighty-five miles north of Rome. Celtic army of Concolitanos and Aneroestos defeat Roman army.
	Battle of Telamon. Major Celtic defeat by Rome. Concolitanos captured and Aneroestos commits suicide.
224	Romans invade and devastate Cisalpine Gaul.
223	Second Roman campaign in Cisalpine Gaul.
222	Celts of Cisalpine Gaul send peace envoys to Rome to ask for terms. Rome rejects negotiations and invades for a third time.
	Battle of Clastidium, major defeat for Celts. Celtic leaders Viridomar (sometimes given as Britomaros) is slain in single combat by Roman commander Marcellus. First emergence in history of the Germanic people, who appear fighting as mercenaries for the Celts.
222–205	Celts still noted serving in Egyptian army.
221	Hamilcar of Carthage, conqueror of Celtic territories in Spain, assassinated by a Celt.
221–218	Hannibal of Carthage continues Spanish conquests. Recruits Celtiberians to his army. Plans war against Rome and seeks Celtic allies in both Gaul and Cisalpine Gaul before beginning his famous march on Rome.
218	Attalos of Pergamum recruits European Celts (Aegosages) to his army.
	Tectosages of Gaul defeated by Hannibal on the Rhône.

	Celtic tribes of the Alpine regions provide Hannibal's army with guides through mountain passes. Hannibal's army is now 50 per cent Celtic.
	Hannibal enters Cisalpine Gaul. 10,000 Cisalpine Celts join him in his war against Rome.
218–207	Celts play prominent role in Hannibal's army, usually occupying the centre position in his battles, as at the battle of Cannae in 216 BC.
217	Massacre of the Celtic Aegosages by Prusias I of Bithynia. 14,000 Celts constitute the major part of the Pharaoh's army at the battle of Raphia between Ptolemy IV and Antiochus II of Syria. It is an Egyptian victory.
216	Roman successes against Carthage in Spain. Some Celtic tribes form an alliance with Rome.
212–211	Carthaginian successes against Rome in Spain.
207	Hannibal's brother Hasdrubal in northern Italy. Joined by Cisalpine Celts but defeated at Metaurus river.
206	Carthaginians driven out of Spain by Rome. Some Celtiberian troops go with them.
203	Battle of Utica. Roman victory over Carthage. Celtic troops stop retreat from becoming a rout.
202	Hannibal recalled from Italy to defend Carthage.
201	Battle of Zama. Hannibal's last battle. Celts hold centre positions in his battle-line. Hannibal defeated by Scipio Africanus.
	Roman army defeated by Celts in Cisalpine Gaul.
198	Rome begins conquest of Cisalpine Gaul.
197	Formal end of Second Punic War. Rome annexes Spain. Cenomani of Cisalpine Gaul defeated.
197–159	Celts of Galatia exert overlordship over Pergamum and form an alliance with Antiochus III of Syria.
196	Insubres of Cisalpine Gaul defeated.
195	Insurrection among Lusitani of Spain.
193	End of Thrace as a Celtic kingdom? Appearance of last Thracian king bearing a Celtic name.
192	Chieftain of Boii (of Cisalpine Gaul) and his family surrender to Rome but are slaughtered by a Roman consul for 'entertainment'.
191	Boii finally defeated.
190	Celts of Galatia serve in army of Antiochus III at battle of Magnesia against Rome. Roman victory.
	Celtic victory over Roman army in Spain.

	Paullus and Roman army achieve victory over Celtiberians.
189	Roman punitive expedition into Galatia.
	Tolistoboii and Troci of Galatia defeated at battle of Olympus.
	Tectosages of Galatia defeated at battle at Ancyra.
187	Cenomani of Cisalpine Gaul disarmed by Rome but protest to senate against violation of treaty agreement.
186–185	Last records of Celts serving in Egyptian army.
186–183	Carni, Transalpine Celtic tribe, try to settle in Po Valley but are driven out by Roman army.
c.181	Rise of Ortagion of the Tolistoboii of Galatia, who attempts to unite the Celtic tribes of Galatia.
c.180	Belgae (Celtic confederation of tribes from Belgium) settle in southern Britain.
179	Carsignatos and Guizatorix lead Celtic alliance of Galatians with Eumenes II of Pergamum.
178–173	3,000 Celts and families try to settle in Cisalpine Gaul but are rounded up and sold into slavery by Rome.
	Rome commences a colonization policy in Cisalpine Gaul. Celtic languages and customs last into imperial times and area produces many writers.
167	Celts of Galatia in alliance with Prusias II of Bithynia.
165	Celts of Galatia expelled from Pergamum territory.
164–160	Celts of Galatia raid Cappadocia.
154	Celtiberian uprising against Rome.
	Celtic Salyes attack Massilia.
153	Roman army besieges Celtic hill-fort of Numantia in Spain for the first time.
151	Roman commander in Spain offers Celts moderate terms for surrender. Agreement reneged upon by senate.
	Roman army under Galba forces Celtic surrender, disarms and massacres them. Survivors sold into slavery.
148	New Celtic insurrection in Spain led by Viriathus. Defeat of Roman army. Roman Governor slain.
141	Viriathus defeats a Roman consular army.
140	Rome agrees treaty with Viriathus but hires a Celtic traitor to assassinate him.
138–132	Celtic resistance to Rome continues in Spain.
136	Roman army besieges Celtic hill-fort of Pallantia in Spain. Celts break siege and put Roman army to flight.

133	Scipio Aemilianus, Roman Consul, sent to Spain to subdue Celts. Siege of Numantia hill-fort (for the second time), defeat by slow starvation and eventual slaughter of all inhabitants and their leader Avarus.
125	Celtic Salyes of Gaul attack Massilia for second time. Roman intervention to protect the city.
122	Roman victory over Salyes. Roman army also attacks Allobriges, allies of the Salyes. Allobriges chieftain Bituitis taken captive to Rome.
	Rome now controls Transalpine Gaul, a province stretching from the Alps to Massilia.
118	Formal extension of the new province (Provence) to Tolosa (Toulouse) and Narbon. New name Gallia Narbonensis.
113	Cimbri attack Boii in Bohemia but are checked.
109	Celts and Dacians form alliance to stop Roman expansion in the east (Rumania) but are defeated.
	Cimbri appear in Gaul with allies, the Teutones. Defeat of Roman army of Silanus.
107	Divico of the Tigurni defeat a Roman army led by Cassius in southern Gaul.
	Caepio and Roman army manage to raise siege of Roman garrison in Tolosa.
105	Cimbri and allies defeats Roman armies of Caepio and of Manlius north of Massilia.
105–102	Cimbri and Teutones raid Spain but are eventually driven out by Celtiberians.
102	Cimbri in Cisalpine Gaul force Roman army of Catalus to fall back from positions in the Po Valley.
	Marius defeats the Teutones at Aquae Sextiae in Gaul.
101	August. Marius defeats the Cimbri and their allies near Vercellae. Some 120,000 members of the Celtic army are slain.
93	Roman commander Didius conducts savage war of repression against Celtiberians in Spain. Celts of Spain finally submit to *pax Romana*.
88	Mithridates V of Pontus assassinates sixty Galatian chieftains at a feast in an attempt to destroy Galatian leadership.
*c.*87	Rise of Deitaros of the Tolistoboii of Galatia. Galatian tribes unite in war against Pontus.
82	Cisalpine Gaul declared a Roman province.

81–73	Celtiberians support revolt of Roman Governor Sertorius against Rome.
74	Deiotaros of Galatia enters alliance with Rome and drives army of Pontus out of Galatia.
71	Sequani Celts of Gaul make alliance with Ariovistus of the Germanic Suebi to help them in a war against their fellow Celts, the Aedui.
66	Deiotaros of Galatia in alliance with Roman General Pompeius (Pompey) and a friend of Cicero.
61	Ariovistus and Germans defeat Aedui. Divitiacos of the Aedui goes to Rome and is allowed to address the senate. He seeks a Roman alliance against the Germans but the senate decides to make an alliance with Ariovistus.
60	Burebista of Dacia launches war of annexation on Celts of the east and defeats the Boii in Bohemia. 32,000 Boii leave Bohemia to join Helvetii in Austria and Switzerland.
58	Helvetii led by Orgetorix and his son-in-law Dumnorix, brother of Divitiacos of the Aedui, form a Celtic alliance and begin plans for a westward migration away from incursions of Germans from the north-east and Romans from the south-east.
	Julius Caesar, given comand of Cisalpine Gaul and Gallia Narbonensis, takes opportunity to intervene in affairs of Gaul proper.
	Helvetii and allies defeated at Bribacte and massacred. Caesar drives Germans back across the Rhine and defeats Ariovistus at Vesontio.
	Caesar begins conquest of Gaul.
57	Roman victory over Belgae on the Sambre.
56	Roman sea power established by victory over Veneti in Morbihan Gulf.
55	Council of all pro-Roman Gaulish chieftains held.
	Caesar checks German incursions near Coblenz.
	Roman reconnaissance of Britain in force. Caesar defeats Cantii army near Walmer/Deal.
54	Roman victory over Indutiomaros of the Treveri in Gaul. Romans kill Dumnorix, their hostage, now regarded as chieftain of the Aedui.
	Roman invasion of Britain. Hill-fort at Bigbury besieged and sacked. Roman victories at Medway, Thames and

	Wheathampstead. Roman withdrawal after submission of main British chieftain, Cassivelaunos.
	Ambiorix leads Gaulish uprising at Tongres. Annihilation of Roman legion commanded by Sabinus and Cotta. Signal for general uprising.
	Ambiorix besieges Roman garrison at Namur but siege is raised by Caesar.
54–53	Winter. Indutiomaros builds up Gaulish army.
	Romans conduct scorched-earth policy. Indutiomaros slain.
	Ambiorix driven across the Rhine.
53–52	Carnutes capture Roman garrison at Cenabum.
52	Vercingetorix of the Averni now commander-in-chief of all Celtic forces in Gaul.
	Caesar massacres inhabitants of Avaricum.
	Vercingetorix defeats Caesar at Gergovia.
	Roman victory over Camulogenos at Agendicum.
	Caesar defeats Vercingetorix at Alesia.
52–51	Winter campaign by Caesar to suppress spirit of insurrection.
51	Romans besiege and destroy last independent Celtic hill-fort, the Aquitani fort of Uxellodunum.
51–50	Atrebates, of the Belgae, settle in Britain under their leader Commios among the Atrebates already settled there. Rise of southern British Atrebate kingdom.
47	Deiotaros of Galatia tried for complicity in plot to kill Caesar, having sided with Pompey in Roman civil war. Defended by Cicero and found not guilty.
46	Vercingetorix publicly beheaded in Rome. Twenty days of celebration held for the conquest of Gaul.
	Bellovaci in insurrection in Gaul.
45–30	Deiotaros II succeeds as King of Galatia. Friend of Mark Antony.
44	Insurrection of Allobriges in Gaul.
42	Cisalpine Gaul official part of the state of Rome.
40	Rome strikes silver *denarius* with head of Vercingetorix as token of complete victory in Gaul.
33–30	Aquitani and Morini of Gaul in insurrection.
c.30	Cassivelaunos of Britain dies and is succeeded by Andoco.
c.25	Amyntas succeeds Deiotaros II in Galatia but Galatia now declared an official province of Rome.

25–7	Series of uprisings against Rome in south-east Gaul. Gaul finally pacified and declared a Roman province.
20	Tasciovanos succeeds Andoco in Britain. The fortress of Wheathampstead is abandoned and new capital is Camulodunum.
7	Strabo speaks of Ireland in his *Geography*.

AD

1–65	Conaire Mór, King in Ireland.
10	Tasciovanos succeeded by Cunobelinos (Cymbeline).
26	Roman plans to invade Britain abandoned.
39–40	Cunobelinos banishes son Adminios, who seeks Roman allies against his father. The mad Roman Emperor Gaius (Caligula) marches legions to seashore of Gaul and tells his soldiers to attack the waves, declaring a 'victory' over Neptune.
40–50	Paul of Tarsus preaches Christianity in Galatia and makes converts. Later Epistle to the Galatians.
40–3	Cunobelinos of Britain dies. Succeeded by son Caratacos.
43	Claudius of Rome orders invasion of Britain. Forces commanded by Aulus Plautius land unopposed. British defeated at Medway and Thames. Claudius arrives in Britain with reinforcements. Siege of Camulodunum. Caratacos escapes to the west but surrender of many British chieftains.
43–51	Celtic resistance to Roman conquest of Britain led by Caratacos.
47	Scapula given command in Britain with orders to step up conquest.
50	Roman victory over Caratacos.
51	Caratacos betrayed to Romans by Cartimandua of the Brigantes of northern Britain. Caratacos, his wife, daughter, brother and their retinue, taken in chains to Rome. Makes a speech to Claudius and senate and is allowed liberty in exile in Rome. Southern British resistance to Roman conquest is ended for the time being.
74	Galatia united with Cappadocia as single province. Separated again in 106 AD by Emperor Trajan. Mention of Galatia existing as a separate province occurs as late as the eighth century AD. In the fourth century AD St Jerome attests that Celtic was still spoken there.

82   Agricola, Governor in Britain, considers a Roman
invasion of Ireland. Crimthann Nía Náir (74–90 AD) is
High King. Agricola welcomes some disgruntled Irish
chieftains to his camp in northern Britain. Invasion plans
are shelved and Ireland continues to avoid a military
conflict with Rome.
With the exception of Ireland, northern Britain
(Caledonia) and the surrounding smaller islands, the
Celtic world, from Galatia in the east to Britain in the
west and south to Cisalpine Gaul and Iberia, is now
under the rule of Rome.

Select Bibliography

Primary sources: the texts of all classical authors quoted are available in English translation in several editions – for example, the Loeb Classical Library, published by Heinemann of London. One particular and excellent translation of Julius Caesar's *De Bello Gallico* is contained in *The Conquest of Gaul*, ed. J. F. Gardner, translated by S. A. Handford, Penguin Books, London, 1982. The work of Livy – *Titus Livius: The History of Rome* – is rendered into an excellent translation by Spillane and Edmunds, G. Bell & Son, London, 1919. Justice in translation is also given to that most trustworthy historian of Rome Polybius in *Polybius: The Histories* by W. R. Paton, Heinemann, London, 1922, and in *Polybius: The Rise of the Roman Empire*, translated by Ian Scott-Kilvert, selected with an introduction by F. W. Walbank, Penguin Books, London, 1979. The works of Tacitus have also been excellently rendered in Tacitus, *Agricola and the Germania*, translated by H. Mattingley, Penguin Books, London, 1970; the *Annals*, translated by F. R. D. Goodyear, Cambridge University Press, 1972; and *Histories*, translated by K. Wellesey, Penguin Books, London, 1972.

ARBOIS DE JUBAINVILLE, MARIE HENRI D'. *Sur l'Histoire des Celtes*, Paris, 1902.

ARBOIS DE JUBAINVILLE, MARIE HENRI D', and DOTTIN, GEORGES. *Le Premiers Habitants de l'Europe*, 2 vols, 1889–94.

ARBOIS DE JUBAINVILLE, MARIE HENRI D', and DOTTIN, GEORGES. *Les Noms gaulois chez Caesar et Hirtius De Bello Gallico*, Paris, 1891.

BENFELD, ERIC. *The Town of Maiden Castle*, Robert Hale, London, 1947.

BERTRAND, ALEXANDRE L. J., and REINACH, SALOMON. *Les Celtes dans les vallées du Pô et du Danube*, Paris, 1894.

BOSCH-GIMPERA, PEDRO. *Los Celtas y la civilización Celtica en le peninsula Iberica*, Madrid, 1923.

BOSCH-GIMPERA, PEDRO. *Two Celtic Waves in Spain*, Proceedings of the British Academy, London, 1939.

BRIARD, JACQUES. *The Bronze Age in Barbarian Europe (from the Megaliths to the Celts)*, trans. Mary Turton, Routledge & Kegan Paul, London, 1979.

BURY, J. B. *History of Greece*, Macmillan, London, 1951.

CARNEY, JAMES, and GREENE, DAVID. *Celtic Studies*, Routledge & Kegan Paul, London, 1968.

CHADWICK, NORA. *The Druids*, University of Wales Press, Cardiff, 1966.

CHADWICK, NORA. *The Celts*, Pelican Books, London, 1970.

CHILDE, V. GORDON. *The Dawn of European Civilization*, Routledge & Kegan Paul, 1957.

CHILVER, G. E. F. *Cisalpine Gaul*, Oxford University Press, London, 1941.

COLES, J. M., and HARDING, A. F. *The Bronze Age in Europe*, Methuen, London, 1979.

COLLINGWOOD, R. G. and MYERS, J. N. L. *Roman Britain and the English Settlements*, Oxford University Press, London, 1936.

COLLIS, JOHN. *European Iron Age*, Batsford, London, 1984.

COTTRELL, LEONARD. *The Great Invasion*, Evans Brothers, London, 1958.

COTTRELL, LEONARD. *Enemy of Rome*, Evans Brothers, London, 1960.

CRAMPTON, PATRICK. *Stonehenge of the Kings*, John Baker, London. 1967.

CUNLIFFE, BARRY. *The Celtic World*, Bodley Head, London, 1978.

CUNLIFFE, BARRY. *Greeks, Romans and Barbarians*, Batsford, London, 1988.

DILLON, MYLES. *The Archaism of Irish Tradition*, Oxford University Press, 1948.

DILLON, MYLES. *Early Irish Literature*, Cambridge University Press, Cambridge, 1948.

DILLON, MYLES. *Early Irish Society*, Cultural Relations Committee, Dublin, 1954.

DILLON, MYLES, and CHADWICK, NORA. *The Celtic Realms*, Weidenfeld & Nicolson, London, 1967.

DIXON, P. *The Iberians of Spain*, Oxford University Press, London, 1940.

DOTTIN, GEORGES. *La Religion des Celtes*, Paris, 1904.

DOTTIN, GEORGES. *La Langue gauloise*, 2 vols. Collection pour l'étude des antiquités nationales, Paris, 1920.

ELLIS, PETER BERRESFORD. *Caesar's Invasion of Britain*, Orbis, London, 1978.

ELLIS, PETER BERRESFORD. *Celtic Inheritance*, Muller, London, 1985.

ELLIS, PETER BERRESFORD. 'Etruria–Celtica: A Rebuttal of the Etruscan –Celtic Theory', *Incorporated Linguist*, Winter 1984. vol. 23, no. 1.

ELLIS EVANS, D. *Gaulish Personal Names*, Oxford University Press, London, 1967.

FEACHAM, R. W. *The North Britons*, Hutchinson, London, 1966.

FELL, R. A. L. *Etruria and Rome*, Cambridge University Press, Cambridge, 1924.

FILIP, JAN. *Celtic Civilization and its Heritage*, Publishing House of the Czechoslovakian Academy of Sciences, Prague, 1962.

GLOTZ, G. *The Aegean Civlization*, Kegan Paul, Trench & Trubner, London, 1925.

GRANT, MICHAEL. *History of Rome*, Faber & Faber, London, 1979.

GREENE, DAVID, and PIGGOT, STUART. 'The Coming of the Celts to Britain and Ireland: An Archaeological–Linguistic Discussion', in *Proceedings of the Sixth International Congress of Celtic Studies*, ed. Prof. Gearóid Mac Eoin, Dublin Institute for Advanced Studies, Dublin, 1983.

GRIFFITH, G. T. *The Mercenaries of the Hellenistic World*, Cambridge University Press, Cambridge, 1935.

GRUPP, GEORG. *Kultur der alten kelten und germanen*, Munich, 1905.

HARBISON, PETER. *Pre-Christian Ireland*. Thames & Hudson, London, 1988.

HATT, JEAN-JACQUES. *Celts and Gallo-Romans*, The Ancient Civilizations series, trans. J. Hogarth, Barrie & Jenkins, London, 1970.

HAWKES, CHARLES FRANCIS CHRISTOPHER. *Camulodunum*, Research Committee of the Society of Antiquities, London, No. 14, 1947.

HAWKES, C. F. C. and S. C. *Greeks, Celts and Romans*, Methuen, London, 1973.

HAWKES, JACQUETTA and CHRISTOPHER. *Prehistoric Britain*, Chatto & Windus, London, 1947.

HOLMES, T. RICE. *Ancient Britain and the Invasion of Julius Caesar*, Oxford University Press, London, 1907.

HUBERT, HENRI. *The Rise of the Celts* and *The Greatness and Decline of the Celts*. Kegan Paul, Trench & Trubner, London, 1934. Published with new Introduction by Professor Gearóid Mac Eoin, Constable, London, 1987.

HULL, ELEANOR. 'Observations of Classical Writers on the Habits of the Celtic Nations', *Celtic Review*, vol. III, 62–76 and 138–54, Edinburgh.

JACKSON, KENNETH H. *Common Gaelic: The Evolution of the Goidelic Languages*, Oxford University Press, London, 1953.

JACKSON, KENNETH H. *Language and History in Early Britain*, Edinburgh University Press, Edinburgh, 1953.

JOYCE, P. W. *A Social History of Ancient Ireland*, 2 vols, Longman, London, 1903.

JULLIAN, CAMILLE. *Vercingetorix*, Paris, 1902 (republished in series Plaisir de l'Histoire, Paris, 1963).

JULLIAN, CAMILLE. *Histoire de la Gaule*, 8 vols, Paris, 1908–26.

KENDRICK, T. D. *The Druids: A Study in Keltic Prehistory*, Methuen, London, 1927.

KILBRIDGE-JONES, H. E. *Celtic Craftsmanship in the Bronze Age*, Croom Helm, London, 1980.

KRUTA, VLADISLAV. *Les Celtes*, Paris, 1978.

KRUTA, V. and FORMAN, W. *The Celts of the West*, Orbis, London, 1985.

LAING, LLOYD. *Celtic Britain*, Routledge & Kegan Paul, London, 1979.

LAING, LLOYD and LAING, JENNIFER. *The Origins of Britain*, Routledge & Kegan Paul, London, 1980.

LEJEUNE, MICHEL. *Celtiberica*, Acta Salamanticensia, series de filosofía y letras, Salamanque, 1955.

LEJEUNE, MICHEL. *Leopontica*, Monographies Linguistiques, Société d'Edition, Paris, 1971.

LIVERSIDGE, JOAN. *Britain in the Roman Empire*, Routledge & Kegan Paul, London, 1968.

MACALISTER, ROBERT ALEXANDER STEWART, and BREMER, W. E. E. F. *Ireland's Place in Prehistoric and Early Historic Europe*, Dublin, 1928.

MACALISTER, R. A. S. *Corpus Inscriptionum Insularium Celticarum*, Irish Manuscripts Commission, Dublin, 1945–9.

MAC CANA, PROINSIAS. *Celtic Mythology*, Hamlyn, London, 1970.

MAC CULLOCH, JOHN A. *The Religion of the Ancient Celts*, T. and T. Clark, Edinburgh, 1911.

MACK, R. P. *The Coinage of Ancient Britain*, Spink & Son, London, 1953.

MAC NAMARA, ELLEN. *Everyday Life of the Etruscans*, B. T. Batsford, London, 1973.

MAC NEILL, EOIN. *Phases of Irish History*, M. H. Gill, Dublin, 1919.

MAC NEILL, EOIN. *Archaism in the Ogham Inscriptions*, Proceedings of the Royal Irish Academy, vol. 39, Dublin, 1931.

MAC NEILL, EOIN, and LESTER, MARTIN. *Celtic Ireland*, Talbot Press, Dublin, 1921.

MAC NIOCAILL, GEARÓID. *Ireland Before the Vikings*, Gill & Macmillan, Dublin, 1972.

MARKLE, JEAN. *Women of the Celts*, trans. A. Mygind, C. Hauch and P. Henry, Gordon Cremonesi, London, 1975.

MEGAW, RUTH and VINCENT. *Celtic Art: From its Beginning to the Book of Kells*, Thames & Hudson, London, 1989.

NASH, DAPHNE. *Coinage in the Celtic World*, B. A. Seaby, London, 1987.

NEWARK, TIM. *Celtic Warriors: 400 BC – 1600 AD*. Blandford Press, Poole, 1986.

NICHOLSON, EDWARD W. B. *Keltic Researches; Studies in the History and Distribution of the Ancient Goidelic Languages and Peoples*, H. Frowde, London, 1904.

NORTON-TAYLOR, DUNCAN. *The Celts*, Time-Life Books, New York, 1975.

O'RAHILLY, THOMAS F. *Early Irish History and Mythology*, Dublin Institute for Advanced Studies, Dublin, 1946.

PEAKE, HAROLD. *The Bronze Age and the Celtic World*, Benn Brothers, London, 1922.

PIGGOT, STUART. *Ancient Europe*, Edinburgh University Press, Edinburgh, 1965.

PIGGOT, STUART, *The Druids*, Thames & Hudson, London, 1968.

POWELL, T. G. E. *The Celts*, Thames & Hudson, London, 1958.

RAFTERY, JOSEPH. *The Celts*, Mercier Press, Cork, 1964.

RANKIN, H. D. *Celts and the Classical World*, Croom Helm, London, 1987.

RAWLINSON, GEORGE. *Ancient History*, 3 vols, C. W. Deacon, London, 1887.

REES, ALWYN and BRINSLEY. *Celtic Heritage*, Thames & Hudson, London, 1961.

RHŶS, SIR JOHN. *Celtic Folklore*, 2 vols, H. Frowde, London, 1901.

RHŶS, SIR JOHN. *Celtic Britain*, 3rd edn, SPCK, London, 1904.

RHŶS, SIR JOHN. *Celtae and Galli*, H. Frowde, London, 1905.

RHŶS, SIR JOHN. *Studies in Early Irish History*, Proceedings of the British Academy, H. Frowde, London, 1905.

RHŶS, SIR JOHN. *The Celtic Inscriptions of France and Italy*. Proceedings of the British Academy, H. Frowde, London, 1905.

RIVET, A. L. F. *Gallia Narbonensis*, B. T. Batsford, London, 1988.

ROBINSON, CYRIL E. *A History of the Roman Republic*, Methuen, London, 1932.

ROSE, H. J. *A Handbook of Greek Literature*, Methuen, London, 1934.

ROSS, ANNE. *Pagan Celtic Britain*, Routledge & Kegan Paul, London, 1967.

ROSS, ANNE. *The Pagan Celts*, B. T. Batsford, London, 1986 (first published as *Everyday Life of the Pagan Celts*, 1970).

ROSS, ANNE, and ROBINS, DON. *The Life and Death of a Druid Prince: The Story of an Archaeological Sensation*, Rider, London, 1989.

SKENE, WILLIAM F. *Celtic Scotland*, 3 vols, Hamilton, Edinburgh, 1876–80.

STEAD, I. M. *Celtic Art*, British Museum Publications, London, 1985.

STRONG, DONALD. *The Early Etruscans*, Evans Brothers, London, 1968.

THURNEYSEN, RUDOLF. *Keltoromanches*, Halle, 1884.

WAGNER, HEINRICH. *Studies in the Origins of the Celts and of Early Celtic Civilization*, Tübingen, 1971.

WEBSTER, GRAHAM. *The Cornovii*, Duckworth, London, 1975.

WEBSTER, GRAHAM. *Rome against Caratacus: The Roman Campaign in Britain*, B. T. Batsford, London, 1981.

WEBSTER, GRAHAM. *The British Celts and Their Gods under Rome*, B. T. Batsford, London, 1986.

WEBSTER, GRAHAM, and DUDLEY, DONALD R. *The Roman Conquest of Britain*, B. T. Batsford, London, 1965.

Index